IARIA

CYBER 2017

The Second International Conference on Cyber-Technologies and Cyber-Systems

November 12 - 16, 2017

Barcelona, Spain

CYBER 2017 Editors

Rainer Falk, Siemens AG, Corporate Technology, Deutschland

Steve Chan, MIT, USA

Juan-Carlos Bennett, SPAWAR Systems Center Pacific, USA

Printed from e-media with permission by:

Curran Associates, Inc.
57 Morehouse Lane
Red Hook, NY 12571

Printed by Curran Associates, Inc. (2017)

International Academy, Research, and Industry Association (IARIA)
412 Derby Way
Wilmington, DE 19810

Phone: (408) 893-6407
Fax: (408) 527-6351

petre@iaria.org

Additional copies of this publication are available from:

Curran Associates, Inc.
57 Morehouse Lane
Red Hook, NY 12571 USA
Phone: 845-758-0400
Fax: 845-758-2633
Email: curran@proceedings.com
Web: www.proceedings.com

Table of Contents

CYBER 2017

Forward

The Second International Conference on Cyber-Technologies and Cyber-Systems (CYBER 2017), held between November 12 - 16, 2017, in Barcelona, Spain, continues the inaugural event covering many aspects related to cyber-systems and cyber-technologies considering the issues mentioned above and potential solutions. It is also intended to illustrate appropriate current academic and industry cyber-system projects, prototypes, and deployed products and services.

The increased size and complexity of the communications and the networking infrastructures are making it difficult the investigation of the resiliency, security assessment, safety and crimes. Mobility, anonymity, counterfeiting, are characteristics that add more complexity in Internet of Things and Cloud-based solutions. Cyber-physical systems exhibit a strong link between the computational and physical elements. Techniques for cyber resilience, cyber security, protecting the cyber infrastructure, cyber forensic and cyber crime have been developed and deployed. Some of new solutions are nature-inspired and social-inspired leading to self-secure and self-defending systems. Despite the achievements, security and privacy, disaster management, social forensics, and anomalies/crimes detection are challenges within cyber-systems.

The event was very competitive in its selection process and very well perceived by the international scientific and industrial communities. As such, it has attracted excellent contributions and active participation from all over the world. We were very pleased to receive a large amount of top quality contributions.

The conference had the following tracks:

- Cyber security
- Cyber crime
- Cyber infrastructure

We take here the opportunity to warmly thank all the members of the CYBER 2017 technical program committee, as well as all the reviewers. The creation of such a high quality conference program would not have been possible without their involvement. We also kindly thank all the authors that dedicated much of their time and effort to contribute to CYBER 2017. We truly believe that, thanks to all these efforts, the final conference program consisted of top quality contributions.

We also gratefully thank the members of the CYBER 2017 organizing committee for their help in handling the logistics and for their work that made this professional meeting a success.

We hope that CYBER 2017 was a successful international forum for the exchange of ideas and results between academia and industry and to promote further progress in the field of cyber-technologies and cyber-systems.

We also hope that Barcelona, Spain, provided a pleasant environment during the conference and everyone saved some time to enjoy the unique charm of the city.

CYBER 2017 Chairs

CYBER Steering Committee

CYBER Industry/Research Advisory Committee

CYBER 2017
Committee

CYBER Steering Committee

Carla Merkle Westphall, Federal University of Santa Catarina (UFSC), Brazil
Cong-Cong Xing, Nicholls State University, USA
Jean-Marc Robert, Polytechnique Montréal, Canada
Steve Chan, Massachusetts Institute of Technology (MIT), USA
Jan Richling, South Westphalia University of Applied Sciences, Germany
Duminda Wijesekera , George Mason University, USA
Francesco Buccafurri, University Mediterranea of Reggio Calabria, Italy
Syed Naqvi, Birmingham City University, UK

CYBER Industry/Research Advisory Committee

Rainer Falk, Siemens AG, Corporate Technology, Germany
Cristina Serban, AT&T Security Research Center, Middletown, USA
Juan-Carlos Bennett, SSC Pacific, USA
Bernard Lebel, Thales Research & Technologies, Canada
Barbara Re, University of Camerino, Italy
Aysajan Abidin, imec-COSIC | KU Leuven, Belgium
Daniel Kaestner, AbsInt GmbH, Germany
George Yee, Carleton University / Aptusinnova Inc., Canada
Yao Yiping, National University of Defence Technology - Hunan, China
Thomas Klemas, SimSpace Corporation, USA

CYBER 2017 Technical Program Committee

Aysajan Abidin, imec-COSIC | KU Leuven, Belgium
Khalid Alemerien, Tafila Technical University, Jordan
Hannan Azhar, Canterbury Christ Church University, UK
Liz Bacon, University of Greenwich, Old Royal Naval College, UK
Pooneh Bagheri Zadeh, Leeds Beckett University, UK
Morgan Barbier, GREYC - ENSICAEN, France
Juan-Carlos Bennett, SSC Pacific, USA
Paul Bogdan, University of Southern California, USA
David Brosset, Naval Academy Research Institute, France
Francesco Buccafurri, University Mediterranea of Reggio Calabria, Italy
Steve Chan, Massachusetts Institute of Technology (MIT), USA
Albert M. K. Cheng, University of Houston, USA
Michal Choras, University of Science and Technology, UTP Bydgoszcz, Poland

Copyright Information

For your reference, this is the text governing the copyright release for material published by IARIA.

The copyright release is a transfer of publication rights, which allows IARIA and its partners to drive the dissemination of the published material. This allows IARIA to give articles increased visibility via distribution, inclusion in libraries, and arrangements for submission to indexes.

I, the undersigned, declare that the article is original, and that I represent the authors of this article in the copyright release matters. If this work has been done as work-for-hire, I have obtained all necessary clearances to execute a copyright release. I hereby irrevocably transfer exclusive copyright for this material to IARIA. I give IARIA permission or reproduce the work in any media format such as, but not limited to, print, digital, or electronic. I give IARIA permission to distribute the materials without restriction to any institutions or individuals. I give IARIA permission to submit the work for inclusion in article repositories as IARIA sees fit.

I, the undersigned, declare that to the best of my knowledge, the article is does not contain libelous or otherwise unlawful contents or invading the right of privacy or infringing on a proprietary right.

Following the copyright release, any circulated version of the article must bear the copyright notice and any header and footer information that IARIA applies to the published article.

IARIA grants royalty-free permission to the authors to disseminate the work, under the above provisions, for any academic, commercial, or industrial use. IARIA grants royalty-free permission to any individuals or institutions to make the article available electronically, online, or in print.

IARIA acknowledges that rights to any algorithm, process, procedure, apparatus, or articles of manufacture remain with the authors and their employers.

I, the undersigned, understand that IARIA will not be liable, in contract, tort (including, without limitation, negligence), pre-contract or other representations (other than fraudulent misrepresentations) or otherwise in connection with the publication of my work.

Exception to the above is made for work-for-hire performed while employed by the government. In that case, copyright to the material remains with the said government. The rightful owners (authors and government entity) grant unlimited and unrestricted permission to IARIA, IARIA's contractors, and IARIA's partners to further distribute the work.

Secure and User-friendly De-Registration of a Vehicle as Off The Road Using Mobile Authentication with German eID Card and a NFC-enabled Smartphone

Michael Massoth
Department of Computer Science
Hochschule Darmstadt – University of Applied Sciences
Darmstadt, Germany
E-mail: michael.massoth@h-da.de

Abstract— **Digitization is as important to public administration as it is to the economy. Therefore, the German authorities currently see an enormous need for action for digitization and cybersecurity. Provided by the German electronic identity (eID) solution, every German citizen has the ability to identify himself against various electronic and mobile government services. In this paper, we will present a new approach for a mobile de-registration of a vehicle as off the road. The new mobile de-registration service of a vehicle as off the road is secure and user-friendly. The new approach implements a strong two-factor authentication with German eID card and the corresponding 6-digits personal identification number (PIN), whereby a Near Field Communication (NFC) enabled Android smartphone will be used as ubiquitous NFC card reader.**

Keywords-mobile authentication; identity management; strong two-factor authentication; high trust level.

I. Introduction and Motivation

Digital identities have gained more and more importance due to the rapid increase of digitalization within our administration, business, industry, and information society. In this paper, we present a new mobile e-government application using the new German National Identity Card with the electronic identity (eID) function for Internet use. In cooperation with the Hessian Ministry of the Interior (Government of the Federal State of Hessen) [10], as well as AUTHADA GmbH [11] and the ekom21 KGRZ Hessen [12], a secure and user-friendly de-registration of a car as off the road mobile e-government service will be presented.

The consumer research company GfK [13] determined in May 2015 that only 5% of all Germans used their eID function of the National Identity Card for online authentication services within the past 12 months [6]. Most probably, there are two main reasons for that disappointing result: First, there are only few services (164 in total, 2015-05) with eID support available on the market. Thus, the German citizen may not see a significant benefit in using eID. Second, for the online authentication, there is a special eID card reader needed, which costs between 30 and 160 Euros. For eID card holders, the need of an expensive card reader may be the biggest barrier. We will overcome this barrier and present a new approach where an NFC-enabled Android smartphone is used as ubiquitous eID card reader.

In order to demonstrate a significant benefit for the citizens and users, we implemented the new approach for a very popular and useful online service, namely, the de-registration of a vehicle as off the road. Therefore, an Android app and a Website were implemented in order to be able to carry out the complete process of the vehicle de-registration in a mobile and user-friendly way in order to provide the Hessian citizens the possibility to avoid the annoying paperwork and the long waiting time. The de-registration of a vehicle as off the road is also a good best-practice example of an electronic government service with required trust level "high". The paper is structured as follows. In Section II, some definitions of terms are given. Section III shows the stationary Internet-based de-registration of a vehicle as off the road. Following this, Section IV introduces the new German National Identity Card with eID function for Internet use. The stationary online authentication process is shown in Section V. In Section VI, the new mobile authentication process is presented in detail. Section VII ends this paper with a conclusion and outlook on future work.

II. Definitions and Fundamentals

Electronic government (e-government) [1] is the use of electronic communications devices, computers and the Internet to provide public services to citizens and other persons in a country or region. Electronic authentication [2] is the process of establishing confidence in user identities, electronically presented to an information system. Digital authentication or e-authentication may be used synonymously when referring to the authentication process that confirms or certifies a person's identity and works.

AUTHADA ID Service [5] is a server operated by the company AUTHADA GmbH. This provides the authentication process via an API, or a software development kit (SDK). The AUTHADA ID service serves as an interface to a certified e-ID server, which is authorized to read the data from the personal ID card. Within the implemented representational state transfer (REST) server [5], a Java library was included, which contains the calls to the AUTHADA service. Near field communication (NFC) [3] is a set of communication protocols which allow the communication between two devices by bringing them within 4 cm of each other. Quick Response Code (QR code) [4] is a machine-readable optical label that contains information about the item to which it is attached. A QR code uses four standardized encoding modes (numeric, alphanumeric, byte/binary, and kanji) to efficiently store data. Representational state transfer (REST) [5] relies on a stateless, client-server, cacheable communications protocol -- and in virtually all cases, the Hypertext Transfer Protocol (HTTP) over Transport Layer Security (TLS) 1.2 is used, also known as HTTP Secure (HTTPS). REST is often used in mobile applications, social networking Web sites, mashup tools and automated business processes. The REST style emphasizes that interactions between clients and services is enhanced by having a limited number of operations (verbs). Flexibility is provided by assigning resources (nouns) their own unique universal resource indicators (URIs).

III. INTERNET-BASED DE-REGISTRATION OF A VEHICLE AS OF THE ROAD

Since January 1st 2015, it is possible to request the de-registration of a motor vehicle (car) as off the road online.

The following prerequisites are hereby necessary:

- New German National Identity card (Figure 5) with activated online eID function for Internet use and a correspondent card reader.
- Certificate of approval Part I ("vehicle registration", in German "Fahrzeugschein") with concealed security code, see Figure 1.
- License plates (front and back) with new stamped chain with concealed security code (vehicles which have been registered or re-registered since January 1st, 2015), see Figure 3.

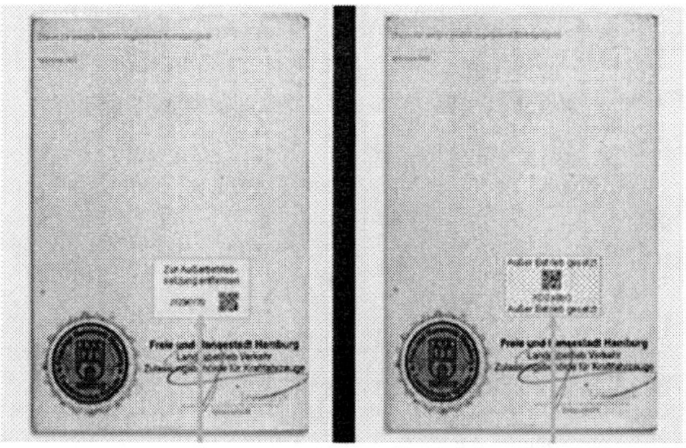

Figure 1. Certificate of Approval Part I ("vehicle registration") with concealed (left) and uncovered (right) security code.

The application is as follows:

(1) Take the Certificate of approval Part I ("vehicle registration", see Figure 1). On the backside of the approval certificate Part I ("vehicle registration") there is a seal label with the concealed security code (a security code example is shown in Figure 2).

(2) Figure 2 shows three different states of scratching and un-coveing the 7-digits security code of the seal label: (On the left) original seal label on Certificate of Approval Part I ("vehicle registration"), (middle) scratched and partly un-covered security code, and (right) the 7-digits security code completely scratched and un-covered.

Figure 2. Seal label on Certificate of Approval Part I ("vehicle registration",)

Figure 3. License plates with seal labels, which contains the concealed 3-digits security codes, and Certificate of Approval Part I ("vehicle registration", see Figure 1) with concealed 7-digits security code.

(3) Take both license plates (front and back) with the seal labels, which contain the concealed security codes. Scratch and un-cover the two 3-digits security codes of the seal labels. (One security code is shown in Figure 4).

Figure 4. Seal label on license plate (left), scratching and un-cover the security code (middle), 3-digits security code (right).

(4) Scan the security code or scan it as a data matrix code (QR code).

(5) Online-Identification of the vehicle owner using the German identity card (eID) with online function, or electronic residence permit (eAT) with online function, on the Website of the central, municipal or national portal.

(6) Enter the vehicle registration code and the three security codes in the application form of the portal.

(7) Pay by ePayment system.

(8) A click and the vehicle is logged off and de-registered as off the road with the date of the processing in the approval authority after the data has been transferred to the relevant approval authority (determined by the indicator).

(9) The statutory off road notification (SORN) is served by electronic mail.

The new German National Identity Card is therefore mandatory for the Internet-based de-registration of a motor vehicle (car) as off the road in order to secure the identity of the car owner.

IV. THE GERMAN NATIONAL IDENTITY CARD

One of the main problems in the implementation and realization of electronic and mobile government services is the secure and user-friendly authentication of the citizens. Many administrative government services still require the written form. However, the Administrative Procedure Act (Verwaltungsverfahrensgesetz VwVfG) §3a allows the written form to be replaced by the electronic form provided that the law does not specify otherwise. A mandatory prerequisite for this is that the sender can be unambiguously identified and the integrity of the data is guaranteed. One possibility for this is the electronic identity-proof using the new German National Identity Card (eID), see Figure 5.

Figure 5. German National eID Card

The new German National Identity Card was introduced on November 1st, 2010.
It looks different from the former ID card

- Smartcard format
- Integrated NFC-chip
- eID function for Internet use, vending machines or terminals
- Stored biometric passport photograph and voluntary storage of fingerprints to clearly match the ID card with the ID card holder
- Electronic signature function to electronically sign binding contracts, applications, documents, etc. (must be purchased separately)
- Enhanced security features
- Special protection of biometric data

A) Data printed on the ID card

Like the former ID card, the national ID card with eID function is an official photo ID with the personal data of the ID card holder printed on the document: family name, name at birth, given names, doctoral degree, date of birth, place of birth, photograph, signature, height, eyes color, address, postal code, citizenship, serial number, religious, stage or pen name if applicable.

B) Data stored in the NFC-Chip

The new German national ID card also contains a contactless, readable biometric passport NFC-chip. This NFC-chip stores all data which are printed on the ID card. Additionally, this NFC-chip stores a biometric passport photograph of the card holder and, if desired the biometric fingerprints. The cardholder decides whether the fingerprint data will be stored on the ID card or not.

C) Applications of the eID Online Function

The eID online function is offered by service providers that wish to make registration procedures easier and more secure for users. This includes, for example, the online services of banks and insurance companies. However, also public authorities offer online identification, for instance when you register your car or apply for child benefits. Users can identify themselves not only on the Internet, but also at vending machines and the self-service terminals in public authorities.

V. STATIONARY ONLINE AUTHENTICATION PROCESS

As prerequisites for the strong two-factor online authentication process of a German citizen there are the following ingredients needed: The new German eID card with an activated online eID function and a corresponding NFC card reader, or an NFC-enabled Android-smartphone.

A secure connection between the user's eID card and the eID authentication system of the service provider is established for online identification. The eID server ensures reciprocal authentication of both sides.

The online authentication process with the eID card is as follows (using the example of a Web service):

(1) The card holder opens the provider's Web service requiring online authentication.

(2) The service transmits the authentication request to the eID server.

(3) A secure channel is established between the eID server,

the client software (e.g. AusweisApp2), the card reader and the ID card's chip, and the authenticity of the service provider and the authenticity and integrity of the eID card (protection against forgery) are checked.

(4) The client software shows the card holder the service provider's authorization certificate and the requested personal data categories. The eID card holder decides which personal data he/she wishes to transmit.

(5) By entering the 6-digits PIN the eID card holder confirms the transmission of his/her data.

(6) The eID card data are sent to the eID server.

(7) The eID server sends an authentication response and the eID card data to the service.

(8) The authentication response and the ID card data are retrieved. The service checks the authentication results and decides whether the authentication was successful. A response is then sent to the user and/or the service is provided.

VI. MOBILE AUTHENTICATION APPROACH IN DETAIL

The high level architecture of the mobile de-registration of a vehicle as off the road service is shown in Figure 6 below. At the beginning of authentication, the user has two options available. Either he performs the complete process through our Android app or he uses our QR Code Website solution.

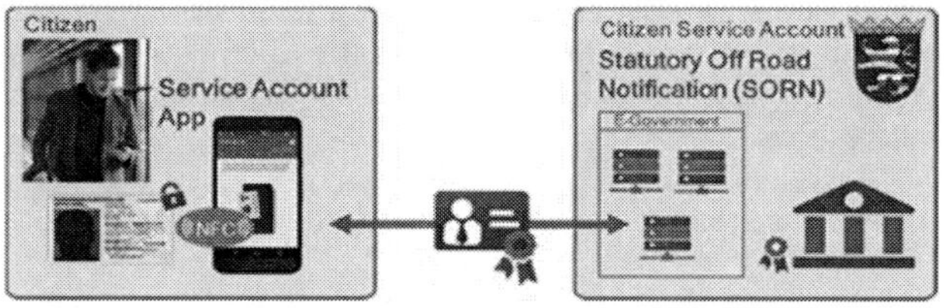

Figure 6. High level overview of the mobile de-registration of a vehicle as off the road service

1. Authentication through our Website

The complete process of de-registration of a vehicle as off the road can be done with our QR code solution. This means that the user performs the actual login process via our Website and uses the app only to scan the generated QR and set the displayed transaction number (TAN) into the corresponding field in the Website.

A) Technical infrastructure

A Linux-based virtual machine from Darmstadt University is used as server platform. A Tomcat Web server was installed on this site, which serves as a container for all developed Web applications. A MariaDB SQL database [14] is used to store the authentication procedures, as well as the vehicle data and log-off procedures. An AUTHADA service is used as a third-party system for identification with the new ID card.

B) Rest – Server

To enable platform-independent communication with various terminals, a REST server based on the Jersey framework [15] was developed as a server application. The task of the REST interface basically consists of two parts. On one hand, it is used to authenticate a customer, using the new ID card. It can also be used to log off a vehicle after successful authentication. Further applications are possible and could be integrated into the architecture. A sequence and message flow of the strong two-factor online authentication of a citizen in order to logout of a vehicle can be seen in Figure 7.

C) Process

The authentication is started at AUTHADA via an integrated library. The obtained data from AUTHADA are first stored in a database and then passed to the caller. With the information obtained, the actual authentication process is now started via the smartphone app or via the Website. The customer identifies himself with his personal ID using the AUTHADA e-Service.

The result of the authentication is a so-called result token. Together with the session information from the first step, the result token is now sent to the server, which in return transfers this information to the AUTHADA e-service and, as a result, receives the read-out customer data from the personal ID card. This data is then stored in the database and linked to the current session. As a result, the REST interface provides only here whether the process was successful or not. In the next step, the customer data that belongs to the respective session can then be retrieved. After this step, the customer's authentication is completed and the vehicle log-off process can be started. In order to request a vehicle cancellation, the vehicle data must first be transmitted together with the session ID. These data must contain at least the label, as well as the necessary security codes. After transmission, the system checks whether the transmitted security codes match the codes stored in the database. For this purpose, some fictitious test codes including security codes were created in the database. Furthermore, it must, of course, be checked whether the authenticated customer is at all entitled to cancel the desired vehicle.

2. Authentication via an NFC-enabled Android app

The complete authentication message flow between the Android App and the eID authentication Server (eID-Server) is shown in detail in Figure 7. The complete process of the de-registration of a vehicle as off the road can also be done with an Android using the AUTHADA SDK and an NFC-enabled mobile, which serves as a reading device to the new German identity card.

After the user decides to execute the login process via the app, he has to accept the privacy policy. Only after this he will be able to do the authentication. After a successful authentication the personal ID data are displayed and the user receives an application form, which must be completed. Before submitting the form, the user's inputs are immediately validated on the client side looking for an error (for example, a security code can only be 3 digits), and the corresponding input validation errors are displayed under the input fields. If the form is valid, the user gets a list of the charges incurred (data coming from the server). If he accepts the costs by touching the button "Compulsory vehicle logout", the log-off process is completed. The user is shown a Success page and then redirected to the start page. In addition, all transactions information (session token) stored until then are removed from the shared preferences (application stored data).

At each step, the user can safely cancel or terminate the vehicle logout by tapping the back button. For this, a dialog is displayed on his mobile terminal with the text "Do you want to terminate the vehicle de-registration?". If the user confirms this dialog with "Yes", he returns to the start page. The session token is also removed from the shared preferences. The following main steps are used to communicate with the eID authentication server (also called eID-Server), see Figure 7:

- Request of an Auth and Session Token
- Transmission of the TAN after successful authentication using the ID card
- Request of the user's read-out ID card data
- Transfer of the input form data
- Confirmation of the vehicle decommissioning

For this purpose, a REST client was implemented, which is able to address the specified REST API of our server. The required data between the app and the server are exchanged in JavaScript Object Notation (JSON) [15] format. Before any request to the server, a check is made as to whether an active Internet connection is available. If this is not the case, the user is shown a message that he must activate his mobile data or WLAN to continue and also he has the possibility to open the settings directly from the app.

All HTTPS connections are implemented and realized with TLS 1.2. If the server is not reachable, or if the response cannot be processed or properly desterilized by the server, the user receives an error message with the request to try again later. From here, he has only the possibility to close the process completely and then reaches the start page. The user is then shown the message that he is not authorized to log off this vehicle and can adjust his inputs again. In order to still be able to use the app in the case of the inadequate availability of our server or to run the logoff process, a mock was developed for test purposes in addition to the real implementation. Before the start of the vehicle logging process, you have the possibility to choose for real or mocked implementation. In the case of the muted variant, the authentication is completely skipped by means of the personal ID card. In addition, the REST requests do not run against our server, but against a mock server [9], which provides static data to successfully test the logoff process.

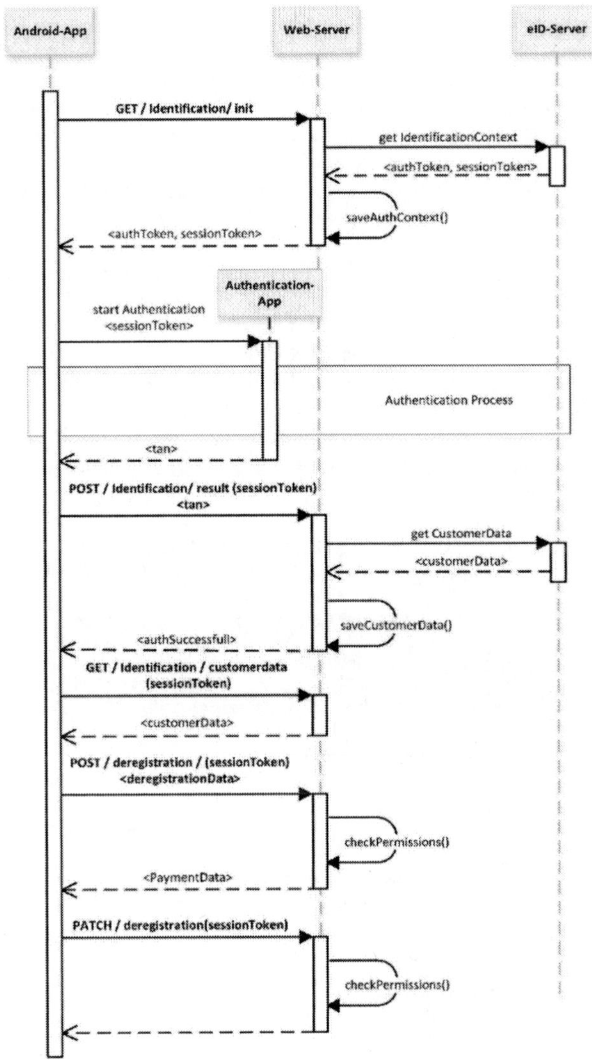

Figure 7. Detailed authentication message flowchart between Android App and eID Authentication Server

VII. CONCLUSION AND OUTLOOK

We presented a new approach for a mobile de-registration of a vehicle as off the road. The new mobile de-registration service of a vehicle as off the road is secure and user-friendly.

The new approach implements a strong two-factor authentication with German eID card and the corresponding 6-digits PIN, whereby a NFC-enabled Android smartphone will be used as ubiquitous NFC card reader. The new solution overcomes the need to buy a specific NFC card reader. Instead, a NFC-enabled Android smartphone will be used.

The big advance for the citizen and users are, in summary: They need not to drive to the government agency, and they save the long waiting times at the agency. So in practice, the citizen save to spend a vacation day for the de-registration of a vehicle as off the road and the Statutory Off Road Notification (SORN). The mobile de-registration service allows the citizens to register their vehicle as off the road (SORN) easily via an Android Smartphone App. In doing so, the electronic identity (eID) of their German eID card will be transmitted via NFC directly via the Android smartphone. Just a few clicks later, the user has registered his/her vehicle as off the road (SORN).

Therefore, here is what the citizen and user needs, in detail: An Android smartphone with enabled NFC functionality, the German eID card with activated online-function and the associated 6-digit PIN, as well as the number/registration plates and vehicle registration license (after 01.01.2015) with three security codes.

The user will find the three security codes on the back of the vehicle registration license, and under the vehicle seal labels on the license plates (front and back).

A strong two-factor authentication ensures the necessary safety and unambiguous identification of the vehicle owner.

Figure 8. Screenshot of App how to enter the vehicle registration code and the three security codes in the application form.
Kennzeicheninformationen =license plate information
Sicherheitscodes = security codes from seal labels on the license plates (front and back), as well as from seal label on Certificate of Approval Part I ("vehicle registration")

A screenshot of the new app, how to enter the vehicle registration code and the three security codes in the application form, is shown in Figure 8. The main advantages of the new mobile government solution (as short overview) are the following:

- Quick and easily Statutory Off Road Notification (SORN) of the Vehicle
- Mobile and secure using the Android smartphone app.
- Strong 2-factor authentication (with eID card + PIN).
- No need for an expensive eID card reader.
- Without biometry, TAN and media breaks.

ACKNOWLEDGMENTS

This work was supported by the Hessian Ministry of the Interior and Sports (HMdIS, Government of the Federal State of Hessen), Project "Mobiles Servicekonto Hessen".

REFERENCES

[1] http://www.egov4dev.org/success/definitions.shtml, last access 4th November 2017.

[2] https://www.cryptomathic.com/news-events/blog/digital-authentication-the-basics, last access 4th November 2017.

[3] http://nearfieldcommunication.org/, last access 4th November 2017.

[4] http://www.investopedia.com/terms/q/quick-response-qr-code.asp, last access 4th November 2017.

[5] http://rest.elkstein.org/, last access 4th November 2017.

[6] GfK SE (2015) http://www.gfk.com/insights/news/fuenf-prozent-nutzen-elektronischen-personalausweis, last access 4th November 2017.

[7] F. Otterbein, T. Ohlendorf, and M. Margraf: "Mobile Authentication with German eID", IFIP Summer School 2016.

[8] AusweisApp2 for download: www.ausweisapp.bund.de, last access 4th November 2017.

[9] http://www.mocky.io, last access 4th November 2017.

[10] https://english.hessen.de, last access 4th November 2017.

[11] https://www.authada.de, last access 4th November 2017.

[12] https://ekom21.de, last access 4th November 2017.

[13] http://www.gfk.com, last access 4th November 2017.

[14] https://mariadb.org, last access 4th November 2017.

[15] https://jersey.github.io, last access 4th November 2017.

[16] http://www.json.org, last access 4th November 2017.

Torrent Forensics: Are your Files Being Shared in the BitTorrent Network?

Ali Alhazmi

Department of Information Systems
Jazan University
Jazan, Saudi Arabia 45142
Email: alihazmi@jazanu.edu.sa

Gabriel Maciá-Fernández

Network Engineering and Security Group, CITIC-UGR
University of Granada
Granada, Spain 18071
Email: gmacia@ugr.es

José Camacho

Network Engineering and Security Group, CITIC-UGR
University of Granada
Granada, Spain 18071
Email: josecamacho@ugr.es

Saeed Salah

Department of Computer Science
Al-Quds University
Abu Dees, Palestine 20002
Email: sasalah@staff.alquds.edu

***Abstract*—BitTorrent is the most common protocol for file sharing nowadays. Due to its distributed nature, monitoring BitTorrent is a difficult task. Under this perception of anonymity, BitTorrent has motivated the rise of criminal activities such as copyright infringement or the sharing of stolen secret documents. This work-in-progress paper focuses on identifying whether a given resource has been shared in the BitTorrent network. We have termed this problem *torrent forensics*. We propose a methodology to solve this problem as well as the design of an operational system to implement the solution. The system is run in two different phases. First, we monitor the network and collect *.torrent* files that describe the resources being shared. Second, a detection module analyzes a given resource and decides if it was observed in the network. We carry out preliminary experiments to support the hypotheses for the design of the system.**

***Keywords*–BitTorrent; P2P; Torrent Forensics.**

I. Introduction

Recently, Recently, peer-to-peer (P2P) has become popular for sharing-files around the world. P2P networks are often used to share diverse digital contents such as movies, music, books, and software. According to Cisco's estimation in 2015, P2P file-sharing users consumed 5,965 petabytes of traffic per month, which was about 15% of all the Internet traffic [1]. BitTorrent is the most common P2P file sharing nowadays. It is estimated to be responsible for more than 50% of file-sharing bandwidth and 3.35% of all total bandwidth [2]. There are millions of users sharing a huge amount of resources everyday. According to [3], BitTorrent had 15-27 million concurrent users at any time in 2013. In addition, BitTorrent Inc. claims that more than 170 million people use BitTorrent products every month [4].

The widespread popularity of BitTorrent has attracted the attention of many researchers, with the aim of studying the nature of shared resources and developing monitoring methodologies to understand the traffic evolution [5]–[8]. Bauer *et al.* [9] proposed active methods to monitor extremely large BitTorrent swarms using trackers. They developed an active probing framework called BitStalker that identifies active peers and collects concrete forensic evidences showing that they were involved in the sharing of a particular resource. Additionally, there exist some works focused on crawling *torrent-discovery sites* [7]. In the previous reference work, five of the most popular torrent-discovery sites were crawled over a nine-month period, identifying 4.6M of torrents and 38,996 trackers. They also obtained peer lists from the Vuze and Mainline Distributed Hash Tables (DHTs) in order to investigate the nature of the exchanged contents. Authors of [10] worked on large-scale monitoring of BitTorrent, crawling resources from two torrent-discovery sites: Pirate Bay and Mininova. They collected 148M of IP addresses and 2M resources over 103 days in order to identify content providers and highly-active users. Other works focus on the crawling of Mainline DHT [5] [11]. Authors in [11] collected 10M magnet links and received over 264M `get_peers` messages from more than 57M unique peers over 10 days in order to provide statistical information. In their resultsthey found that, for example, Russian and China were playing dominant roles in Mainline DHT, contributing 35% of peers, and that 5% Internet users using Mainline came from Europe.

The major contribution of this work-in-progress paper is different from those in the mentioned works. It focuses on the specific problem of identifying whether a given resource has been shared in the BitTorrent network. We have termed this problem *torrent forensics*, due to its forensic nature. To our knowledge, there is no previous published research on this topic. From a cyber security perspective, many participants can take advantage of a solution to this problem. The most widespread interest comes from end users, who may be interested in identifying

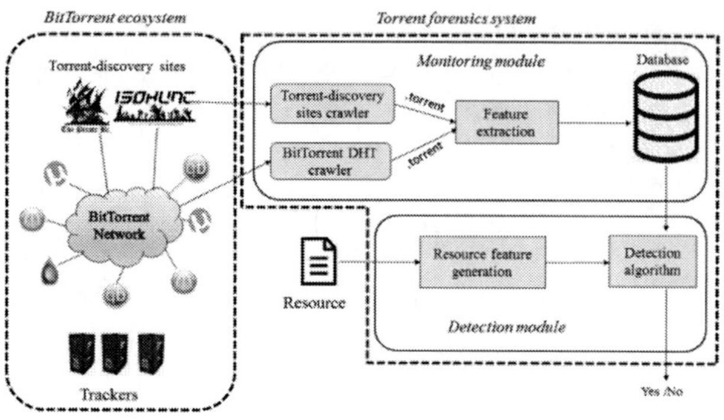

Figure 1. Architecture of the torrent forensics system.

if their private files or images are being shared in the BitTorrent network; another example is that of companies that have confidential documents and could also be interested in monitoring possible information leakages; finally, identifying the sharing of copyright materials is essential for many industries.

We propose a methodology to solve the problem of *torrent forensics* and an operational system to implement this solution. The proposed system considers two different phases. First, *.torrent* files that describe the resources being shared in the network are collected by monitoring both torrent-discovery sites and the BitTorrent DHT network. Subsequently, we build a database with the relevant features of the resources previously monitored. A main advantage of this approach is that only metadata of the resources, and not the resources themselves, need to be downloaded from the network. This saves time and storage space. In a second phase, we design a module capable of analyzing a given document and deciding if it is present in our database by comparing its features with those in the database. In this work-in-progress paper, there are some preliminary experiments to validate the main hypotheses under which our system is built.

The remainder of this paper is organized as follows. Section II discusses the design of our system and explains its components. Section III describes the experiments to evaluate the main hypotheses our system is based on. Finally, we draw conclusions and outline some future work in Section IV.

II. Torrent Forensics System

Here, we describe the design of the torrent forensics system and discuss the details and hypotheses in which it is based on. As shown in Figure 1, the system contains two main modules:

- *A monitoring module:* It is responsible for monitoring the BitTorrent network in order to obtain *.torrent* files of the resources being shared in the network. This module is also in charge of extracting some features from these files and building a database containing the monitored information.
- *A detection module:* It runs in parallel with the other module. It takes a given document as input, processes it and detects if it has been shared in the network by comparing its features with those saved in the database of monitored resources.

A. Monitoring Module

The monitoring module for our system is based on three submodules: (a) a torrent-discovery sites crawler, (b) a BitTorrent DHT crawler and (c) a feature extraction module.

1) Torrent-Discovery Sites Crawler: The purpose of the torrent-discovery sites crawler is to obtain *.torrent* files of resources that are being published in the BitTorrent network. Recall that torrent-discovery sites publish *.torrent* files that are previously uploaded by users or transferred from other torrent discovery sites. These sites usually have a query interface that allows users to get information by using an Application Program Interface (API).

In order to obtain *.torrent* files from these sites, two different strategies follow:

- Passive search: when available, Rich Site Summary (RSS) feeds to get updated information from the site about new *.torrent* files announced in the network.
- Active search: it is possible to use active crawling navigation of the web pages of the torrent-discovery sites or use APIs provided by these sites to query for existing *.torrent* files.

2) BitTorrent DHT Crawler: The main goal of this module is to obtain *.torrent* files of resources being announced in the BitTorrent DHT. For this module, we use a similar strategy to that used by the authors in [12], namely, we adapt the crawling mechanism to enable the collection of features that are used in our detection algorithm. Note that the process followed is specific for Mainline DHT, although minor modifications can be extended to the Vuze DHT [13].

The crawling process is as follows. It first gets a list of the active nodes in a specific zone of the network by sending `find_node` messages to a list of bootstrap nodes. Bootstrap nodes are used to join the network initially. Their addresses can either be hardcoded in the client software or looked up in a known directory. Subsequently, we keep active communications with them by sending `ping` messages periodically. Then, a great amount of sybil nodes are inserted as neighbors in the chosen zone of the network, in order to be included in the routing tables of known nodes in that zone. At this point, when legitimate nodes share a resource, they send `announce_peer` messages periodically, containing the *infohash* for that resource.

Once a new infohash is observed, the associated *.torrent* file must be collected. For this purpose, we send a `get_peers` message for that *infohash*, obtaining the list of peers in the swarm. Then, we query those peers so that they send us the *.torrent* file. For this purpose, the BitTorrent extension for peers to send metadata files [14] is used, in a similar way as magnet links are used to download a resource.

3) Feature Extraction: This module takes *.torrent* files as inputs from the crawling modules, and extract some features from them. A parser processes these files to read bencoded information and extract these features: (i) the *name* of the resource as identified in the *.torrent* file; (ii)

```
function GENERATE_SHA1_LIST(resource)
    Initialize piece_size_list
    SHA1_list = ∅
    for piece_size in piece_size_list do
        pieces ← split(resource,piece_size)
        SHA1_list + = SHA-1(pieces)
    end for
    return SHA1_list
end function
```

Figure 2. Algorithm to generate *SHA1_list* for a given resource.

the *length* of the resource in bytes; (iii) the *piece_size*; and (iv) a Secure Hash Algorithm *SHA1_list*, *i.e.*, a list of SHA-1 hashes, one for every piece that forms the resource. Finally, all this information is logged into a database, where each record includes the mentioned features for every *.torrent* file.

B. Detection module

The main aim of this module is to identify if the features obtained for a given resource are present in the monitored resources database. It is composed of two submodules: a *resource feature generation* module and a *detection algorithm* module.

1) Resource Feature Generation: This module takes the resource of interest, that is the one we are looking, as an input. In it, we emulate the data processing prior to uploading the file to the Bittorrent network. The goal is to generate the set of features that will allow the next module (detection algorithm) to find if the resource is present in the database or not. Obtaining the *length* and the *name* of the resource is straightforward. In order to obtain the *SHA1_list*, the resource is needed to be split into pieces of *piece_size* bytes and the corresponding hashes need to be calculated. The problem here is that the *piece_size* that was used in case the resource was uploaded to the network is unknown. As a matter of fact, as we will show later, the same resource may have been uploaded several times to the network with different *piece_size* values. For this reason, a list of possible candidate values for *piece_size* is selected and an *SHA1_list* is generated for every considered value. The final *SHA1_list* is compiled by joining all these SHA1 lists into a single one (see Figure 2). In Section III, we discuss a selection method for the candidate values for *piece_size*.

2) Detection algorithm: The main aim of this module is to detect whether the set of features obtained by the previous module are present in the monitored resources database. The algorithm used is shown in Figure 3. Recall that our database contains, for every resource, a record with the *name*, *length*, *piece_size* and *SHA1_list* features. *length* and *piece_size* will first be used to narrow our search and speed up the searching process, selecting only those resources with exact match. Note also that the *SHA1_list* is considered instead of the *infohash* of the resource. The main reason is that, as it is shown in Section III, BitTorrent clients might generate different *infohashes* even for a same resource. On the contrary, the *SHA1_list* remains unaltered when generating a *.torrent* file with different BitTorrent clients. Observe that the *name* is not considered in the search. Actually this feature is included to add semantic information in case a resource was renamed before being shared in BitTorrent.

Finally, our proposed system is highly dependent on two algorithms i.e. generate *SHA1_list* and search algorithm. Therefore, if any of two algorithms does not work for any reason, the proposed system will be useless.

```
function SEARCH(length,piece_size,SHA1_list)
    records ← getRecordsFromDB(length,piece_size)
    for record in records do
        if record.SHA1-l in SHA1_list then
            return True
        end if
    end for
    return False
end function
```

Figure 3. Algorithm to search in the database for features extracted of a given resource.

III. PRELIMINARY EXPERIMENTS

As indicated in our introduction, in this work-in-progress paper we are only interested in verifying that the main hypotheses for the design of our torrent forensic system are validated by experimental support.

First, we check how *infohashes* for a same resource are distinct when different BitTorrent clients are used and the reasons behind that. This supports our design decision to search information in the database based on the *SHA1_list* instead of using *infohashes*.

Nowadays, there exist more than 50 BitTorrent clients that are freely available [15]. To check that *infohashes* generated by different clients for a single resource are not necessarily the same, the four most used BitTorrent clients have been selected [16] in their current versions: uTorrent v3.5 [17], Deluge v1.3.12 [18], Vuze v5.7.5.0/4 [19], and bitComet v1.45 [20]. Then, a PDF file with size 96 MB has been uploaded to every selected BitTorrent client. We choose 128 KB as piece size for all clients, obtaining the corresponding *.torrent* files with the values shown in Table I. The table shows that the *infohashes* are different.

TABLE I. INFOHASHES FOR A 96MB PDF FILE

BT client	Infohash
uTorrent	C31527AA36F7F27744C653E216B9C175223E8672
Deluge	381B9A152F902FAF16A39BEBD1A72CC56F946756
Vuze	B36F6AA3FBED37108A0AF3EB07F4D8B7C139C38A
BitComet	FEB8AAA48EAC7A6A33C61270459194F2FEB233DA

We have investigated the reasons behind these differences in the *infohashes* among BitTorrent clients. We found that there are some differences in the `info` section generated for the *.torrent* file. First, a private parameter is added in Deluge client, even when the torrent is not private. Second, the name of the file is inserted by the Vuze client in a different place than in the others, locating it after the *SHA1_list* of hashes. Finally, the order of other parameters, such as the name, length and piece's length also lead to different *infohashes* for our selected

BitTorrent clients. In conclusion, these minor differences in the `info` section lead to different *infohashes*. Yet, in all our experiments, we have checked that the *SHA1_list* for all the pieces remains the same with all the clients. Therefore, *infohashes* cannot be used for torrent forensics, while the *SHA1_list* can.

The second hypothesis that this paper is interested to validate is with regard to the need of generating different *SHA1_lists* for every piece size in the 'document feature generation' module. The selection of a value for the piece size is a matter of optimizing the transfer speed for the download of the resource. According to the recommendation in [21], a torrent should have 1000-1500 pieces in order to get reasonably small torrent file pieces and an efficient download. In many clients, there is an auto-size option that generates *.torrent* files choosing the *piece size* parameter automatically. In our experiment, we check if all the BitTorrent clients implement the auto-size option in a similar way or they differ. We upload a file of size 175 MB to the same selected BitTorrent clients except Deluge because it does not have the auto-size option. The results from this experiment show that Vuze splits our file by 128 KB while uTorrent and BitComet choose to split it by 256KB even though the size of the file is the same. Thus, we confirm the need to generate different *SHA1_lists* for every possible piece size in the 'document feature generation' module.

Finally, regarding the initialization of the `piece_size_candidate_list` parameter in Figure 2, we consider that a good set of values are those offered to the users by these set of BitTorrent clients, *i.e.*, the set given by $j \cdot 16KB, j \in [1, 11]$ (most common clients) and $j \cdot 48\ KB, j \in [1, 7]$ (only Vuze client).

IV. Conclusions and Future Work

In this paper, we have suggested a methodology and designed a system to identify whether a given resource has been shared in the BitTorrent network. The system is based on two main modules:(i) a monitoring module to crawl the network and obtain *.torrent* files of shared resources, extracting features and saving them in a database; and (ii) a detection module, that finds if a given resource has been observed during the monitoring of the network.

Our system is currently a prototype that shows the feasibility of a partial solution for the Torrent Forensics problem. Some scale experiments should be done to complete the conclusions obtained in this paper. In addition, as future work, we plan to deal with the problem when the resources are modified before being shared in the network.

Acknowledgment

This work is supported by Jazan University through the Saudi Arabian Cultural Mission in Spain, the Spanish Ministry of Economy, and FEDER funds through project TIN2014-60346-R.

References

[1] "White paper: Cisco vni forecast and methodology 2015-2020," http://www.cisco.com/c/en/us/solutions/collateral/service-provider/visual-networking-index-vni/complete-white-paper-c11-481360.html, [retrieved: September, 2017].

[2] M. Scanlon and H. Shen, "An analysis of bittorrent cross-swarm peer participation and geolocational distribution," in Computer Communication and Networks (ICCCN), 2014 23rd International Conference on. IEEE, 2014, pp. 1–6.

[3] L. Wang and J. Kangasharju, "Measuring large-scale distributed systems: case of bittorrent mainline dht," in Peer-to-Peer Computing (P2P), 2013 IEEE Thirteenth International Conference on. IEEE, 2013, pp. 1–10.

[4] "Bittorrent." [Online]. Available: http://www.bittorrent.com/company/about [retrieved: September, 2017].

[5] R. A. Rodríguez-Gómez, G. Maciá-Fernández, L. Sánchez-Casado, and P. García-Teodoro, "Analysis and modelling of resources shared in the bittorrent network," Transactions on Emerging Telecommunications Technologies, vol. 26, no. 10, 2015, pp. 1189–1200.

[6] N. Andrade, E. Santos-Neto, F. Brasileiro, and M. Ripeanu, "Resource demand and supply in bittorrent content-sharing communities," Computer Networks, vol. 53, no. 4, 2009, pp. 515–527.

[7] C. Zhang, P. Dhungel, D. Wu, and K. W. Ross, "Unraveling the bittorrent ecosystem," IEEE Transactions on Parallel and Distributed Systems, vol. 22, no. 7, 2011, pp. 1164–1177.

[8] P. K. Hoong, I. K. Tan, and C. Y. Keong, "Bittorrent network traffic forecasting with arma," arXiv preprint arXiv:1208.1896, 2012.

[9] K. Bauer, D. McCoy, D. Grunwald, and D. Sicker, "Bitstalker: Accurately and efficiently monitoring bittorrent traffic," in Information Forensics and Security, 2009. WIFS 2009. First IEEE International Workshop on. IEEE, 2009, pp. 181–185.

[10] S. L. Blond, A. Legout, F. L. Fessant, W. Dabbous, and M. A. Kaafar, "Spying the world from your laptop–identifying and profiling content providers and big downloaders in bittorrent," arXiv preprint arXiv:1004.0930, 2010.

[11] Z. Xinxing, T. Zhihong, and Z. Luchen, "A measurement study on mainline dht and magnet link," in Data Science in Cyberspace DSC, IEEE International Conference on. IEEE, 2016, pp. 11–19.

[12] R. A. Rodríguez-Gómez, G. Maciá-Fernández, P. García-Teodoro, M. Steiner, and D. Balzarotti, "Resource monitoring for the detection of parasite p2p botnets," Computer Networks, vol. 70, 2014, pp. 302–311.

[13] S. Wolchok and J. a. Halderman, "Crawling bittorrent dhts for fun and profit," Proc 4th USENIX Workshop on Offensive Technologies, 2010, pp. 1–8.

[14] G. Hazel and A. Norberg, "Bittorrent specification. extension for peers to send metadata files," 2017. [Online]. Available: http://bittorrent.org/beps/bep_0009.html [retrieved: September, 2017].

[15] "Bittorrent clients." [Online]. Available: http://en.wikipedia.org/wiki/BitTorrent_client [retrieved: September, 2017].

[16] W. Mazurczyk and P. Kopiczko, "Understanding bittorrent through real measurements," China Communications, vol. 10, no. 11, 2013, pp. 107–118.

[17] "utorrent." [Online]. Available: http://www.utorrent.com/ [retrieved: September, 2017].

[18] "Deluge." [Online]. Available: http://deluge-torrent.org/ [retrieved: September, 2017].

[19] "Vuze." [Online]. Available: http://www.vuze.com/ [retrieved: September, 2017].

[20] "Bitcomet." [Online]. Available: https://www.bitcomet.com/en/downloads [retrieved: September, 2017].

[21] "Torrent piece size." [Online]. Available: http://wiki.vuze.com/w/Torrent_Piece_Size [retrieved: September, 2017].

Citizen Sensing for Environmental Risk Communication

Action Research on $PM_{2.5}$ Air Quality Monitoring in East Asia

Yang Ishigaki and Kenji Tanaka
Graduate School of Informatics and Engineering
University of Electro-Communications
Tokyo, Japan
Email: pokega@tanaka.is.uec.ac.jp

Yoshinori Matsumoto
Faculty of Science and Technology
Keio University
Kanagawa, Japan
Email: matsumoto@appi.keio.ac.jp

Harrizki Arie Pradana
STMIK Atma Luhur Pangkalpinang
Bangka Island, Indonesia
Email: harrizkiariep@atmaluhur.ac.id

Yasuko Yamada Maruo
Department of Environment and Energy
Tohoku Institute of Technology
Miyagi, Japan
Email: y-y-maruo@tohtech.ac.jp

***Abstract*— Air pollution is becoming a serious global health issue. We propose a risk communication method called 3D (detection, data sharing and discussion) to ensure risk awareness for environmental hazards for individual citizens. This paper presents a prototype system of a sensor connected to smartphone which detects $PM_{2.5}$ (Particle Matter with aerodynamic diameters $\leq$ 2.5 *u*m). Preliminary field tests showed that $PM_{2.5}$ concentration levels differed in the regions we tested in the East-Asian countries. As a next step, we plan to a conduct risk communication experiment through social media discussion involving local residents, experts and public sector, to ensure risk awareness and education of individuals.**

Keywords - participatory sensing; AQI (Air Quality Index).

I. INTRODUCTION

WHO (World Health Organization) estimated that 6.5 million people are dying annually from air pollution [1]. Nearly 90% of the deaths occur in low- and middle-income countries in the South-East Asia and Western Pacific regions, as shown in Figure 1. Also, in 28 countries in Europe, around 400 thousand premature deaths still occur each year due to long-term exposure to PM2.5 [3]. The transboundary health impacts of PM2.5 pollution associated with global trade are greater than those associated with long-distance atmospheric pollutant transport [4].

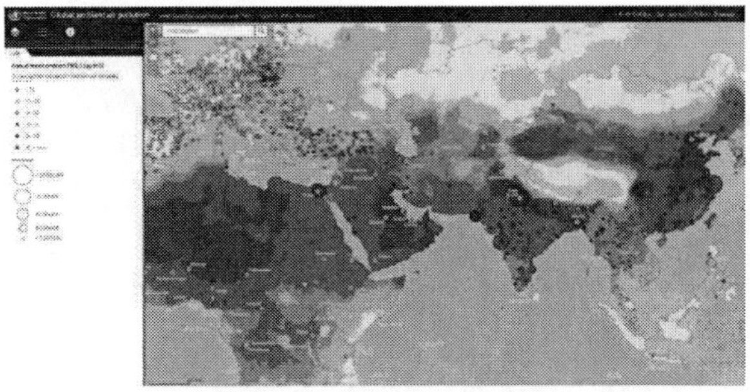

Figure 1. Air Pollution Mapping [2]

Simultaneously, coal use is expanding rapidly, especially in Asia, for cheaper power generation. Koplitz et al. estimated that 15 thousand deaths will occur annually if all of the projected plants become operational in Indonesia by 2030 [5].

II. APPROACH

Town-scale pollution mapping is vital for risk awareness in individuals from the local community, since $PM_{2.5}$ concentration levels differ, even in small areas, depending on the terrain, building structures or vegetation. Further, scientific communication is essential to educate citizens to take appropriate risk avoiding actions, involving public sectors and experts such as meteorologists, environmentalists or medical doctors. To ensure such citizen-centered and autonomous risk communication, we propose the '3D' method as shown in Figure 2 (left).

- *Detection* of environmental pollution by smartphone connected sensors for citizens under open source technology, which is mobile and cost-effective.
- *Data sharing* for swift risk awareness using IoT (Internet of Things) and free cloud system to show clear evidence based on Web-based visualization.
- *Discussion* on healthcare risk, hazard protection or reduction plan including citizens, public sector and experts through democratic social media.

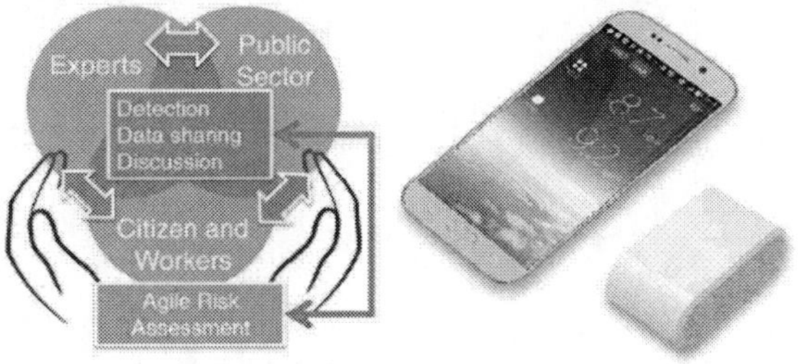

Figure 2. 3D method (left) and Poket $PM_{2.5}$ Sensor (Right)

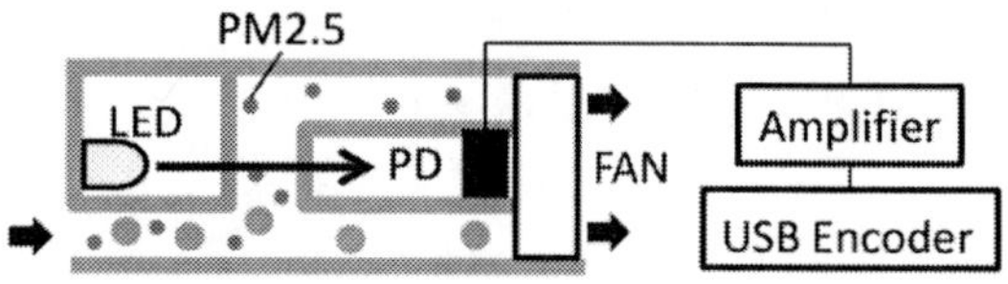

Figure 3. Principle of Pocket $PM_{2.5}$ Sensor Module

We developed 'Pocket $PM_{2.5}$ Sensor' as shown in Figure 2 (right) to demonstrate the 3D in real situation. A free App is capable to generate log data in CSV (Comma-Separated Values) or Google KML (Keyhole Markup Language) format, including GPS (Global Positioning System) information. The sensor has a laser LED (Light Emitting Diode), a PD (photodiode) sensor, a fan, amplifier and USB (Universal Serial Bus) encoder, as shown in Figure 3.

III. Preliminary Results From Field Experiments

A. Mobile Sensing

Figure 4 shows pollution mapping results in Japan, China and Korea using a prototype of Pocket $PM_{2.5}$ Sensor. In Tokyo, Japan, the Pocket $PM_{2.5}$ Sensor showed a reading of 22.5-25 *ug/m*^{3} in an area close to a public pollution measurement instrument installed by the local government, which reported 21 *ug/m*^{3}. The two readings are considered as almost same. We found a high concentration level (60-83 *ug/m*^{3}) in smoking and grill restaurants zones, which we call 'hotspots'. In Weihai, China, the $PM_{2.5}$ concentration was around 28-36 *ug/m*^{3} at the seaside and, in contrast, it was 44-57 *ug/m*^{3} in downtown. Also, we found a hotspot (94 *ug/m*^{3}) close to an exhaust connected to underground restaurants. In Seoul, Korea, $PM_{2.5}$ concentration was 47-47 *ug/m*^{3} in downtown, and 30-35 *ug/m*^{3} in a garden area. The difference seems to be related to vegetation.

B. Fixed Monitoring

We conducted 24/7 continuous monitoring using the Pocket $PM_{2.5}$ sensors combined with solar cells and 3G/4G network. The monitors have been installed in the vicinity of public pollution measurement instruments, as shown in Figure 5, in cooperation with the local government. The comparative experiments will provide accuracy and reliability assurance continuously.

Figure 5. Installation of Pocket $PM_{2.5}$ Solar Monitoring system

IV. Conclusion

Pocket $PM_{2.5}$ Sensor has a great potential for mobile citizen sensing and visualization. Its accuracy seems sufficient, but more assurance is needed by performing regular cross-checking with public monitoring instruments. We plan to conduct a data sharing and risk communication experiment through social media discussion involving local residents, experts and public sector, to ensure monitoring, risk awareness and education of individuals based on the 3D method.

Acknowledgment

This research is funded by Grants-in-Aid for Scientific Research (KAKENHI) of Japan Society for the Promotion of Science (JSPS) under Grant Number 15H01788.

References

[1] United Nations Report, "Vast majority of world – 6.76 billion people – living with excessive air pollution", 7 Sept, 2016. [Online]. Available from: http://www.un.org/apps/news/story.asp?NewsID=55138#.WXWnFYjyhaQ (2017.7.24).

[2] http://maps.who.int/airpollution/ (Accessed on 2017.7.24).

[3] European Environment Agency, "Air quality in Europe — 2016 report", EEA Report No 28/2016, ISSN 1977-8449, 23 Nov 2016. [Online]. Available from: https://www.envir.ee/sites/default/files/air_quality_in_europe_2016_report_thal16027enn.pdf (2017.7.24)

[4] Q. Zhang, et al., "Transboundary health impacts of transported global air pollution and international trade", 30 Mar, Vol. 543, pp.705-709, Nature, 2017

[5] S. Koplitz, et al.: Burden of disease from rising coal emissions in Asia, presentation on *GEOS-Chem Meeting (IGC7)*, Harvard University, May 4-7, 2015.

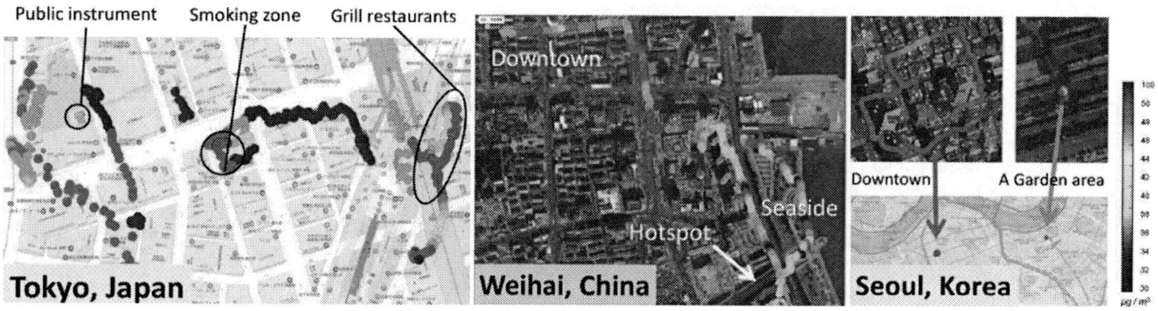

Figure 4. Pollution mapping results in Tokyo, Japan (left), Weihai, China (mid) and Seoul, Korea (right).

Global Information Privacy Infringement Index (GPI)

Hyunmin Suh and Myungchul Kim
School of Computing
Korea Advanced Institute of Science and Technology
Daejeon, Republic of Korea
e-mail: {hyunmin088, mck}@kaist.ac.kr

Abstract - **The proliferation of the Internet has attracted much attention with regard to the leakage of online private/personal information, as exposed information is being used for criminal purposes. In this regard, a criterion for information privacy must be clarified for governments and other public institutions as well as private enterprises in order to curtail information privacy violations and criminal activity. In order to apply such an information privacy criterion, we propose a global-scale information privacy infringement index, known as the Global Information Privacy Infringement Index (GPI). The GPI examines the level of information privacy infringement by measuring the factors, such as types, records, sources, characteristics, and actions based on infringed records for each country. Our approach can be a useful guide for governments, the public and private enterprises in their efforts to enhance information privacy.**

Keywords-information privacy; information privacy infringement; index.

I. INTRODUCTION

The number of Internet users stands at nearly 3.4 billion as of July, 2016, meaning that 40 percent of the world population is currently connected to the Internet [1]. The emergence of the Internet of Things (IoT) has also contributed to the rapid proliferation of mobile Internet users such that the Internet has now become absolutely inseparable tool from the lives of people.

Despite the great benevolent intention of the Internet, the leakage of online private/personal information has been a significant issue around the world. The security burden of protecting personal information applies to all countries. Currently, companies in the US are experiencing losses of more than 525 million US dollars annually due to cybercrime based on malicious codes [2]. The increase in cybercrime has had profound effects on consumers. The largest infringes of information amount to more than 130 million user accounts. The potential targets of phishing attacks are mostly online brands such as PayPal and EBay, an online payment provider and online auction site, respectively [2].

The importance of maintaining reasonable expectations of privacy does not literally mean only preserving personal information, but also, the respecting human rights. For instance, the Identity Card Act [3] was proposed in the UK in 2006. The Identity Card Act was proposed to facilitate a reliable and secure record of individual registrations in the UK. It also promises a useful means for individuals to prove their identities. Initially, it was created to protect Britain against terrorism, organized crime, and to prevent identity theft, illegal immigration and illegal employment. However, the Identity Card Act was repealed due to criticism related to privacy and human rights issues. Privacy campaigner, who stood against the Act, argued that the identity database is a likely target for abuse. For instance, members of the witness protection program, celebrities and victims of domestic violence can be targeted as vulnerable groups in that their personal information can be stolen and sold. Moreover, on 2 February 2005, the UK Parliament's Joint Committee on Human Rights challenged the compatibility of the Bill in consideration of Article 8 of the European Convention on Human Rights and Article 14, both from the Human Rights Act 1998 [4]. Thus, many in Britain believed that Identity Cards Act was in violation of the right to privacy and the right to non-discrimination, as encompassed in the Human Rights Act.

In South Korea, three major credit card companies were targeted by malicious outsiders, leading to the leakage of 104 million instances of information, specifically cardholders' personal and financial information, in 2013 [5]. After this major leak from the card companies, billions stolen from NongHyup Bank, one of the major banks in South Korea, it was assumed that hackers used pharming attack with the victims' personal information [6]. According to Statistics Korea (KOSTAT), 152,151 records were reported as undergoing an information privacy infringement in 2015. These instances are classified into unauthorized collections of personal information, unauthorized abuses of personal information, illegal uses of personal identification numbers, cases not subject to the law, and others. In the records, the illegal use of personal identification numbers accounts for the largest proportion of information privacy infringements, at 77,598 records, i.e., 51 percent of the entire number of records [7].

Therefore, it is essential to make the conditions of the online environment safer and more secure by encouraging the involvement of the public and of the government. In this regard, a criterion pertaining to information privacy must be clarified by the government, public and private enterprises in order to curtail online privacy violations and criminal activity. In order to apply a criterion of privacy, we propose an information privacy index, which works on a global scale, known as the GPI. The GPI examines the level of information privacy by measuring the factors such as types, records, sources, characteristics, and actions based on infringed records which have occurred in the country. This approach can be a useful guide to the public and to government and private organizations as they attempt to enhance information privacy.

The contributions of this paper are as follows:

First, we propose the GPI as a means of measuring the level of information privacy for each country. With regard to the GPI, we successfully quantified the level of information privacy, making it much easier for people to increase their self-awareness of information privacy in their country of residence.

Second, we attempt to provide an empirical analysis on the basis of publicly available data. In this way, we do not provide any ambiguous or estimated data about the privacy level in near future but rather give information about the present based on the publicly disclosed records.

Last, we demonstrate the GPI for five countries as case studies by applying our method using infringed records from around the globe.

This paper is organized as follows. Section II consists of the basic concepts of the GPI. In this section, we clarify the definition and provide background information. Related work with regard to the GPI is presented in Section III. In Section IV, a description of GPI is given in detail. The GPI is measured and evaluated in Section V. We finalize the paper in Section VI.

II. Basic Concepts

This section presents the definition of privacy and information privacy and background information related to GPI.

A. *Privacy, Information Privacy and Personal Information*

Privacy is ambiguous in that includes a broad range of concepts, such as freedom of thought, control over personal information, and others. According to the United Nation (UN), "Privacy can be defined as the presumption that individuals should have an area of autonomous development, interaction and liberty, a 'private sphere' with or without interaction with others, free from State intervention and from excessive unsolicited intervention by other uninvited individuals. The right to privacy is also the ability of individuals to determine who holds information about them and how that information is used" [8].

Privacy has become a controversial issue which has a profound impact around the globe. Protecting privacy is now a subjective goal for nearly every nation, with numerous statutes, constitutional rights, and judicial decisions affecting these efforts. Most nations around the globe note privacy in their constitutions for the protection of citizens. Even if privacy is not mentioned in constitutions, many countries are aware of the importance of constitutional rights to privacy, including Canada, France, Germany, Japan, and India [9].

Information privacy is an emerging topic with the advent of the Internet, as personal information is digitalized on the Internet for many purposes. The definition of information privacy must encompass an important feature to refer also to the privacy of digitalized personal data which is stored on a computer system. Information privacy concerns the collection and dissemination of data, technology, legal and political issues surrounding them.

There is great ambiguity in the way 'personal information' is used. In the context of privacy or academic research, personal information refers to information that is sensitive and any information that can designate or identify a person [10]. Personal information, under the law of South Korea, is defined as a personal information related to a natural person whom he or she must be alive. Personal information means an information that can designate or identify an alive person. If collected information does not identify a person, it still counts as a personal information when collected information can be easily combined with other information [11]. In the European Union Directive, "personal data shall mean any information relating to an identifiable person is one who can be identified, directly or indirectly, in particular by reference to an identification number or to one or more factors specific to his physical, physiological, mental, economic, cultural or social identity [12]." Personal information can appear in online and offline environments. This paper focuses on digitalized personal information that is acquired, stored on, abused, and/or removed from a computer system.

B. *Personal Identification Number*

The definition of a 'personal identification number' [13] differs for each country. Such numbers are termed national identification number, national identity number, national insurance number, personal identification number, or resident registration number. The governments of many countries use personal identification number as means of tracking citizens and permanent/temporary residents. Personal identification numbers can be given to foreigners for guidance and to differentiate them from citizens. Moreover, personal identification numbers can be used for tracking for the purposes of employment, taxation, governmental benefits, health care, and other government related functions. They are not widely used in relation to violations of human rights, but some countries still maintain the system for convenience in managing citizens.

Various personal identification number systems are implemented among countries; however, most nations issue an identification number when citizens are born or when they reach a certain age (or legal age). For noncitizens, identification numbers can be issued when they enter the country and/or when they are granted a temporary/permanent resident permit, but the numbers will be issued with a different logic from that used with citizens. Many countries have attempted to issue identification numbers for singular purposes, but many of these efforts have been halted due to strong resistance from human rights movements. In fact, personal identification number system is still used in some countries.

C. *A Comparison of Personal Identification Number Systems*

As noted above, personal identification number systems vary across among countries. In this subsection, we provide more detailed information about the personal identification number among five countries; the United States, the United Kingdom, Germany, Japan, and South Korea. In addition, we analyze the domain of personal identification number in five sector; Passport Issuance, Driver License, Taxation, Social Insurance, and Finance summarized in Table 1. These five sectors are critical in that each nation uses a different approach to authenticate users and collect personal information.

The United States developed its Social Security Number (SSN) [14] system for the organization of social security related benefits. However, the number is now used for other purposes, working as a personal identification number system. For passport issuance, a person needs to prove his or her citizenship (such as proof of birth, certification of citizenship, or certification of naturalization), and the SSN must be given [15]. For a driver's license, proof of birth and identification documents must be given along with the SSN [16]. For taxation, four types of taxation numbers exist; Taxpayer Identification Number (TIN), Employer Identification Number (EIN), Individual Taxpayer Identification Number (ITIN), and Preparer Taxpayer Identification Number (PTIN) [17]. For finance, the SSN is not necessarily a required condition.

In the United Kingdom, there is no official personal identification number system and legal requirement to possess any types of identification document to prove one's identity. However, there is the National Insurance Number (NIN) [18], which is issued to all citizens in the United Kingdom for the purpose of insurance. The NIN is issued when legal age is turned 16. The NIN is not mandatory to possess, and driver's license is generally used as proof of identity. In order to issue a driver's license, proof of identification must be submitted such as proof of birth or a passport. When applying online, the driver's license issuing institution may collect the NIN [19]. For taxation, the NIN is needed in order to issue a Unique Tax Reference (UTR). Employers collect the NINs of employees for taxation related purposes [20]. For finance, the NIN is rarely used, whereas driver's licenses and passports are mostly used as proof of address and identity [21].

In Germany, there is the Neuer Personalausweis (nPA), but it does not function as a personal identification number. The nPA, which is known as an ID card system, is heavily regulated in terms of its usage. Almost every sector issues a unique number that each sector such as passport, driver license, taxation, social insurance, and finance has its own unique number. The nPA is used as an authentication method but storing or wiring nPA information with the unique number is regulated. This ID card system nPA is implemented in 2010 that is an electronic high-tech ID card using, for instance, Radio-Frequency ID (RFID), cryptographic technique, secure storage, and others. Validation using the nPA lasts 10 years, and a new number is issued when the card is lost or reissued. The collection of the nPA by private institution is illegal. For the protection of personal information, there is no unified number that grants access to social security services in Germany. There are unique numbers for each social security services wiring these numbers with the nPA is illegal [22][23].

My Number [24] of Japan is a newly emerging personal identification number system which started in 2016. My Number is a 12 digits number issued to all residents of Japan, including temporary and permanent residents with valid permits. The previous personal identification number system was only used for taxation, social insurance, and medical insurance purposes. However, the Japanese government has stepped forward to centralize the system with a number for nearly every sector, to eventually become a unique number for the entire system. Thus, My Number will be used for taxation, social security, driver's license, and a passport [25].

In South Korea, the Resident Registration Number (RRN) [26] is a 13-digit number issued to all residents of the country. The system started on November of 1968 for the purpose of identifying spies. The RRN is used in nearly every sector not only as an authentication method but also as a key number with which to make inquiries into the system. Even up to August of 2012, the RRN was ruthlessly collected by public and private institutions for convenience [27]. There are critical problems which have long occurred in South Korea associated with the extensive use of the RRN. First, the South Korean government has implemented an e-government system and there are at least 1,100 information systems under 47 administrative agencies which are linked in a single integrated government network [28]. These distributed information systems are integrated instantly when the RRN is entered into the system. Thus, personal information in every sector can be easily acquired by the government which can lead to the serious problem of state surveillance. Secondly, the meaningless collection of the RRN by private companies has led to many accidents, such as leakages of RRN. Moreover, the most critical problem related to the RRN is that leaked RRNs cannot be changed during the course of one's lifetime once they are issued.

TABLE I. A COMPARISON OF PERSONAL IDENTIFICATION NUMBER SYSTEMS

	Taxation	Passport	Driver's License	Social Insurance	Finance	Change of Personal Identification Number
U.S (SSN)	Δ	O	O	O	Δ	Cannot be changed (except in cases of error)
U.K (NIN)	O	X	X	O	X	Cannot be changed
Germany (nPA)	X	X	X	X	X	Changed in every 10 years
Japan (My Number)	O	O	O	O	X	Cannot be changed
South Korea (RRN)	O	O	O	O	O	Cannot be changed

* O: Must, Δ: Optional, X: Not required

III. RELATED WORKS

In this section, we briefly survey the works that are relevant to the GPI.

A. *The Breach Level Index*

The Breach Level Index [29] aims to provide the overall breach severity level by tracking publicly known breaches to allow organizations to measure their own risk assessment. The Breach Level Index does not set an upper limit, but the largest breach scores are 10 thus far. The Index is in logarithmic (base 10) scales used similar to the scales for volcanoes and earthquakes [30][31]. However, the Breach Level Index is designed to provide a risk assessment tool specifically targeting enterprises. The GPI tends to complement the weaknesses of the Breach Level Index to provide a national level scale to acknowledge the level of information privacy infringement.

B. *The Global Cybersecurity Index*

The Global Cybersecurity Index [32] is a project that aims to measure each nation's level of commitment to cybersecurity. The final goal of the GCI is to advocate for a global culture of cybersecurity and its integration in terms of information and communication technologies. The Global Cybersecurity Index covers the five areas of legal measures, technical measures, organizational measures, capacity building, and cooperation. These five areas have a profound impact on cybersecurity with regard to assessing national capabilities as they form the building blocks of national capabilities. The GCI covers various fields but their global ranking of cybersecurity index is relatively impractical. The GCI only focuses on the existence of national structures in place rather than actual cybersecurity level for a particular country. Ironically, the GCI has reported that the United States of America is placed at first in their cybersecurity index; however, the U.S. is happened to be the country with highest number of cybersecurity related accidents according to the Breach Level Index. GPI scale aims to provide information based on infringed records that focuses more on evidence rather than the infrastructure. Thus, GPI is based on the fact itself as well as the details occurred in the specific country.

C. *The Global Conflict Risk Index*

The Global Conflict Risk Index (GCRI) [33] was developed by the Joint Research Center. The GCRI is designed to assist with decision making about long-term conflict risk by providing accessible and objective open sources. The contributions of the GCRI are described as follow: It clarifies the definitions of 'risk' and 'risk conflict' which derived from existing methodologies of conflict research. In addition, five risk areas for each state are presented for a quick overview of the structural conditions of the state. Moreover, it provides an evaluation and an assessment of a particular country's risk. The GCRI is focused on the risk that can occur in a certain country. However, the GPI is more focused on infringement level as opposed to the level of risk in a country.

D. *The Crime Rate*

The crime rate represents the number of offenses per certain number of people. The Federal Bureau of Investigation (FBI) [34] releases crime statistics, dividing the number of crimes by 100,000 inhabitants. The GPI has benchmarked the concept of the crime rate as the number of infringed records per the number of data production. Moreover, we attempt to provide a level of information privacy infringement at present based on the publicly disclosed records.

IV. The Description of the GPI

This section presents a description of the GPI with regard to categories and methodology.

A. Categories

The GPI model deals with five factors, as seen in Table 2. 'N' represents the total number of infringement records, specifically representing when private information has been leaked. For instance, the number of records infringed was 24 million in the case of Zappos, when they were hacked by a malicious hacker [35]. We measure the total IP traffic of the country as 'I', as indicated. Since the amount of data production is not publicly available, the total IP traffic brought by Cisco VNI [36] is used to consider the amount of data produced in a certain country. The type of data in the records 't' ranging from 1 (least) to 5 (most) covering all types of data, ranging from less important information to the most important information. Identity theft, which is ranked 4 in Table 2, has been developed from the conventional type specifically noting what types of identification were infringed. It is important to consider what caused the information to be leaked. In this regard, 's' represents the source of the infringement ranging from 1 to 5 and covering a lost/stolen device, malicious insider/outsider, and state sponsored attacker. Leaked information can be replaced or reissued but particular information is an exception. For example, if a user's email address is leaked, it can be easily replaced with another email address. The user may experience inconvenience when replacing his lifelong email address but it may not harm his personal life. However, an information like RRN, a type of personal identification number in South Korea, is permanent and unique number and being used for multiple purposes as a method of online/offline authentication. As a consequence, leaked RRN has been adversely abused for pharming attack, phishing, and various types of fraud. In this sense, it is vital to measure the value of personal identification number system as noted 'c' as characteristics of personal identification number system in the GPI. The 'c' is ranging from 1 to 5 with regard to the personal identification number system. Leaked information can be used for the secondary purposes as well. Stolen identity can be used to target the victim, or it can be used to access their financial account. The type of actions denoted by 'A' in the GPI refers to instances of the secondary use of data.

TABLE II. Categories of the GPI

N = the total number of infringement records	
I = Total IP traffic information according to the Cisco Visual Networking Index (Cisco VNI), an ongoing initiative to track and forecast the impact of visual networking applications	
t = the type of data in the records	
values	
1	Email addresses
2	Online account access (username/passwords to social media, websites, etc.)
3	Financial access (bank account credentials, credit card data)
4	Identity theft (such as personal identification Number, driver's license number, etc.)
5	Confidential information (highly sensitive information on a national scale)
s = source of the infringement	
values	
1	Lost device (such as a laptop, OTP or USB)
2	Stolen device
3	Malicious insider
4	Malicious outsider
5	State sponsored
c = characteristic	
values	
1	Lost personal identification number can be replaced, reissued or recovered easily, and no harm done
2	Lost personal identification number can be replaced, reissued or recovered, it may be used for humiliation, but not financially damaging
3	Lost personal identification number can be replaced, reissued or recovered, but it may be used for secondary purposes
4	Lost personal identification number cannot be replaced, reissued or recovered, and it can be used to gain financial access
5	Lost personal identification number cannot be replaced, reissued or recreated, and it can cause serious damage or be used for secondary purposes
A = whether secondary actions are taken (for criminal or humiliation purposes)	
values	
1	No action
2	Publication of embarrassing information or used for humiliation
3	Publication of harmful information such as hacker logs, etc.
4	Access to financial websites or private websites
5	Use of financial identity to obtain financial funds or any damage to finances

B. Methodology

The methodology of our approach for the GPI relies on publicly disclosed infringed records. The equation of the GPI is presented below.

$$\mathrm{GPI} = \sum_{x=1}^{n}[\log(\frac{N}{I} * t * s * c * A)]_x$$

The GPI aims to cover all infringed or leaked information occurring at a national level. We divide the total number of infringement records 'N' by 'I' denoting the IP traffic of a country. After multiplying each category of the data, we use the logarithm (base 10) scale to make it as simple as the system used in the Breach Level Index. In the equation, 'x' represents an event of each infringed record which occurs in a particular country. The sum of 'n' number of records will represent the entire set of infringed information occurring in a certain country. Finally, the score of the GPI does not set the upper limit as benchmarked from the crime rate.

V. Evaluation

We evaluate the GPI based on the methodology introduced in the previous section. We used the sets of infringed records derived from Breach Level Index [29] for five countries such as the United States, the United

Kingdom, Japan, Germany, and South Korea and obtained their privacy levels.

TABLE III. RESULT OF THE GPI

Country	Contents		
	Infringed Records (2014)	*GPI*	*Rank*
United States	1,257	933.7	1
United Kingdom	135	159.4	2
South Korea	12	73.4	3
Japan	12	30.7	4
Germany	10	14.1	5

Among many other countries, the United States accounts for the largest amount of infringed information around the world. There are 1,257 infringed records for the period from January 1st, 2014 to December 31st, 2014. However, due to the exceeding number of records, we discard the records scoring below 6 in the Breach level Index. The data of the United States implies that more information infringements are likely to occur in the United States, as much more information is produced there than in any other country. The total amount of IP traffic produced within the United States was 18.1 exabytes in 2014, clearly higher than those figures for other countries. As a result, the United States scored 934 on the GPI. Various causes can explain why the United States is the country with the greatest amount of infringed information, but this does not mean that the level of privacy is low there. It is arguable that the United States may report the infringement records more transparently than other countries.

Similar to the United States, the total number of infringed records was 135 in 2014 in the UK. We discarded information which scored under 6 points from the dataset for the same reason given in the previous case. We accumulated all of the infringed record of the United Kingdom in 2014 as well as the total IP traffic in 2014, which was 2.4 exabytes. The United Kingdom does not have a personal identification number, with individual identification numbers issued from different institutions. In this sense, most of the identification numbers in the UK can be replaced or reissued easily, but information there can still be used to identify a person. As a result, the United Kingdom scored 159 on the GPI.

In South Korea, there are 12 infringed records in 2014. Although South Korea has fewer infringed records, they scored 73. In 2014, the three largest credit companies had 104 million records of personal information stolen and leaked, including RRN. Unlike other countries, South Korea is the only country using a RRN, a personal identification number system for which the number cannot be replaced or reissued once it is issued. The RRN can be used as an online and offline as a means of authentication, and it is used extensively in many sectors in South Korea. Most phishing and pharming attacks are initiated by identifying a person through their RRN. Thus, the RRN is a critical factor which violates the privacy level in South Korea, and this resulted in a higher GPI score.

In Germany, there are ten infringed records in 2014. Compared to the United States and the United Kingdom, there are relatively few records. Germany's GPI is 38. Germany has a strong regulation on the usage of personal identification number system that the domain of ID card is far lower than any other countries. The nPA, an ID card system of Germany, can easily be replaced and reissued that it has absolutely no harm on citizens in Germany.

In Japan, since there are 12 infringed records in 2014, the GPI is 31. The GPI score is low, but several factors should be considered. Japan has adopted an electronic national identification number system known as 'My Number' that can be used to identify a person. The system can lead to serious phishing or pharming attacks, as shown in the case of South Korea. However, the infringed information in 2014 does not include any information from the 'My Number' system, resulting in a score for Japan that was relatively low compared to those of other countries.

VI. CONCLUSION AND FURTHER WORK

The GPI aims to provide a useful criterion when dealing with information privacy infringement issues on a global scale. The GPI can be enhanced in various forms, such as through a regression analysis, a multi-year data analysis, and others. The model can be advanced if we consider the cost aspects of information privacy infringement. Moreover, multi-year data of the cost is publicly disclosed, our model can be much developed.

Our initiative of providing information about the level of information privacy infringement on a global scale is certainly a valuable means of alerting to the world. We continue to complement our GPI methodology to cover every country around the world for a brighter and more secure future.

ACKNOWLEDGEMENT

This work was supported by a grant from the National Research Foundation of Korea (NRF) funded by the Korean government (MSIP) (No. 2017R1A2B4005865).

REFERENCES

[1] Internet Live Stats., [Online]. Available from: http://www.internetlivestats.com/internet-users/ [Last access: March, 2016]

[2] Statista., "Statistics and Market Data on Cyber Crime" [Online]. Available from: http://www.statista.com/markets/424/topic/1065/cyber-crime/ [Last access: March 2016]

[3] The Guardian., [Online]. Available from: http://www.theguardian.com/commentisfree/libertycentral/2009/jan/15/identity-cards-act [Last access: March, 2016]

[4] European Commision. "UK's ID Cards Bill wins parliamentary vote despite Human Rights concerns" [Online]. Available from: http://ec.europa.eu/idabc/servlets/Docee17.pdf?id=21693 [Last access: March, 2016]

[5] Joongangdaily., [Online]. Available from: http://koreajoongangdaily.joins.com/news/article/article.aspx?aid=2983762 [Last access: March, 2016]

[6] Koreabang., [Online]. Available from: http://www.koreabang.com/2014/stories/hackers-steal-billions-from-nonghyup-bank-is-not-responsible.html [Last access: March, 2016]

[7] Statistics Korea., [Online]. Available from: http://www.index.go.kr/potal/main/EachDtlPageDetail.do?idx_cd=1366 [Last access: March, 2016]

[8] Techopedia., "Information Privacy." [Online]. Available from: https://www.techopedia.com/definition/10380/information-privacy [Last access: April, 2016]

[9] D., Solove, "Understanding Privacy," Harvard University Press, 2008.

[10] H., Nissenbaum, "Privacy in Context: Technology, Policy, and the Integrity of Social Life," Stanford University Press, 2010.

[11] Ministry of Interior., "Persoanl Information Protection Act, Article 2," [Online]. Available from: https://www.privacy.go.kr/eng/laws_policies_list.do [Last access: April, 2016]

[12] Data Protection Commissioner (DPC), "EU Directive 95/46/EC – The Data Protection Directive, Chapter 1 – General Provision," 2016.

[13] Record Union., "What is a national identification number?," [Online]. Available from: http://helpdesk.recordunion.com/FAQ/what-is-a-national-identification-number [Last access: April, 2016]

[14] Social Security., "The Story of the Social Security Number," [Online]. Available from: https://www.ssa.gov/policy/docs/ssb/v69n2/v69n2p55.html [Last access: April, 2016]

[15] U.S. Passports & International Travel, "First Time Applicants," 2016 [Online]. Available from: https://travel.state.gov/content/passports/en/passports/first-time.html [Last access: April, 2016]

[16] California Department of Motor Vehicles. "Social Security Number (FFDL 8)," 2016 [Online]. Available from: https://www.dmv.ca.gov/portal/dmv/detail/pubs/brochures/fast_facts/ffdl08 [Last access: April, 2016]

[17] Internal Revenue Service, "Taxpayer Identification Number (TIN)," 2016 [Online]. Available from: https://www.irs.gov/individuals/international-taxpayers/taxpayer-identification-numbers-tin [Last access: May, 2016]

[18] UK Government, "National Insurance," [Online]. Available from: https://www.gov.uk/national-insurance/your-national-insurance-number [Last access: May, 2016]

[19] UK Government, "Apply for your first provisional driving license," 2016 [Online]. Available from: https://www.gov.uk/apply-first-provisional-driving-licence [Last access: May, 2016]

[20] Unique Taxpayer Reference Government, "How to get u UTR Number if Self Employed," [Online]. Available from: http://utr.org.uk/home [Last access: May, 2016]

[21] Barclays, "Identification for bank accounts," 2016 [Online]. Available from: http://www.barclays.co.uk/validid [Last access: May, 2016]

[22] German-way.com, "The Identity Card –der Ausweis," [Online]. Available from: http://www.german-way.com/for-expats/living-in-germany/the-identity-card-der-ausweis/ [Last access: May, 2016]

[23] M., Margraf, "The New German ID Card," [Online]. Available from: http://www.personalausweisportal.de/SharedDocs/Downloads/EN/Paper_new_German_ID-card.pdf?__blob=publicationFile

[24] Cabinet Secretariat, [Online]. Available from: http://www.gov-online.go.jp/tokusyu/mynumber/ad/?sec1_kojin_2-2 [Last access: May, 2016]

[25] M., King, "My Number system: a worring glimpse of the future," 2015 [Online]. Available from: http://www.japantoday.com/category/opinions/view/my-number-system-a-worrying-glimpse-of-the-future [Last access: May, 2016]

[26] OECD, "Information on Tax Identification Numbers Section," [Online]. Available from: https://search.oecd.org/tax/automaticexchange/tinsandtaxresidency/taxidentificationnumberstins/Korea-TIN.pdf [Last access: May, 2016]

[27] Koreabang, "Korean Government Reorganizes National ID System After Leaks," 2014 [Online]. Available from: http://www.koreabang.com/2014/stories/korean-government-reorganizes-resident-registration-number-system.html [Last access: May, 2016]

[28] Ministry of Public Administration and Security, "e-Government in South Korea" [Online]. Available from: http://unpan1.un.org/intradoc/groups/public/documents/UNGC/UNPAN043625.pdf [Last access: May, 2016]

[29] BreachlevelIndex.com, [Online]. Available from: http://breachlevelindex.com/#!breach-database [Last access: May, 2016]

[30] S., Huler, "Defining the Wind: The Beaufort Scale and How a 19th-Century Admiral Turned into Poetry," 2014.

[31] Melaragno, M., "Severe Storm Engineering for Structural Design, " 1996.

[32] The Global Cybersecurity Index, [Online]. Available from: http://www.itu.int/en/ITU-D/Cybersecurity/Pages/GCI.aspx [Last access: May, 2016]

[33] The Global Conflict Risk Index, "The Global Conflict Risk Index (GCRI) a Quantitative Model," 2014.

[34] FBI., "FBI Releases 2014 Crime Statistics" [Online]. Available from: https://www.fbi.gov/news/pressrel/press-releases/fbi-releases-2014-crime-statistics [Last access: May, 2016]

[35] CNN Money., "Zappos hacked, 24 million accounts accessed" [Online]. Available from: http://money.cnn.com/2012/01/16/technology/zappos_hack/ [Last access: May, 2016]

[36] Cisco.com., "The Zettabyte Era – trends and Analysis" [Online]. Available from: http://www.cisco.com/c/en/us/solutions/collateral/service-provider/visual-networking-index-vni/VNI_Hyperconnectivity_WP.html [Last access: May, 2016]

An Investigation on Forensic Opportunities to Recover Evidential Data from Mobile Phones and Personal Computers

Philip Naughton and M A Hannan Bin Azhar
Computing, Digital Forensics and Cybersecurity
Canterbury Christ Church University
Canterbury, United Kingdom
Email: {p.naughton78, hannan.azhar}@canterbury.ac.uk

Abstract— **This paper is a summary of experiments conducted to explore forensic opportunities available to the Law Enforcement Agency in the recovery of artefacts resulting from criminal use of popularly chosen applications. The experiments were conducted using forensic examination tools and techniques on a mobile phone running an Android operating system (OS) and another using Apple's OS, as well as a computer running Windows 10 OS. These examinations involved the forensic acquisition and analysis of artefacts resulting from simulated criminal use of common messaging applications, running on both mobile smart phones and personal computers. Many of the complexities and factors effecting successful forensic data acquisition, such as encryption and ephemeral burn functions were also explored together with data analysis.**

Keywords- Digital forensics; data acquisition; messaging applications; mobile phones and PCs .

I. INTRODUCTION

Increased data download speeds have made it possible for new social media applications (Apps), delivering rich content between users, to work effectively in a way that was not previously possible. By 2016, the improvements in mobile data speeds had resulted in 71% of all adults in the UK owning a smartphone, up from 66% in 2015 [1]. This growth in smart phone ownership combined with improvements in 4G network coverage across the UK and ever more sophisticated Apps in terms of functionality and content delivery, explains why there is continuous high demand for Apps from both the Apple and Google stores.

Data recovered from digital devices is vital in identifying a suspect's on-line activity to prove or disprove his/her alleged involvement in a criminal offence. Police forces utilise all their available intelligence sources to inform their decision making in order to prioritise which of the thousands of devices seized every day during criminal investigations will be examined for evidence. They also must make decisions, based on demand pressures, which devices will not be examined at all, despite the potential possibility of evidence being on them. When reviewing forensic examination processes, Her Majesty's Inspector of Constabulary (HMIC) reported negatively that during a review of a UK force, there were significant delays caused to investigations because computers and other media submitted to Digital Forensic Examiner (DFEs) were taking too long to forensically examine [2]. Despite all the best efforts of an intelligence led forensic prioritisation approach, the delays in examinations were potentially impacting negatively on the efficiency of serious crime investigations. So further studies were required to identify which platforms and Apps would offer more forensic opportunities to the Law Enforcement Agencies (LEAs) while recovering evidential data from a collection of suspect devices. This in turn could potentially assist the LEAs in their decision making and prioritising of the many devices submitted to them for forensic examination, which eventually would help with the case load management. This paper reports forensically sound analysis and results in gathering evidential data from the Apps commonly used in criminal activities and installed on both smart phones and personal computers (PCs).

Section 2 of this paper reviews existing work by academic and subject matter experts in relation to the topic of this research paper. A brief explanation on the methodology used will be discussed in Section 3. Results and analysis will be reported in Section 4. Finally, Section 5 concludes the paper.

II. LITERATURE REVIEW

The literature review sought to identify known challenges and opportunities that tend to frustrate or enhance forensic opportunities for LEAs to recover digital evidence from devices (mobile smart phones and PCs). This paper considered a digital forensic opportunity to mean when a file or chat log sent by a criminal between devices could be acquired from these devices by employing forensic examination software tools to recover these artefacts. The topics covered in the research ranged from the scope and limitations of the forensic tools available to potential future hardware and software developments, such as cloud based technology. Understanding the differences between App types available on the market and any built-in anti-forensic features was important to be able to assess how their difference might impact on the results of this paper's experiments.

A. App types

There are three main App types: Native, Web and Hybrid. 'Native Apps' are built with a mix of platform-specific technologies running in most cases on either Android or iOS platforms. Each platform uses different technologies. Android programmers for example mainly build their Apps with Java [3], making occasional use of Python, whereas iOS developers use the Objective-C programming language. Secondly, 'Web Apps', which run on a device's browser are rendered HTML web pages and look like an App. The third type of App is called a Hybrid. Here, developers build a standard Web App, primarily built using HTML5 and JavaScript, then insert it inside a thin native container that provides access to native platform features that allows it to function like a native App. WhatsApp reported that over 60 million recent downloads were made of their native Apps [4]. The constant 'on' state of native Apps may potentially result in creating more opportunities for DFE from devices that are capturing more records of user activity, for example location data. Although native Apps usually performs better than Web Apps, a recent empirical study [5] reported that in about 31% of the situations, Web apps perform much better than the native apps, when providing the same functionality.

As Apps have become widely used, so too have the public's concerns regarding security. This has led to several App developers incorporating additional features to protect user data. Although data security is a good thing, it can however often frustrate DFE efforts to pursue criminals. WhatsApp for example has now built in end-to-end encryption anti-forensic features. Others such as Snapchat reportedly provide users with ephemeral messaging, which is described as the mobile-to-mobile transmission of multimedia messages that automatically disappeared from the recipient's screen after the message had been viewed [6]. That is to say they were automatically and permanently deleted from the user's device. However, other researchers were sceptical about Apps such a Snapchat's claims to permanently delete messages, photos and videos contesting that at best, the data is recorded, used, saved and then deliberately deleted; but at worst, the ephemeral nature is faked [7].

B. *Law Enforcements' ability to acquire digital evidence*

LEAs rely on physical and software inspection tools to conduct their forensic data acquisition and analysis of evidential data from digital devices. Commercially available forensic examination tools are constantly having to play catch up with the high frequency of App developer updates, as seen in Table 1, and this causes ongoing challenges in recovering evidential data from devices.

TABLE I. APPS UPDATE VERSION HISTORY.

Apps	Number of times App updated	
	Android	*iOS*
WhatsApp	13	4
Facebook messenger	5	4
Google photos	5	4
Skype	5	1
Twitter	5	5
Instagram	4	6
Kik	3	5
Dropbox	2	3
Snapchat	1	5

There is a general lack of hardware, software, and/or interface standardization within the industry ranging from the storage media and file system to the OS [8]. Each manufacturer develops their very own bespoke versions of the android OS specific to its hardware, which means that App developers must ensure that their product will work with every Android phone OS version in addition to iOS devices. Individual Apps, as seen in Table 1, do not get upgraded at the same time or frequency across platforms. From Table 1, it can be seen that the Android version for WhatsApp was updated thirteen times in just two months (January and February, 2017), whereas the Apple iOS version of the same App was updated four times in the same period. App updates for PCs tend to be far fewer and less frequent.

There are two types of physical data acquisition tools for mobile phones. They are used infrequently by LEAs due to the costs, both in conducting the processes and in replacing phones damaged during these processes, which tend to be destructive to the device. The first of these two techniques is called Chip-off, which is the process as involving the physically removing flash memory chips from a suspect's mobile phone and then acquiring the raw data using specialized equipment [9]. The second physical technique used called Joint Test Action Group (JTAG) is the process of soldering wires directly to the test access ports [10] on a device's circuit board. Again, this process is not widely used because of the risk of damage resulting from soldering contacts to the phone.

C. *Cloud based technology*

Cloud computing is the act of storing, accessing and sharing data Apps in remote locations [11]. In order to cope with the problem of limited storage capacity, mobile phone devices manufacturers recognise the need to use services which can seamlessly offload some of the tasks of a mobile application from the handset to servers [12]. However, others believe that because smartphones aren't expected to do as many things as PCs can, and what they can do they must do on less power, that this is the real driver for the use of cloud technologies [13]. Accessing cloud data may produce different but no less significant challengers for DFEs. As a consequence, many of the forensic software tool companies, at the time of this paper, were tasking their developers to work on cloud data acquisition tools.

PCs do not share the same storage issues as mobile phones. They typically stores several terabytes (TB) of data [14]. A PC with a storage drive of 3TB can hold roughly 360 videos, 750,000 songs or 600,000 images. The sheer volume of the potential data on a drive of this capacity can cause DFE challenges when reviewing the data recovered during an examination of a suspect's PC. Despite PCs not having the same storage issues, they still make some use of cloud storage to make backups of their contents or user data, such as photos sent and received via Apps.

The Acquisition and Disclosure of Communications Data - Regulation of Investigatory Powers Act 2000 [15] governs UK LEAs' powers to acquire data. Although DFEs can technically acquire data from a cloud server in a foreign country using a suspect's device via a connection with that server, they may breach laws in that jurisdiction because UK courts cannot authorise such action in foreign countries.

III. METHODOLOGY

During the experiments, a set of test files and chat messages were sent between the devices via a set of test Apps known to be commonly used to simulate potential communications between criminals. Experienced and qualified. Law enforcement forensic examiners were consulted in the planning and designing the experiments, so that the experiments were realistic and in accordance with what the professionals have to deal with in practice. To capture a representative sample of policing across the UK, fifteen forces were chosen to cover all the countries in the British Isles representing the diversity in policing experiences. The findings and conclusions from the experiments would therefore be comparable to those in real investigations.

Oracle's open source software VirtualBox [16] was used to create a virtual machine (VM) in a PC to be one of the three test devices. It was used rather than a physical machine because the VM PC had the advantage of only having a fresh Windows OS installed on it and the Apps needed for these experiments, which are detailed in Table 2. Therefore, the results found during the forensic examination of the device could not have been influenced by other software previously installed as could have been the case on an old re-used physical PC.

TABE II. VM PC SETUP AND CONFIGURATION.

Machine Type	*Specifications*		
	Operating system	*Installed software*	
PC – Oracle VM created and running on host machine Acer Aspire Laptop Intel Core i3	Windows 10 64 bit	Clean install Windows 10 with only the following Apps installed on the PC (VM). Current versions used as of 6th January 2017	
		Dropbox	Google photos
		Google search	Skype
		Twitter	WhatsApp
		Blue Stacks Android Emulator – used to install and run the Apps listed below. Current versions used as of 6th January 2017	
		Facebook Messenger	Instagram
		Kik	Snap Chat

The two mobile smart phones were also used during the experiments and are detailed in Table 3. The current versions of the same Apps detailed in Table 2 were also installed on both phones as of 6th January 2017. The iPhone was not jailbroken, neither was the Samsung rooted because these experiments did not involve the use of alternative Apps available outside of Apple or Android stores. No device OS or disk encryption were enabled on any of the test devices.

TABLE III. MOBILE SMART PHONES CONFIGURATIONS.

Phone types	**Specifications**		
	Model	***OS version***	***Kernel version***
Samsung Galaxy J3	SM-J320FN	Android 5.1.1	3.10.65.8870959
iPhone 5c	A1507	IOS 10.1.1	XNU based on Darwin 16

Two forensic workstations were set up to facilitate the forensic examination of all three devices being investigated. Forensic software tools were then used to examine devices to acquire and analyse the test sample data from them. One of the workstations used for investigation had Cellebrite UFED [17] software tool installed, which was used for examining all the Apps on both smart phone devices. Its job was to acquire artefact evidence from the mobile phones and analyse the recovered data. The second workstation had an open source forensic acquisition and analysis tool installed called Autopsy version 4.3.0 [18]. Autopsy is a digital forensics platform and graphical interface to digital forensics tools.

The forensic examinations were conducted following the guidelines set by the Association of Chief Police Officers (ACPO) [19] namely the first principle, by not taking action to change the data, and the third principle, by keeping an audit trail, so that an independent third party could examine the procedures and achieve the same result. Tools which pose risks in breaching these principles were not used in the experiment. One example of such tools was RetroScope [20], which can recreate multiple previous screens of an Android App in the order they were displayed from the phone's memory. But use of such tools may be considered as the breach of the first principle of the ACPO guidelines [19] due to the restructure of data and hence were not used in the study.

The test files used during the experiments were selected to represent common illegal communications between criminals, such as the distribution of child pornography or documents detailing stolen bank account details. While consulting with the law enforcement processionals, it was found that MD5 (message-digest algorithm) was widely used in their forensic laboratories. All test files used in the experiments had their MD5 hash value calculated before they were sent. These hashes were used to conduct keyword searching during the examination in order to manually trace and locate the test data files on the devices, which might not have otherwise been recovered during the use of a forensic tool's automated examination process and in its basic reporting mechanism.

Every time the forensic examination software located one of the sent test files and messages on the devices, which could be attributed to one of the test Apps, then a count was recorded for the App and its device. Once the first examinations were completed, the test data was deleted from each device, as is commonly done by criminals to hide their activity and incriminating files. Only the App's general user interfaces were used during this data deleting phase. The forensic examination of each device was then repeated and once again test files recovered and attributable to test Apps were counted. The totals of the successfully recovered files were calculated and considered as positive forensic opportunities because each recovered test file represented a crime having been committed and therefore the recovery of such a file could potentially lead to the prosecution of an offender.

IV. RESULTS AND ANALYSES

This section outlines the results and analysis from the experiments conducted during this research exploring the difficulties and opportunities in forensically acquiring evidential data from Apps running on both phones and PCs.

A. *Cloud technology challenges*

Apps like Instagram store most of the users' images and messages in the cloud and store cached links on the device to these images so that the user can find them again. The difficulty here for DFE is that the images may no longer be stored on the device itself for recovery via examination. None of the test files were recovered from the Instagram App across all three devices.

B. Web forensic opportunities on PCs

Web based Apps, such as Dropbox on PCs are now offering more evidence than in the past because of backups of files, documents and images from mobile phones and other devices being synchronised via the internet to the PC. This leaves a copy of the data, which can be potentially recovered by forensic examination of the PC. Only Dropbox and WhatsApp were found to offer consistent forensic opportunities to recover test files from across all three device types.

C. App developer updates issues

The forensic tools tended to check one App at a time for potential digital evidence as they worked through fully examining the mobile devices. If it came to an App that had been updated the tool could no longer recover data from it (because the data is was now stored in a different location on a different SQLite database than previously), and tended to finish the examination. Forensic tools data acquisition processes appear sensitive to the versions of operating software used on a device. On occasions data was found but not reported by the tool. These issues with the commercial forensic tools get fixed regularly, but until the glitch does get fixed evidential data could potentially be missed.

The situation is however less severe with App updates on PCs because Microsoft regulate their operating systems and for Apps to run on them they have to comply with the operating system and fit with its controls. Therefore, there is not as much variance on PCs as on Android phones in particular and also iPhone.

D. Ephemeral messaging challenges

Snapchat, on both mobile phones and PCs, does not store images. After a very short period of time they are deleted by the software automatically. None of the test files were recovered, either pre or post file deletion, from this App. The recovery of data is low and only occurring when the message has not been already read. Although some users often screen capture the Snapchat message and store it on their device, this is often recoverable by examiners.

It is noteworthy that phones back up files to a PC through a process of synchronisation. This process takes place so that the phone's data can be later restored back to the phone if necessary, for example if it encounters an OS issue. Although not tested during these experiments, this synchronisation function facilitates opportunities to recover data that was once on a mobile phone, not from examining the phone itself, but from examining the PC where the phone's data was backed up. This approach by forensic examiners may capture user data, which may no longer be recoverable from the mobile phone itself because the user deleted it.

E. Encrypted services

WhatsApp was the only App tested during this paper's experiments that purported to provide users with end to end encryption. Encryption is more common on mobile phones than on PCs but does not totally frustrate DFE. For example, sometimes thumb nail pictures still exist on a device, which can be viewed even if the criminal were to subsequently encrypt the photo. Despite WhatsApp encryption services, it was found to offer forensic opportunities across all three device types.

F. Duplication of test files

Large numbers of duplicate copies of the test data were found during the forensic examinations across all three devices both pre and post file deletion. There appeared to be duplicate files stored within all the Apps examined as well as in other locations on the devices not easily attributable to any App. The Apps themselves and/or the devices' OS appeared to be creating and storing duplicates of the test data that had been sent. Duplicate video files for example were found to be part copied and stored in the device's cached memory resulting from what appears to be user video playback activity on the device.

During the iPhone examination, significant numbers of files were recovered that had been saved in UNIX executable format. This occurs when files are originated from a non-Apple operating system and no extension is put on the file. However, on some occasions this did not happen with files that were received on the iPhone from the PC because the files were received with extensions. Even though such files had lost their information of resource forks (type/creator codes, specifically) during transmission from the PC to the iPhone, iOS could still use the extensions to associate the specific file types. In such scenario, both the UNIX and reconstructed files were stored on the iPhone and could both be recovered. Both files had the same time stamps on them indicating that they were the same file as the one sent from the PC.

Some of the recovered files on the iPhone had been saved within the "thumbs.db" files, which were created by Windows OS without user's knowledge as per default settings. This type of file generates a quick preview of the content of a folder using a thumbnail cache. During experiments, such cache files appeared to have been sent along with the test video and picture files. Recovered artefacts from these files could be used to prove that illicit photos were previously stored on a suspect's hard drive even after the deletion of the content.

Backups of media contents in both Kik and WhatsApp were found to cause duplicates of photos and videos. For example, the exact same file was recovered from the Kik App stored in the folders "content_manager/data_chache" and also "attachments" within the path "Backup/Applications/group.com.kik.chat/cores/private/41b3f76b03e54d9dac449d1c1ab5955b/". Photographs received from WhatsApp were found to be stored into Apple's photos as well as in the App's databases. During this process files stored in "bmp" and "gif" appeared to be duplicated into a "jpg" format before being stored in Apple's photos.

G. Device type factor

Table 4 is a summary of the positive forensic examination results found by device type during experiments. The second column from the left shows the number of test files sent to the device and therefore could have been potentially recovered from it. Every time one of the test files was found that could be attributable to one of the test App, a note was recorded. This was done, pre and post deletion, for each of the devices.

TABLE IV. POSITIVE FORENSIC EXAMINATION RESULTS BY DEVICE TYPE.

	Total test files that could be potentially recovered	Pre - deletion files actually recovered	Post - deletion files actually recovered	Actual links to files stored in the cloud recovered Pre -deletion	Actual links to files stored in the cloud recovered Post - deletion	Grand totals of files recovered
PC	266	29	29	10	10	78-30%
iOS	210	14	12	22	17	65-30%
Android	218	18	14	2	0	34-16%

The remaining columns in Table 4 show the actual number of files found both pre and post deletion. As can be seen in the column on the far right of Table 4, the PC appeared to offer DFE the most forensic opportunities with 30% of the test sample files being recovered, which is similar to the number recovered from the iPhone. Only 16% of the test files were recovered from the android phone.

Most PCs run Microsoft operating systems. The file structures and OS run on these devices' hard drives are all the same despite the PCs and the hard drives being manufactured by numerous different companies. This may explain why, at 78 files and 30% recovery, the PC offered most opportunities compared with the android phone. This is likely to be as a result of the frequency of upgrade of the android operating system, as shown in Table 1, and the lack of regulation and uniformity around its development between phone manufacturers.

All the forensic examination tools used have had development updates since the experiments were conducted. However, the experiments were not repeated with the updated forensic software tools so it is not possible to say whether the updates to the tools may have improved the recovery of the test files, improving positive forensic opportunities.

H. App type factor

None of the test files recovered could be attributable to Instagram or Snap chat, which is likely to be because of their ephemeral security features. Table 5 shows the ranking of the Apps, in terms of the number of test files recovered on each device and across all devices. It was observed that across all devices, Google Photos, Dropbox and WhatsApp were the top three Apps which offered the most forensic opportunities to recover the test files.

TABLE V. POSITIVE FORENSIC EXAMINATION RANKS BY APP TYPE.

PC		
App		Recovered files
1st	Google photos	20
2nd	Dropbox	18
3rd	Skype	16
4th	Twitter	10
5th	Whatspp	8

Iphone		
App		Recovered files
1st	Google photos	22
2nd	Drop box	17
3rd	WhatsApp	12
4th	Kik	10
5th	Twitter	4

Samsung		
App		Recovered files
1st	WhatsApp	11
2nd	kik	10
3rd	DropBox	6
4th	Skype	4
5th	Facebook Messenger	3

All devices		
App		Recovered files
1st	Google Photos	42
2nd	Dropbox	41
3rd	WhatsApp	31
4th	Skype	20
5th	Kik	20
6th	Twitter	14
7th	Facebook Messenger	3

TABLE VI. POSITIVE FORENSIC EXAMINATION RESULTS BY FILE TYPE.

Test File types	Files recovered
Jpeg	50
Chat logs	23
MS Word document	20
Bitmap	19
MP4	17
GIF	16
Avi	12
Mpeg	11
Winzip	5
3GP mobile phone images	4
Total files succesfully sent	177

Table 6 shows that Jpeg was the most widely recovered of all the test files. Jpeg files have two sub-formats, one of which is JFIF (Jpeg File Interchange Format). JFIF is often used on the web. In the mandatory JFIF APP0 marker [21], segment parameters of the image are specified and this is where an uncompressed thumbnail can be embedded. Because of the embedding of a thumbnail, the hash value for the file is changed, which explains why duplicates of the files look the same to the user but are in fact not identical.

V. CONCLUSIONS

Although some files could no longer be recovered after they had been deleted during the experiments, a significant number could still be recovered again. It was not possible to send all the test files to the smart phones. The iPhone was only capable of receiving 210 of the test files compared with 266 to the PC because of OS and App differences. Of the test files that were successfully sent to the iPhone, 30% of those were successfully recovered. It was possible to send slightly more test files, in total 218, to the Samsung phone than the iPhone but only 16% were recovered.

Duplicates of the test files resulting from OS and App processes were also recovered during the experiments. A law court may decide to take these into consideration, if found on a suspect's device, even though these files may not always be easily associated with any particular App because, for example, they may be stored in unallocated space on the device's memory. However, because of hash value differences between the file sent from one suspect's device with that duplicate file recovered on the second suspect's device, the DFE would need to be able to explain how and why the file had been altered to prove it actually came from the first suspect, thereby linking them together.

None of the test files sent using ephemeral Apps, Snap chat and Instagram, were recovered. However, they may be recoverable using specific forensic examination processes [22]. This causes additional complexities for DFEs. If mobile phones, and in particular Android based phones, were to consistently offer fewer opportunities to recover evidence both now and in the future, then that would potentially represent a degradation in LEAs' capabilities, given that large numbers of criminals are moving to using their phones as the primary device to connect to the internet.

In future, a more longitudinal study will be necessary to take into account the impact of updates by OS and App developers on the tools. It will be worth conducting a statistical analysis to determine if the ability to retrieve data is related to the number of updates of the operating platform made by the developer. Establishing whether the OS continues to create and save duplicate files to the cloud despite the auto save function being disabled would be useful. Knowing the effects that such an action may have on the numbers of recoverable duplicate files and their storage locations, such as cache, would be helpful.

REFERENCES

[1] OFCOM, "Communications Market Report (UK)", 2016, Available online: https://www.ofcom.org.uk/__data/assets/pdf_file/0024/26826/cmr_uk_2016.pdf, Last accessed September 2017.

[2] HMIC, "National Child Protection Inspections", 2014, Available online:https://www.justiceinspectorates.gov.uk/hmicfrs/wp-content/uploads/greater-manchester-national-child-protection-inspection.pdf, Last accesed September 2017.

[3] S. Bommisetty, R. Tamma, and H. Mahalik, "Practical Mobile Forensics", Packt Publishing, 2014.

[4] AppBrain, "WhatsApp Inc. summary", Available online: http://www. appbrain.com/dev/WhatsApp+Inc./, Last accessed September 2017.

[5] Y. Ma, X. Liu; Yi. Liu; Yu. Liu and G. Huang "A Tale of Two Fashions: An Empirical Study on the Performance of Native Apps and Web Apps on Android", IEEE Transactions on Mobile Computing, ISSN: 1536-1233, doi: 10.1109/TMC. 2017.2756633, in press.

[6] J. B. Bayer, N. B. Ellison, S. Y. Schoenebeck and E. B. Falk, "Sharing the Small Moments: Ephemeral Social Interaction on Snapchat", Information, Communication & Society, vol. 19, pp. 956-977, 2016.

[7] F. Roesner, B. T. Gill and T. Kohno, "Sex, Lies, or Kittens? Investigating the Use of Snapchat's Self-Destructing Messages", Financial Cryptography and Data Security, Lecture Notes in Computer Science, vol. 8437. Springer, 2014.

[8] J. Lessard and G. C. Kessler, "Android Forensics: Simplifying Cell Phone Examinations", Small Scale Digital Device Forensics Journal, vol. 4, no. 1, pp. 1-12, ISSN: 1941-6164, September 2010.

[9] V. Rao and A.S.N. Chakravarthy, "Survey on Android Forensic Tools and Methodologies", International Journal of Computer Applications, vol. 154, no. 8, pp.17-21, 2016.

[10] M. F. Breeuwsma, Forensic imaging of embedded systems using JTAG (boundary-scan), Digital Investigation, vol. 3, pp. 32–42, 2006.

[11] D. T. Hoang, C. Lee, D. Niyato and P. Wang, "A survey of mobile cloud computing: architecture, applications, and approaches", Wireless Communications and Mobile Computing, vol. 13, pp. 1587-1611, 2013.

[12] K. Yang, S. Ou and H. Chen, "On effective offloading services for resource-constrained mobile devices running heavier mobile Internet applications", IEEE Communications Magazine, vol. 46, pp. 56-63, January 2008.

[13] M. Lai, J. Wang, T. Song, N. Liu, Z. Qi and W. Zhou, "VSP: A Virtual Smartphone Platform to Enhance the Capability of Physical Smartphone", IEEE Trustcom, BigDataSE & ISPA, pp.1434-1441, August 2016.

[14] A. Klein, "Hard Drive Stats for Q2 2017", Available online: https://www.backblaze.com/blog/hard-drive-failure-stats-q2-2017/,Last accessed September 2017.

[15] Legistlation.gov.uk. "Regulation of Investigatory Powers Act 2000", 2000, Available online: http://www.legislation.gov.uk/ukpga/2000/23/contents, Last accessed September 2017.

[16] VirtualBox tool, Available online: https://www.virtualbox.org, Last accessed September 2017.

[17] Cellebrite UFED tool, Available online: http://www.cellebrite.com/Mobile-Forensics/Solutions, Last accessed September 2017.

[18] Autopsy tool, Available online: https://www.sleuthkit.org, Last accessed September 2017.

[19] Association Of Chief Police Officers, "ACPO Good Practice Guide for Digital Evidence v5", 2012, Available online: http://www.digital-detective.net/digital-forensics-documents/ACPO_Good_Practice_Guide_for_Digital_Evidence_v5.pdf, Last accessed September 2017.

[20] B. Saltaformaggio, R. Bhatia, X. Zhang, D. Xu., G. Richard III, "Screen after Previous Screens: Spatial-Temporal Recreation of Android App Displays from Memory Images". In Proc. 25th USENIX Security Symposium (Security'16), Austin, TX, 2016.

[21] Jpeg file format, Available online: https://www.w3.org/Graphics/JPEG/jfif3.pdf, Last accessed September 2017.

[22] M. A. H. B. Azhar, and T. Barton, "Forensic Analysis of Secure Ephemeral Messaging Applications on Android Platforms" In: Jahankhani H. et al. (eds) Global Security, Safety and Sustainability - The Security Challenges of the Connected World. ICGS3 2017. Communications in Computer and Information Science, vol. 630, pp. 27-41, Springer, 2017.

Detecting Safety- and Security-Relevant Programming Defects by Sound Static Analysis

Daniel Kästner, Laurent Mauborgne, Christian Ferdinand

AbsInt GmbH
Science Park 1, 66123 Saarbrücken, Germany
Email: kaestner@absint.com, mauborgne@absint.com, ferdinand@absint.com

***Abstract*—Static code analysis has evolved to be a standard technique in the development process of safety-critical software. It can be applied to show compliance to coding guidelines, and to demonstrate the absence of critical programming errors, including runtime errors and data races. In recent years, security concerns have become more and more relevant for safety-critical systems, not least due to the increasing importance of highly-automated driving and pervasive connectivity. While in the past, sound static analyzers have been primarily applied to demonstrate classical safety properties they are well suited also to address data safety, and to discover security vulnerabilities. This article gives an overview and discusses practical experience.**

Keywords–static analysis; abstract interpretation; runtime errors; security vulnerabilities; functional safety; cybersecurity.

I. Introduction

Some years ago, static analysis meant manual review of programs. Nowadays, automatic static analysis tools are gaining popularity in software development as they offer a tremendous increase in productivity by automatically checking the code under a wide range of criteria. Many software development projects are developed according to coding guidelines, such as MISRA C [1], SEI CERT C [2], or CWE (Common Weakness Enumeration) [3], aiming at a programming style that improves clarity and reduces the risk of introducing bugs. Compliance checking by static analysis tools has become common practice.

In safety-critical systems, static analysis plays a particularly important role. A failure of a safety-critical system may cause high costs or even endanger human beings. With the growing size of software-implemented functionality, preventing software-induced system failures becomes an increasingly important task. One particularly dangerous class of errors are runtime errors which include faulty pointer manipulations, numerical errors such as arithmetic overflows and division by zero, data races, and synchronization errors in concurrent software. Such errors can cause software crashes, invalidate separation mechanisms in mixed-criticality software, and are a frequent cause of errors in concurrent and multi-core applications. At the same time, these defects are also at the root of many security vulnerabilities, including exploits based on buffer overflows, dangling pointers, or integer errors.

In safety-critical software projects, obeying coding guidelines such as MISRA C is strongly recommended by all current safety standards, including DO-178C [4], IEC-61508 [5], ISO-26262 [6], and EN-50128 [7]. In addition, all of them consider demonstrating the absence of runtime errors explicitly as a verification goal. This is often formulated indirectly by addressing runtime errors (e.g., division by zero, invalid pointer accesses, arithmetic overflows) in general, and additionally considering corruption of content, synchronization mechanisms, and freedom of interference in concurrent execution. Semantics-based static analysis has become the predominant technology to detect runtime errors and data races.

Abstract interpretation is a formal methodology for semantics-based static program analysis [8]. It supports formal soundness proofs (it can be proven that no error is missed) and scales to real-life industry applications. Abstract interpretation-based static analyzers provide full control and data coverage and allow conclusions to be drawn that are valid for all program runs with all inputs. Such conclusions may be that no timing or space constraints are violated, or that runtime errors or data races are absent: the absence of these errors can be guaranteed [9]. Nowadays, abstract interpretation-based static analyzers that can detect stack overflows and violations of timing constraints [10] and that can prove the absence of runtime errors and data races [11][12], are widely used for developing and verifying safety-critical software.

In the past, security properties have mostly been relevant for non-embedded and/or non-safety-critical programs. Recently due to increasing connectivity requirements (cloud-based services, car-to-car communication, over-the-air updates, etc.), more and more security issues are rising in safety-critical software as well. Security exploits like the Jeep Cherokee hacks [13] which affect the safety of the system are becoming more and more frequent. In consequence, safety-critical software development faces novel challenges which previously only have been addressed in other industry domains.

On the other hand, as outlined above, safety-critical software is developed according to strict guidelines which effectively reduce the relevant subset of the programming language used and improve software verifiability. As an example dynamic memory allocation and recursion often are forbidden or used in a very limited way. In consequence, for safety-critical software much stronger code properties can be shown than for non-safety-critical software, so that also security vulnerabilities can be addressed in a more powerful way.

The topic of this article is to show that some classes of defects can be proven to be absent in the software so that exploits based on such defects can be excluded. On the other hand, additional syntactic checks and semantical analyses become necessary to address security properties that are orthogonal to safety requirements. Throughout the article we will focus on software aspects only, without addressing safety or security properties at the hardware level. While we focus on the programming language C, the basic analysis techniques described in this article are applicable to other programming languages as well.

The article is structured as follows: Section II discusses the relation between *safety* and *security* requirements. The role of coding standards is discussed in Section II-A, a classification of vulnerabilities is given in Section II-B, and Section II-C focuses on the analysis complexity of safety and security properties. Section III gives an overview of abstract interpretation and its application to runtime error analysis, using the sound analyzer Astrée as an example. Section IV gives an overview of control and data flow analysis with emphasis on two advanced analysis techniques: program slicing (cf. Section IV-A) and taint analysis (cf. Section IV-B). Section V concludes.

II. Security in Safety-Critical Systems

Functional safety and security are aspects of dependability, in addition to reliability and availability. *Functional safety* is usually defined as the absence of unreasonable risk to life and property caused by malfunctioning behavior of the software. The main goals of *information security* or *cybersecurity* (for brevity denoted as "*security*" in this article) traditionally are to preserve *confidentiality* (information must not be disclosed to unauthorized entities), *integrity* (data must not be modified in an unauthorized or undetected way), and *availability* (data must be accessible and usable upon demand).

In safety-critical systems, safety and security properties are intertwined. A violation of security properties can endanger the functional safety of the system: an information leak could provide the basis for a successful attack on the system, and a malicious data corruption or denial-of-service attack may cause the system to malfunction. Vice versa, a violation of safety goals can compromise security: buffer overflows belong to the class of critical runtime errors whose absence have to be demonstrated in safety-critical systems. At the same time, an undetected buffer overflow is one of the main security vulnerabilities which can be exploited to read unauthorized information, to inject code, or to cause the system to crash [14]. To emphasize this, in a safety-critical system the definition of functional safety can be adapted to define cybersecurity as absence of unreasonable risk to life and property caused by malicious misusage of the software.

The convergence of safety and security properties also becomes apparent in the increasing role of data in safety-critical systems. There are many well-documented incidents where harm was caused by erroneous data, corrupted data, or inappropriate use of data – examples include the Turkish Airlines A330 incident (2015), the Mars Climate Orbiter crash (1999), or the Cedars Sinai Medical Centre CT scanner radiation overdose (2009) [15]. The reliance on data in safety-critical systems has significantly grown in the past few years, cf. e.g., data used for decision-support systems, data used in sensor fusion for highly automatic driving, or data provided by car-to-car communication or downloaded from a cloud. As a consequence of this there are ongoing activities to provide specific guidance for handling data in safety-critical systems [15]. At the same time, these data also represent safety-relevant targets for security attacks.

A. Coding Guidelines

The MISRA C standard [1] has originally been developed with a focus on automotive industry but is now widely recognized as a coding guideline for safety-critical systems in general. Its aim is to avoid programming errors and enforce a programming style that enables the safest possible use of C. A particular focus is on dealing with undefined/unspecified behavior of C and on preventing runtime errors. As a consequence, it is also directly applicable to security-relevant code.

The most prominent coding guidelines targeting security aspects are the ISO/IEC TS 17961 [16], the SEI CERT C Coding Standard [2], and the MITRE Common Weakness Enumeration CWE [3].

The ISO/IEC TS 17961 C Secure Coding Rules [16] specifies rules for secure coding in C. It does not primarily address developers but rather aims at establishing requirements for compilers and static analyzers. MISRA C:2012 Addendum 2 [17] compares the ISO/IEC TS 17961 rule set with MISRA C:2012. Only 4 of the C Secure rules are not covered by the first edition of MISRA C:2012 [1], however, with Amendment 1 to MISRA C:2012 [18] all of them are covered as well. This illustrates the strong overlap between the safety- and security-oriented coding guidelines.

The SEI CERT C Coding Standard belongs to the CERT Secure Coding Standards [19]. While emphasizing the security aspect CERT C [2] also targets safety-critical systems: it aims at "developing safe, reliable and secure systems". CERT distinguishes between rules and recommendations where rules are meant to provide normative requirements and recommendations are meant to provide general guidance; the book version [2] describes the rules only. A particular focus is on eliminating undefined behaviors that can lead to exploitable vulnerabilities. In fact, almost half of the CERT rules (43 of 99 rules) are targeting undefined behaviors according to the C norm.

The Common Weakness Enumeration CWE is a software community project [3] that aims at creating a catalog of software weaknesses and vulnerabilities. The goal of the project is to better understand flaws in software and to create automated tools that can be used to identify, fix, and prevent those flaws. There are several catalogues for different programming languages, including C. In the latter one, once again, many rules are associated with undefined or unspecified behaviors.

B. Vulnerability Classification

Many rules are shared between the different coding guidelines, but there is no common structuring of security vulnerabilities. The CERT Secure C roughly structures its rules according to language elements, whereas ISO/IEC TS 17961 and CWE are structured as a flat list of vulnerabilities. In the following we list some of the most prominent vulnerabilities which are addressed in all coding guidelines and which belong to the most critical ones at the C programming level. The presentation follows the overview given in [14].

1) Stack-based Buffer Overflows: An array declared as local variable in C is stored on the runtime stack. A C program may write beyond the end of the array due to index values being too large or negative, or due to invalid increments of pointers pointing into the array. A runtime error then has occurred whose behavior is undefined according to the C semantics. As a consequence the program might crash with bus error or segmentation fault, but typically adjacent memory regions will be overwritten. An attacker can exploit this by manipulating the return address or the frame pointer both of which are stored on the stack, or by indirect pointer overwriting, and thereby gaining control over the execution flow of the program. In the first case the program will jump to code injected by the attacker into the overwritten buffer instead of executing an intended function return. In case of overflows on array read accesses confidential information stored on the stack (e.g., through temporary local variables) might be leaked. An example of such an exploit is the well-known W32.Blaster.Worm [20].

2) Heap-based Buffer Overflows: Heap memory is dynamically allocated at runtime, e.g., by calling $malloc()$ or $calloc()$ implementations provided by dynamic memory allocation libraries. There may be read or write operations to dynamically allocated arrays that access beyond the array boundaries, similarly to stack-allocated arrays. In case of a read access information stored on the heap might be leaked – a prominent example is the Heartbleed bug in OpenSSL (cf. CERT vulnerability 720951 [21]). Via write operations attackers may inject code and gain control over program execution, e.g., by overwriting management information of the dynamic memory allocator stored in the accessed memory chunk.

3) General Invalid Pointer Accesses: Buffer overflows are special cases of invalid pointer accesses, which are listed here as separate points due to the large number of attacks based on them. However, any invalid pointer access in general is a security vulnerability – other examples are null pointer accesses or dangling pointer accesses. Accessing such a pointer is undefined behavior which can cause the program to crash, or behave erratically. A dangling pointer points to a memory location that has been deallocated either implicitly (e.g., data stored in the stack frame of a function after its return) or explicitly by the programmer. A concrete example of a dangling pointer access is the double free vulnerability where already freed memory is freed a second time. This can be exploited by an attacker to overwrite arbitrary memory locations and execute injected code [14].

4) Uninitialized Memory Accesses: Automatic variables and dynamically allocated memory have indeterminate values when not explicitly initialized. Accessing them is undefined behavior. Uninitialized variables can also be used for security attacks, e.g., in CVE-2009-1888 [22] potentially uninitialized variables passed to a function were exploited to bypass the access control list and gain access to protected files [2].

5) Integer Errors: Integer errors are not exploitable vulnerabilities by themselves, but they can be the cause of critical vulnerabilities like stack- or heap-based buffer overflows. Examples of integer errors are arithmetic overflows, or invalid cast operations. If, e.g., a negative signed value is used as an argument to a $memcpy()$ call, it will be interpreted as a large unsigned value, potentially resulting in a buffer overflow.

6) Format String Vulnerabilities : A format string is copied to the output stream with occurrences of %-commands representing arguments to be popped from the stack and expanded into the stream. A format string vulnerability occurs, if attackers can supply the format string because it enables them to manipulate the stack, once again making the program write to arbitrary memory locations.

7) Concurrency Defects: Concurrency errors may lead to concurrency attacks which allow attackers to violate confidentiality, integrity and availability of systems [23]. In a race condition the program behavior depends on the timing of thread executions. A special case is a write-write or read-write data race where the same shared variable is accessed by concurrent threads without proper synchronization. In a Time-of-Check-to-Time-of-Use (TOCTOU) race condition the checking of a condition and its use are not protected by a critical section. This can be exploited by an attacker, e.g., by changing the file handle between the accessibility check and the actual file access. In general, attacks can be run either by creating a data race due to missing lock-/unlock protections, or by exploiting existing data races, e.g., by triggering thread invocations.

Most of the vulnerabilities described above are based on undefined behaviors, and among them buffer overflows seem to play the most prominent role for real-live attacks. Most of them can be used for denial-of-service attacks by crashing the program or causing erroneous behavior. They can also be exploited to inject code and cause the program to execute it, and to extract confidential data from the system. It is worth noticing that from the perspective of a static analyzer most exploits are based on potential runtime errors: when using an unchecked value as an index in an array the error will only occur if the attacker manages to provide an invalid index value. The obvious conclusion is that safely eliminating all potential runtime errors due to undefined behaviors in the program significantly reduces the risk for security vulnerabilities.

C. Analysis Complexity

While semantics-based static program analysis is widely used for safety properties, there is practically no such analyzer dedicated to specific security properties. This is mostly explained by the difference in complexity between safety and security properties. From a semantical point of view, a safety property can always be expressed as a trace property. This means that to find all safety issues, it is enough to look at each trace of execution in isolation.

This is not possible any more for security properties. Most of them can only be expressed as set of traces properties, or hyperproperties [24]. A typical example is non-interference [25]: to express that the final value of a variable x can only be affected by the initial value of y and no other variable, one must consider each pair of possible execution traces with the same initial value for y, and check that the final value of x is the same for both executions. It was proven in [24] that any other definition (tracking assignments, etc) considering only one execution trace at a time would miss some cases or add false dependencies. This additional level of sets has direct consequences on the difficulty to track security properties soundly.

Other examples of hyperproperties are secure information flow policies, service level agreements (which describe acceptable availability of resources in term of mean response time or percentage uptime), observational determinism (whether a system appears deterministic to a low-level user), or quantitative information flow.

Finding expressive and efficient abstractions for such properties is a young research field (see [26]), which is the reason why no sound analysis of such properties appear in industrial static analyzers yet. The best solution using the current state of the art consists of using dedicated safety properties as an approximation of the security property in question, such as the taint propagation described in Section IV-B.

III. Proving the Absence of Defects

In safety-critical systems, the use of dynamic memory allocation and recursions typically is forbidden or only used in limited ways. This simplifies the task of static analysis such that for safety-critical embedded systems it is possible to formally prove the absence of runtime errors, or report all potential runtime errors which still exist in the program. Such analyzers are based on the theory of abstract interpretation [8], a mathematically rigorous formalism providing a semantics-based methodology for static program analysis.

A. Abstract Interpretation

The semantics of a programming language is a formal description of the behavior of programs. The most precise semantics is the so-called concrete semantics, describing closely the actual execution of the program on all possible inputs. Yet in general, the concrete semantics is not computable. Even under the assumption that the program terminates, it is too detailed to allow for efficient computations. The solution is to introduce an abstract semantics that approximates the concrete semantics of the program and is efficiently computable. This abstract semantics can be chosen as the basis for a static analysis. Compared to an analysis of the concrete semantics, the analysis result may be less precise but the computation may be significantly faster.

A static analyzer is called *sound* if the computed results hold for any possible program execution. Abstract interpretation supports formal correctness proofs: it can be proved that an analysis will terminate and that it is sound, i.e., that it computes an over-approximation of the concrete semantics. Imprecision can occur, but it can be shown that they will always occur on the safe side. In runtime error analysis, soundness means that the analyzer never omits to signal an error that can appear in some execution environment. If no potential error is signaled, definitely no runtime error can occur: there are no false negatives. If a potential error is reported, the analyzer cannot exclude that there is a concrete program execution triggering the error. If there is no such execution, this is a false alarm (false positive). This imprecision is on the safe side: it can never happen that there is a runtime error which is not reported.

B. Astrée

In the following we will concentrate on the sound static runtime error analyzer Astrée [12][27]. It reports program defects caused by unspecified and undefined behaviors according to the C norm (ISO/IEC 9899:1999 (E)), program defects caused by invalid concurrent behavior, violations of user-specified programming guidelines, and computes program properties relevant for functional safety. Users are notified about: integer/floating-point division by zero, out-of-bounds array indexing, erroneous pointer manipulation and dereferencing (buffer overflows, null pointer dereferencing, dangling pointers, etc.), data races, lock/unlock problems, deadlocks, integer and floating-point arithmetic overflows, read accesses to uninitialized variables, unreachable code, non-terminating loops, violations of optional user-defined static assertions, violations of coding rules (MISRA C, ISO/IEC TS 17961, CERT, CWE) and code metric thresholds.

Astrée computes data and control flow reports containing a detailed listing of accesses to global and static variables sorted by functions, variables, and processes and containing a summary of caller/called relationships between functions. The analyzer can also report each effectively shared variable, the list of processes accessing it, and the types of the accesses (read, write, read/write).

The C99 standard does not fully specify data type sizes, endianness nor alignment which can vary with different targets or compilers. Astrée is informed about these target ABI settings by a dedicated configuration file in XML format and takes the specified properties into account.

The design of the analyzer aims at reaching the zero false alarm objective, which was accomplished for the first time on large industrial applications at the end of November 2003. For keeping the initial number of false alarms low, a high analysis precision is mandatory. To achieve high precision Astrée provides a variety of predefined abstract domains, e.g.: The interval domain approximates variable values by intervals, the octagon domain [28] covers relations of the form $x \pm y \leq c$ for variables x and y and constants c. The memory domain empowers Astrée to exactly analyze pointer arithmetic and union manipulations. It also supports a type-safe analysis of absolute memory addresses. With the filter domain digital filters can be precisely approximated. Floating-point computations are precisely modeled while keeping track of possible rounding errors.

To deal with concurrency defects, Astrée implements a sound low-level concurrent semantics [29] which provides a scalable sound abstraction covering all possible thread interleavings. The interleaving semantics enables Astrée, in addition to the classes of runtime errors found in sequential programs, to report data races, and lock/unlock problems, i.e., inconsistent synchronization. The set of shared variables does not need to be specified by the user: Astrée assumes that every global variable can be shared, and discovers which ones are effectively shared, and on which ones there is a data race. After a data race, the analysis continues by considering the values stemming from all interleavings. Since Astrée is aware of all locks held for every program point in each concurrent thread, Astrée can also report all potential deadlocks.

Thread priorities are exploited to reduce the amount of spurious interleavings considered in the abstraction and to achieve a more precise analysis. A dedicated task priority domain supports dynamic priorities, e.g., according to the Priority Ceiling Protocol used in OSEK systems [30]. Astrée includes a built-in notion of mutual exclusion locks, on top of which actual synchronization mechanisms offered by operating systems can be modeled (such as POSIX mutexes or semaphores).

Programs to be analyzed are seldom run in isolation; they interact with an environment. In order to soundly report all runtime errors, Astrée must take the effect of the environment into account. In the simplest case the software runs directly on the hardware, in which case the environment is limited to a set of volatile variables, i.e., program variables that can be modified by the environment concurrently, and for which a range can be provided to Astrée by formal directives written manually, or generated by a dedicated wrapper generator. More often, the program is run on top of an operating system, which it can access through function calls to a system library. When analyzing a program using a library, one possible solution is to include the source code of the library with the program. This is not always convenient (if the library is complex), nor possible, if the library source is not available, or not fully written in C, or ultimately relies on kernel services (e.g., for system libraries). An alternative is to provide a stub implementation, i.e., to write, for each library function, a specification of its possible effect on the program. Astrée provides stub libraries for the ARINC 653 standard, and the OSEK/AUTOSAR standards. In case of OSEK systems, Astrée parses the OIL (OSEK Implementation Language) configuration file and generates the corresponding C implementation automatically.

Practical experience on avionics and automotive industry applications are given in [12][31]. They show that industry-sized programs of millions of lines of code can be analyzed in acceptable time with high precision for runtime errors and data races.

IV. Control and Data Flow Analysis

Safety standards such as DO-178C and ISO-26262 require to perform control and data flow analysis as a part of software unit or integration testing and in order to verify the software architectural design. Investigating control and data flow is also subject of the Data Safety guidance [15], and it is a prerequisite for analyzing confidentiality and integrity properties as a part of a security case. Technically, any semantics-based static analysis is able to provide information about data and control flow, since this is the basis of the actual program analysis. However, data and control flow analysis has many aspects, and for some of them, tailored analysis mechanisms are needed.

Global data and control flow analysis gives a summary of variable accesses and function invocations throughout program execution. In its standard data and control flow reports Astrée computes the number of read/write accesses for every global or static variable and lists the location of each access along with the function from which the access is made and the thread in which the function is executed. The control flow is described by listing all callers and callees for every C function along with the threads in which they can be run. Indirect variable accesses via pointers as well as function pointer call targets are fully taken into account.

More sophisticated information can be provided by two dedicated analysis methods: program slicing and taint analysis. Program slicing [32] aims at identifying the part of the program that can influence a given set of variables at a given program point. Applied to a result value, e.g., it shows which functions, which statements, and which input variables contribute to its computation. Taint analysis tracks the propagation of specific data values through program execution. It can be used, e.g., to determine program parts affected by corrupted data from an insecure source. In the following we give a more detailed overview of both techniques.

A. Program Slicing

A slicing criterion of a program P is a tuple (s, V) where s is a statement and V is a set of variables in P. Intuitively, a slice is a subprogram of P which has the same behavior than P with respect to the slicing criterion (s, V). Computing a statement-minimal slice is an undecidable problem, but using static analysis approximative slices can be computed. As an example, Astrée provides a program slicer which can produce sound and compact slices by exploiting the invariants from Astrée's core analysis including points-to information for variable and function pointers. A dynamic slice does not contain all statements potentially affecting the slicing criterion, but only those relevant for a specific subset of program executions, e.g., only those in which an error value can result.

Computing sound program slices is relevant for demonstrating safety and security properties. It can be used to show that certain parts of the code or certain input variables might influence or cannot influence a program section of interest.

B. Taint Analysis

In literature, taint analysis is often mentioned in combination with unsound static analyzers, since it allows to efficiently detect potential errors in the code, e.g., array-index-out-of-bounds accesses, or infeasible library function parameters [2], [16]. Inside a sound runtime error analyzer this is not needed since typically more powerful abstract domains can track all undefined or unspecified behaviors. Inside a sound analyzer, taint analysis is primarily a technique for analyzing security properties. Its advantage is that users can flexibly specify taints, taint sources, and taint sinks, so that application-specific data and control flow requirements can be modeled.

In order to be able to leverage this efficient family of analyses in sound analyzers, one must formally define the properties that may be checked using such techniques. Then it is possible to prove that a given implementation is sound with respect to that formal definition, leading to clean and well defined analysis results. Taint analysis consists of discovering data dependencies using the notion of taint propagation. Taint propagation can be formalized using a non-standard semantics of programs, where an imaginary taint is associated to some input values. Considering a standard semantics using a successor relation between program states, and considering that a program state is a map from memory locations (variables, program counter, etc.) to values in $\mathcal{V}$, the *tainted* semantics relates tainted states which are maps from the same memory locations to $\mathcal{V} \times \{\text{taint}, \text{notaint}\}$, and such that if we project on $\mathcal{V}$ we get the same relation as with the standard semantics.

To define what happens to the *taint* part of the tainted value, one must define a *taint policy*. The taint policy specifies:

Taint sources which are a subset of input values or variables such that in any state, the values associated with that input values or variables are always tainted.

Taint propagation describes how the tainting gets propagated. Typical propagation is through assignment, but more complex propagation can take more control flow into account, and may not propagate the taint through all arithmetic or pointer operations.

Taint cleaning is an alternative to taint propagation, describing all the operations that do not propagate the taint. In this case, all assignments not containing the taint cleaning will propagate the taint.

Taint sinks is an optional set of memory locations. This has no semantical effect, except to specify conditions when an alarm should be emitted when verifying a program (an alarm must be emitted if a taint sink may become tainted for a given execution of the program).

A sound taint analyzer will compute an over-approximation of the memory locations that may be mapped to a tainted value during program execution. The soundness requirement ensures that no taint sink warning will be overlooked by the analyzer.

The tainted semantics can easily be extended to a mix of different hues of tainting, corresponding to an extension of the taint set associated with values. Then propagation can get more complex, with tainting not just being propagated but also changing hue depending on the instruction. Such extensions lead to a rather flexible and powerful data dependency analysis, while remaining scalable.

V. Conclusion

In this article, we have given an overview of code-level defects and vulnerabilities relevant for functional safety and security. We have shown that many security attacks can be traced back to behaviors undefined or unspecified according to the C semantics. By applying sound static runtime error analyzers, a high degree of security can be achieved for safety-critical software since the absence of such defects can be proven. In addition, security hyperproperties require additional analyses to be performed which, by nature, have a high complexity. We have given two examples of scalable dedicated analyses, program slicing and taint analysis. Applied as extensions of sound static analyzers, they allow to further increase confidence in the security of safety-critical embedded systems.

Acknowledgment

This work was funded within the project ARAMiS II by the German Federal Ministry for Education and Research with the funding ID 01—S16025. The responsibility for the content remains with the authors.

References

[1] MISRA (Motor Industry Software Reliability Association) Working Group, MISRA-C:2012 Guidelines for the use of the C language in critical systems, MISRA Limited, Mar. 2013.

[2] Software Engineering Institute SEI – CERT Division, SEI CERT C Coding Standard – Rules for Developing Safe, Reliable, and Secure Systems. Carnegie Mellon University, 2016.

[3] The MITRE Corporation, "CWE – Common Weakness Enumeration." [Online]. Available: https://cwe.mitre.org [retrieved: Sep. 2017].

[4] Radio Technical Commission for Aeronautics, "RTCA DO-178C. Software Considerations in Airborne Systems and Equipment Certification," 2011.

[5] IEC 61508, "Functional safety of electrical/electronic/programmable electronic safety-related systems," 2010.

[6] ISO 26262, "Road vehicles – Functional safety," 2011.

[7] CENELEC EN 50128, "Railway applications – Communication, signalling and processing systems – Software for railway control and protection systems," 2011.

[8] P. Cousot and R. Cousot, "Abstract interpretation: a unified lattice model for static analysis of programs by construction or approximation of fixpoints," in Proc. of POPL'77. ACM Press, 1977, pp. 238–252. [Online]. Available: http://www.di.ens.fr/~cousot/COUSOTpapers/POPL77.shtml [retrieved: Sep. 2017].

[9] D. Kästner, "Applying Abstract Interpretation to Demonstrate Functional Safety," in Formal Methods Applied to Industrial Complex Systems, J.-L. Boulanger, Ed. London, UK: ISTE/Wiley, 2014.

[10] J. Souyris, E. Le Pavec, G. Himbert, V. Jégu, G. Borios, and R. Heckmann, "Computing the worst case execution time of an avionics program by abstract interpretation," in Proceedings of the 5th Intl Workshop on Worst-Case Execution Time (WCET) Analysis, 2005, pp. 21–24.

[11] D. Delmas and J. Souyris, "ASTRÉE: from Research to Industry," in Proc. 14th International Static Analysis Symposium (SAS2007), ser. LNCS, no. 4634, 2007, pp. 437–451.

[12] D. Kästner, A. Miné, L. Mauborgne, X. Rival, J. Feret, P. Cousot, A. Schmidt, H. Hille, S. Wilhelm, and C. Ferdinand, "Finding All Potential Runtime Errors and Data Races in Automotive Software," in SAE World Congress 2017. SAE International, 2017.

[13] Wired.com, "The jeep hackers are back to prove car hacking can get much worse," 2016. [Online]. Available: https://www.wired.com/2016/08/jeep-hackers-return-high-speed-steering-acceleration-hacks/ [retrieved: Sep. 2017]

[14] Y. Younan, W. Joosen, and F. Piessens, "Code injection in c and c++ : A survey of vulnerabilities and countermeasures," Departement Computerwetenschappen, Katholieke Universiteit Leuven, Tech. Rep., 2004.

[15] SCSC Data Safety Initiative Working Group [DSIWG], "Data Safety (Version 2.0) [SCSC-127B]," Safety-Critical Systems Club, Tech. Rep., Jan 2017.

[16] ISO/IEC, "Information Technology – Programming Languages, Their Environments and System Software Interfaces – Secure Coding Rules (ISO/IEC TS 17961)," Nov 2013.

[17] MISRA (Motor Industry Software Reliability Association) Working Group, MISRA-C:2012 – Addendum 2. Coverage of MISRA C:2012 against ISO/IEC TS 17961:2013 "C Secure", MISRA Limited, Apr. 2016.

[18] MISRA (Motor Industry Software Reliability Association) Working Group , MISRA-C:2012 Amendment 1 – Additional security guidelines for MISRA C:2012, MISRA Limited, Apr. 2016.

[19] CERT – Software Engineering Institute, Carnegie Mellon University, "SEI CERT Coding Standards Website." [Online]. Available: https://www.securecoding.cert.org [retrieved: Sep. 2017].

[20] Wikipedia, "Blaster (computer worm)." [Online]. Available: https://en.wikipedia.org/wiki/Blaster_(computer_worm) [retrieved: Sep. 2017].

[21] CERT – Vulnerability Notes Database, "Vulnerability Note VU#720951 – OpenSSL TLS heartbeat extension read overflow discloses sensitive information." [Online]. Available: http://www.kb.cert.org/vuls/id/720951 [retrieved: Sep. 2017].

[22] NIST – National Vulnerability Database, "CVE-2009-1888: SAMBA ACLs Uninitialized Memory Read." [Online]. Available: https://nvd.nist.gov/vuln/detail/CVE-2009-1888 [retrieved: Sep. 2017].

[23] J. Yang, A. Cui, J. Gallagher, S. Stolfo, and S. Sethumadhavan, "Concurrency attacks," in In the Fourth USENIX Workshop on Hot Topics in Parallelism (HOTPAR12), 2012.

[24] M. R. Clarkson and F. B. Schneider, "Hyperproperties," Journal of Computer Security, vol. 18, 2010, pp. 1157–1210.

[25] A. Sabelfeld and A. C. Myers, "Language-based information-flow security," IEEE Journal on Selected Areas in Communications, vol. 21, no. 1, 2003, pp. 5–19.

[26] M. Assaf, D. A. Naumann, J. Signoles, E. Totel, and F. Tronel, "Hypercollecting semantics and its application to static analysis of information flow," CoRR, vol. abs/1608.01654, 2016. [Online]. Available: http://arxiv.org/abs/1608.01654 [retrieved: Sep. 2017].

[27] A. Miné, L. Mauborgne, X. Rival, J. Feret, P. Cousot, D. Kästner, S. Wilhelm, and C. Ferdinand, "Taking Static Analysis to the Next Level: Proving the Absence of Run-Time Errors and Data Races with Astrée," Embedded Real Time Software and Systems Congress ERTS^2.

[28] A. Miné, "The Octagon Abstract Domain," Higher-Order and Symbolic Computation, vol. 19, no. 1, 2006, pp. 31–100.

[29] A. Miné, "Static analysis of run-time errors in embedded real-time parallel C programs," Logical Methods in Computer Science (LMCS), vol. 8, no. 26, Mar. 2012, p. 63.

[30] OSEK/VDX, OSEK/VDX Operating System. Version 2.2.3., http://www.osek-vdx.org, 2005.

[31] A. Miné and D. Delmas, "Towards an Industrial Use of Sound Static Analysis for the Verification of Concurrent Embedded Avionics Software," in Proc. of the 15th International Conference on Embedded Software (EMSOFT'15). IEEE CS Press, Oct. 2015, pp. 65–74.

[32] M. Weiser, "Program slicing," in Proceedings of the 5th International Conference on Software Engineering, ser. ICSE '81. IEEE Press, 1981, pp. 439–449.

Evaluations of Maximum Distance Achieved Using the Three Stage Multiphoton Protocol at 1550 nm, 1310 nm, and 850 nm

Majed Khodr
Electrical, Electronics and Communications Department
American University of Ras Al Khaimah
Ras Al Khaimah, UAE
e-mail: majed.khodr@aurak.ae

Abstract—**This paper presents an initial investigation of practical realization of quantum secure communication using the three-stage multi-photon tolerant protocols. The secret raw key was optimized and used to calculate the maximum achievable distance at three different wavelengths, i.e., 1550 nm, 1310 nm, and 850 nm assuming lossless fiber optics channel length. The maximum achievable distances for the three wavelengths were around 200 km, 140 km, and 25 km, respectively.**

Keywords-quantum communication; fiber channel; three stage protocol; multi-photon.

I. INTRODUCTION

Quantum cryptography is an emerging field in network security that relies on quantum mechanics proofs [1, 2] rather than on the complexity of solving a mathematical problem as in the case of classical cryptography. It is mainly used for secret key distribution, called quantum key distribution (QKD). The BB'84 protocol is the first QKD distribution protocol [1] and it was proposed by Bennett and Brassard in 1984. BB'84 is based on encoding the bits of a random key using a single photon for each bit. The major drawbacks associated with the BB'84 protocol are due to the constraint of using a single photon per encoded bit to provide a provably secure QKD scheme. Therefore, this protocol is vulnerable to photon number splitting attacks (PNS) in cases where more than a single photon is generated per bit transmission.

The three stage multi-photon tolerant protocol investigated in this paper does not require any prior agreement between a sender Alice and a receiver Bob [3-5]. This protocol is based on the use of unitary transformation known only to the party applying them. The transformation applied to the message in transit is the key that provides it with quantum level security. As shown in Figure 1, for each transmission, Alice and Bob use a new set of transformations.

Coherent non-decoying quantum states are used in this paper in order to transfer the encoded bits from Alice to Bob. The studied multi-photon, multi-stage protocol is considered quantum secure as long as less than N photons are used for communication [5] [6]. Therefore, in this paper, it is assumed that a light source can be constructed such that its Poisson photon-number distribution is truncated to a maximum number of photons. Although, this type of light source does not exit practically at this time, current and future developments in this field can lead to such sources and hence validate this research in a practical setup. Based on this and the formulations obtained, the maximum achievable distance for the three wavelengths of interest were evaluated at: 1550 nm, 1310 nm, and 850 nm.

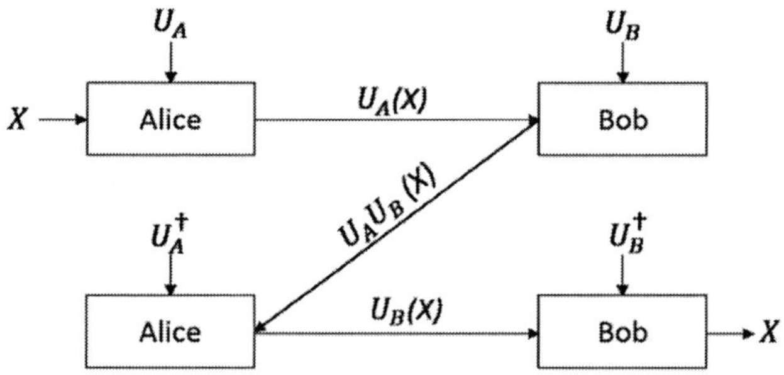

Figure 1. Schematic of the three-stage protocol [3].

Significantly, this is the first research that has ever been done on the three stage protocol that estimates key results such as maximum distance that can be achieved at three key communication wavelengths, and then compares the data to existing results. Moreover, the three stage multi-photon protocol eliminates the need for the sifting step that is needed in the BB'84 protocol. In section II, the BB'84 formulations were adopted to fit the three stage protocol under study. Section III include the theoretical data and results obtained, while section IV is the conclusion.

II. FORMULATION METHOD

A sender, Alice, has in her possession a list of symbols (called raw key); she wishes to share them with Bob using the three stage quantum protocol. To extract a short secret key from the raw key, one-way post-processing is required. The optimal one–way post processing consists of two steps. The first step is error correction (EC), also called information reconciliation, at the end of which the raw key becomes shorter and symbols perfectly correlated. The second step is privacy amplification (PA), and it is aimed at diminishing Eve's knowledge of the reference raw key. The length of the final secret key depends on Eve's information about the raw keys.

However, for practical setups, a practical parameter must also be taken into account as well: namely the raw key rate (R) rather than the raw key. This rate depends on the protocol used and on details of the implementation setup: the source used, losses in the channel, efficiency, and type of detectors. Hence, to assess the performance of practical single-stage protocol, a secret key rate is defined as [7]:

$$K = Rr \tag{1}$$

Based on the suggestions from references [6] and [7], the protocol is secure as long as the number of photons are less than a threshold maximum value $N_{max.}$. We express the raw key rate R by the following equation:

$$R=v_s P_{Bob}(N_{max})=v_s \sum_{n=1}^{N_{max}} p_A(n)\left[1-\left(1-\eta_{det}\eta_{qc}\right)^n\right] \tag{2}$$

The factor v_s is the repetition rate of the source used, and $P_{Bob}(N)$ is Bob's detection probability. Under the no-truncation assumption (i.e. $N_{max} \to\infty$), Alice's photon-number distribution for a polarized-modulated pulse that she uses to send a single bit is according to Poissonian statistics of mean $\mu = \langle n\rangle$, $p_A(n) = \frac{\mu^n}{n!}e^{-\mu}$. Because of the truncation assumption at N_{max}, $p_A(n)$, it was properly normalized so that Alice's average photon number is represented correctly by $\mu = \langle n\rangle$. η_{det} is the quantum efficiency of the detector (typically 10% at telecom wavelengths), and η_{qc} is the attenuation due to losses in the quantum channel. For fiber optics link with length D, η_{qc} is given by

$$\eta_{qc}=10^{\frac{-\alpha D}{10}}, \tag{3}$$

where α is the attenuation coefficient in dB/km at telecom wavelengths of interest. In this paper, we consider three communication wavelengths λ=1550 nm, 1310 nm, and 850 nm with attenuation coefficients of 0.25, 0.35, and 2 dB/km respectively.

The second parameter in (1) is defined as the secret fraction r, and can be written in terms of quantities that are known from calibration or from the parameter estimation of the protocol as [7]:

$$r=\left(1-\frac{\mu}{2\eta_{det}\eta_{qc}}\right)\{1-h(2Q)\}-h(Q), \tag{4}$$

Where Q is the expected error rate QBER and h is the binary entropy.

As a first step, set in (2) was an assumed maximum number of photons $N_{max} = 12$ that was encoded by Alice and sent to Bob at a fixed optics link length D to calculate the secret key rate K as a function of μ. A maximum K value will be obtained at an optimum value of μ referred to in this paper as μ_{opt}. Since the attenuation in (3) depends on the D and α, used, in this first step, is a laboratory short distance ($D \approx 0$) for the calculation of μ_{opt} where the attenuation is equal to 1.00 regardless of the wavelength used.

As a second step, using this optimum value of μ_{opt}, one can calculate the secret key rate K from (1) as a function of the optical length D for each of the three communication wavelengths under investigations. The maximum optical link length or distance that can be achieved at each wavelength can then be determined. Varying the optics link length will affect the attenuation in (3), and hence will reduce the value of the maximum secret key rate from its peak value at D≈ 0.

III. RESULTS

As shown in Figure 2, the secret key rate from (1) as a function of μ for $N_{max} = 12$. One notices that the maximum K value occurs at $\mu_{opt} = 7.22$. This value can then be used to calculate the maximum secret key as a function of D. As we increase D, the maximum secret key rate starts to decrease linearly until we reach a maximum possible distance ($D_{max.}$). The maximum possible distances (D_{max}) that can be achieved at μ_{opt} can be found from Figure 3 at the fall off K values due to the effects of error correction and privacy amplifications for a no-decoy state at $\mu_{opt} = 7.22$ as a function of distance. It can be noted from the linear relationship that these effects are small for short distances and small losses. However as we approach the maximum possible distance the channel losses increase; thus EC and PA have more severe effects on K. This leads to a sharp drop in the secret key rate at the distance of about 200 km for the 1550 nm wavelength. This distance is comparable and even better theoretically from the currently used protocols in the market where the maximum distance achieved is around 100 km. The influence of the wavelength through the attenuation coefficients on the secret key rate values for $\mu_{opt} = 7.22$ at 1310 nm and 850 nm are also shown in Figure 3. The maximum distances that can be achieved at 1310 nm and 850 nm are 140 km and 25 km, respectively. The maximum achievable distance is higher at $\lambda = 1550$ nm that is due to the low attenuation of the medium at this wavelength.

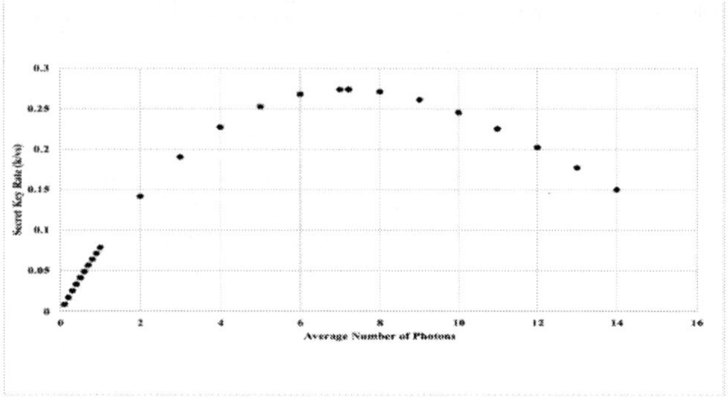

Figure 2. Plot of the secret key rate key rate as the function of average number of photons per pulse sent by Alice μ.The maximum secret key rate occurs at μ_{opt} = 7.22.

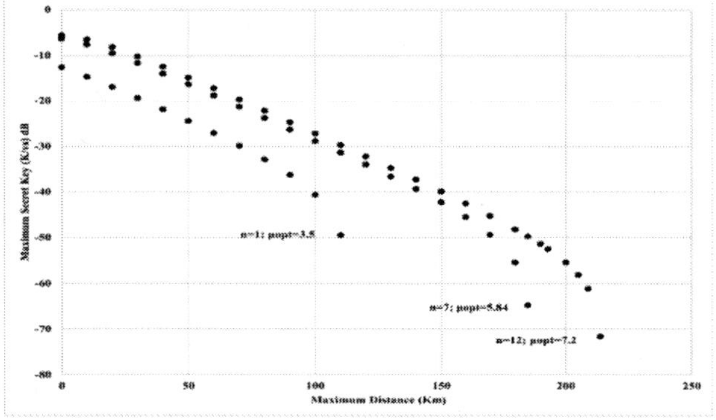

Figure 3. Plot of the secret key rate as a function of Optics Link length D for μ_{opt}=7.22

IV. CONCLUSION

This theoretical study was the first one toward determining key parameters and results to validate the use of the three stage multi-photon protocol in a practical setup. One of the key parameters that was determined is the maximum optical link length or maximum distance that the three stage multi-photon protocol can achieve to securely distribute a secret key between Alice and Bob at three communication wavelengths. Namely: 1550 nm, 1310 nm, and 850 nm. It is concluded that the maximum achievable distance using the three stage multi photon can reach 200 km at 1550 nm, theoretically, exceeding the single photon BB'84 protocol. This is an important result that needs to be proved in a practical setup. Operating at the other two wavelengths, where the fiber attenuation is higher, and decreases the maximum distance in a noticeable way.

Future work is required to validate this study. A starting point is to develop a laboratory setup were the fiber distance can be can considered zero and hence the maximum secret key rate can be determined and compared with the findings in this paper. Potential future research includes the use of fiber link lengths and wavelengths as parameters to determine the maximum distance that can be achieved practically with the use of this protocol. In addition, it can include developing a light source that can be truncated to a maximum number of photons per pulse.

ACKNOWLEDGMENT

The author would like to extend his gratitude to the support of this research by the Oklahoma University Quantum Communications group.

REFERENCES

[1] C. Kollmitzer and M. Pivk, Applied Quantum Cryptography. Springer 2010.

[2] C. H. Bennett and G. Brassard, "Quantum Cryptography: Public Key Distribution and Coin Tossing, in Proceedings of IEEE International Conference on Computers, Systems, and Signal Processing, Bangalore, India (IEEE, New York, 1984), p. 175.

[3] S. Kak,"Three-stage Quantum Cryptography Protocol," Foundations of Physics Letters 2006, 19, pp. 293-296

[4] S. Mandal, et al., "Implementation of Secure Quantum Protocol using Multiple Photons for Communication," arXiv preprint arXiv:1208.6198, 2012.

[5] Y. Chen, et al.,"Multi-photon tolerant secure quantum communication—From theory to practice," IEEE International Conference on Communications (ICC) 2013, pp. 2111-2116.

[6] K. W. Chan, M. El Rifai, P. K. Verma, S. Kak. and Y. Chen, "Multi-Photon Quantum Key Distribution Based on Double-Lock Encryption," arXiv: 1503. 05793 [quant-ph] 2015.

[7] V. Scarani, et al, "The security of practical quantum key distribution," Rev. Mod. Phys.2009, 81, pp. 1301-1350.

Enhancing Integrity Protection for Industrial Cyber Physical Systems

Rainer Falk and Steffen Fries
Corporate Technology
Siemens AG
Munich, Germany
e-mail: {rainer.falk|steffen.fries}@siemens.com

Abstract—**Cyber physical systems are technical systems that are operated and controlled using information technology. Protecting the integrity of cyber physical systems is a highly important security objective to ensure the correct and reliable operation and to ensure high availability. A comprehensive protection concept of the system integrity involves several axes: the component level ranging from sensors/actuator devices up to control and supervisory systems, planning and configuration management, and the system life cycle. It allows detecting integrity violations on system level reliably by analyzing integrity measurements from a multitude of independent integrity sensors, capturing and analyzing integrity measurements of the physical world, on the field level, and of control and supervisory systems.**

Keywords–system integrity, device integrity; cyber physical systems; Internet of Things, embedded security; cyber security.

I. INTRODUCTION

With ubiquitous machine-oriented communication, e.g., the Internet of Things and interconnected cyber physical systems (CPS), the integrity of technical systems is becoming an increasingly important security objective. Information technology (IT) security mechanisms have been known for many years, and are applied in smart devices (Internet of Things, Cyber Physical Systems, industrial and energy automation systems, operation technology) [1]. Such mechanisms target authentication, system and communication integrity and confidentiality of data in transit or at rest. System integrity takes a broader approach where not only the integrity of individual components (device integrity) and of communication is addressed, but where integrity shall be ensured at the system level of interconnected devices. This purpose is in particular challenging for dynamically changing cyber physical systems, that come with the industrial Internet of Things (IIoT) and Industrie 4.0. Cyber systems will become more open and dynamic to support flexible production down to lot size 1 (plug-and-work reconfiguration of manufacturing equipment), and flexible adaptation to changing needs (market demand, individualized products).

The flexibility starts on the device level where smart devices allow for upgrading and enhancing device functionality by downloadable apps. But also the system of interconnected machines is reconfigured according to changing needs.

Classical approaches for protecting device and system integrity target at preventing any changes, and compare the current configuration to a fixed reference policy. More flexible approaches are needed to protect integrity for flexibly reconfigurable and self-adapting CPSs.

This paper describes an integrated, holistic approach for ensuring CPS integrity. After summarizing system security requirements coming from relevant industrial security standard IEC62443 [1] in Section II, an overview for protecting device integrity and system integrity is described in Sections III and IV. The presented approach for integrity monitoring is an extensible framework to include integrity information from IT-based functions and the physical world of a CPS. This allows integrating integrity information from the digital and the physical world. A new approach for integrity monitoring of encrypted communications is described in Section V. An approach for evaluation in an operational security management setting is outlined in Section VI. Related work is summarized in Section VII, and Section VIII concludes the paper.

II. SYSTEM INTEGRITY REQUIREMENTS

A. *Overview IEC62443 Industrial Security Standard*

The international industrial security standard IEC 62443 is a security requirements framework defined by the International Electrotechnical Commission (IEC) and can be applied to different automation domains, including energy automation, process automation, building automation, and others. The standard has been created to address the specific requirements of industrial automation and control systems. It covers both organizational and technical aspects of security. In the set of corresponding documents, security requirements are defined, which target the solution operator and the integrator but also the product vendor.

As shown in Figure 1, different parts of the standard are grouped into four clusters covering

- common definitions and metrics;
- requirements on setup of a security organization (ISMS related, comparable to ISO 27001 [2]), as well as solution supplier and service provider processes;
- technical requirements and methodology for security on system-wide level, and

– requirements on the secure development lifecycle of system components, and security requirements to such components at a technical level.

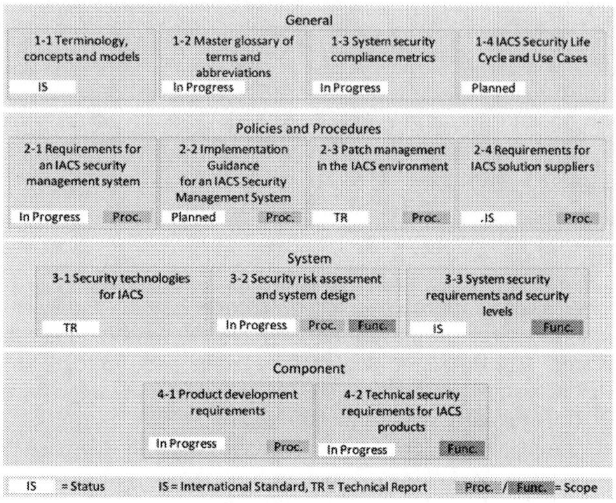

Figure 1. IEC 62443 Overview and Status

According to the methodology described in IEC 62443-3-2, a complex automation system is structured into zones that are connected by and communicate through so-called "conduits" that map for example to the logical network protocol communication between two zones. Moreover, this document defines Security Levels (SL) that correlate with the strength of a potential adversary as shown in Figure 2 below. To reach a dedicated SL, the defined requirements have to be fulfilled.

4 Security Level (SL)	
SL 1	Protection against **casual or coincidental** violation
SL 2	Protection against **intentional violation** using **simple means** with low resources, generic skills and low motivation
SL 3	Protection against intentional violation using **sophisticated means** with **moderate resources**, IACS specific skills and moderate motivation
SL 4	Protection against intentional violation using sophisticated means with **extended resources**, IACS specific skills and high motivation

Figure 2. IEC 62443 defined Security Level

B. *IEC62443 Integrity Requirements*

Part 3.3 of IEC62443 [3] defines seven foundational security requirements, including a specific foundational requirement on integrity.

IEC 62443 part 3-3 defines seven foundational requirements group specific requirements of a certain category:

– FR 1 Identification and authentication control
– FR 2 Use control
– FR 3 System integrity
– FR 4 Data confidentiality
– FR 5 Restricted data flow
– FR 6 Timely response to events
– FR 7 Resource availability

For each of the foundational requirements there exist several concrete technical security requirements (SR) and requirement enhancements (RE) to address a specific security level. In the context of communication security, these security levels are specifically interesting for the conduits connecting different zones.

Integrity requirements cover in particular the following areas:

– Overall system integrity
– Communication integrity
– Device integrity

The following examples from IEC 62443-3-3 [3] illustrate some of the foundational requirements:

– FR3, SR3.1 Communication integrity: "The control system shall provide the capability to protect the integrity of transmitted information".
– FR3, SR3.4 Software and information integrity: "The control system shall provide the capability to detect, record, report and protect against unauthorized changes to software and information at rest."
– FR3, SR3.8 Session integrity: "The control system shall provide the capability to protect the integrity of sessions. The control system shall reject any usage of invalid session IDs."
– FR5, SR 5.2 Zone boundary protection: "The control system shall provide the capability to monitor and control communications at zone boundaries to enforce the compartmentalization defined in the risk -based zones and conduits model."

III. PROTECTING DEVICE INTEGRITY

The objective of device integrity is to ensure that a device is not manipulated in an unauthorized way. This includes the integrity of the device firmware, of the device configuration, but also the physical integrity. Main technologies to protect device integrity are:

– Secure boot: A device loads at start-up only unmodified, authorized firmware.
– Measured boot: The loaded software modules are checked when they are loaded. Usually, a cryptographic hash value is recorded in a platform configuration register of a hardware of firmware trusted platform module (TPM) [4][5]. The configuration information can be used to grant access to keys, or it can be attested towards thirds parties.

- Protected firmware update: When the firmware of a device is updated, the integrity and authenticity of the firmware update is checked. The firmware update image can be digitally signed.
- Runtime integrity checks: During operation, the device performs self-test of security functionality and integrity checks to verify whether it is operating as expected. Integrity checks can verify the integrity of files, configuration data, software modules, and or runtime data as process list.
- Process isolation, kernel-based mandatory access control (MAC): Hypervisors or kernel MAC systems like SELinux [6], AppArmor [7], or SMACK [8], can be used to isolate different classes of software (security domains). An attack or malfunction one security domain does not affect other security domains on the same device.
- Tamper evidence, tamper protection: The physical integrity of a device can be protected, e.g., by security seals or by tamper sensors that detect opening or manipulation of the housing.
- Device integrity self test: A device performs a self-test to detect failures. The self-test is performed typically during startup and is repeated regularly during operation. Operation integrity checks: measurements on the device can be compared with the expected behavior in the operative environment. An example is the measurement of connection attempts to/from the device. Based on a Management Information Base (MIB) setting.

The functionality of some devices can be extended by extensions (App). Here, the device integrity has to cover also the App runtime environment: Only authorized, approved apps can be downloaded and installed. Apps are isolated during execution (managed runtime environment, hypervisor, container)

The known approaches to protect device integrity focus on the IT-related functionality of a device (with the exception of tamper protection). Also, a strong tamper protection is not common on device level. The main protection objective for device integrity shall ensure that the device's control functionality operates as designed. However, the integrity of input/output interfaces, sensors, and actuators are typically out of scope. In typical industrial environments, applying a strong tamper protection to the each control device, sensor, and actuator would not be economically feasible. So, protecting device integrity alone would be too limited to achieve the goal of protection the integrity of an overall CPS.

IV. System Integrity Monitoring

The next level of integrity is on the system level comprising a set of interconnected devices. The main approaches to protect system integrity are collecting and analyzing information on system level:

- Device inventory: Complete and up-to-date list of installed devices (including manufacturer, model, serial number version, firmware version, current configuration, installed software components, location)Centralized Logging: Devices provide logdata, e.g., using Open Platform Communication Unified Architecture (OPC UA) protocol [9], SNMP [10], or syslog protocol [11], to a centralized logging system.
- Runtime device integrity measurements: A device integrity agent provides information gathered during the operation of the device. It collects integrity information on the device and provides it for further analysis. Basic integrity information are the results of a device self-test, and information on the current device configuration (firmware version, patches, installed applications, configuration). Furthermore, runtime information can be gathered and provided for analysis (e.g., process list, file system integrity check values, partial copy of memory).
- Network monitoring: The network communication is intercepted, e.g., using a network tap or a mirror port of a network switch. A challenge is the fact that network communication is increasingly encrypted.
- Physical Automation process monitoring: Trusted sensors provide information on the physical world that can be used to cross-check the view of the control system on the physical world.
- Physical world integrity: trusted sensors (of physical world). Integrated monitoring of embedded devices and IT-based control systems, and of the technical process. Allow now quality of integrity monitoring as physical world and IT world are checked together.

The captured integrity information can be used for runtime integrity monitoring to detect integrity violations in real-time. Operators can be informed, or actions can be triggered automatically. Furthermore, the information is archived for later investigations. So, integrity violations can probably be detected later, so that corresponding counter-measures can be initiated (e.g., plan for an additional quality check of produced goods). The integrity information can be integrated in or linked to data of a production management system, so that it can be investigated under which integrity conditions certain production steps have been performed. Product data is enhanced with integrity monitoring data related to the production of the product.

A. *System Overview*

Agents on the system components acting as integrity sensors collect integrity information and optionally determine an integrity attestation of the collected information. To allow for flexibility in CPS, the approach puts more focus on monitoring integrity and acting when integrity violations are detected, than on preventing any change that has not been pre-approved by a static policy.

The approach is based on integrity sensors that provide integrity related measurements. An intelligent analysis platform analysis this data using data analysis (e.g., statistical analysis, big data analysis, artificial intelligence) and to trigger suitable respondence actions (e.g., alarm, remote wipe of a device, revocation of a device, stop of a production site, planning for additional test of manufactured goods).

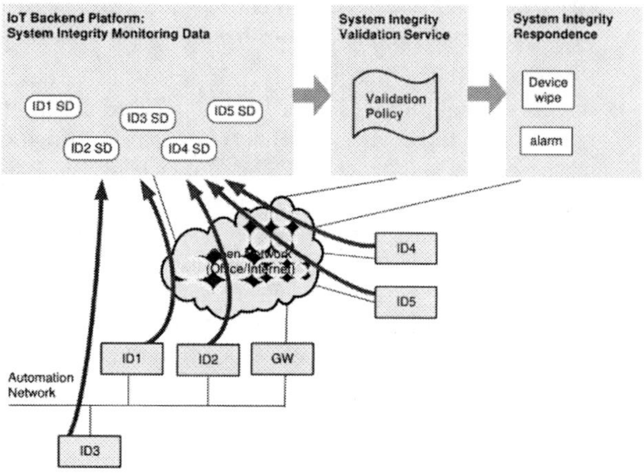

Figure 3. Validation of Device Monitoring Data

Figure 3 shows an example for an IoT system with IoT devices (ID1, ID2, etc.) that communicate with an IoT backend platform. The devices provide current integrity monitoring information to the backend platform. The devices can be automation devices that include integrity measurement functionality, or dedicated integrity sensor devices. The device monitoring system itself has to be protected against attacks itself, following IEC62443.

An integrity data validation service checks the obtained integrity measurement data for validity using a configurable validation policy. If a policy violation is detected, a corrective action is triggered: For example, an alarm message can be displayed on a dash board. Furthermore, an alarm message can be sent to the IoT backend platform to terminate the communication session of the affected IoT device. Moreover, the device security service can be informed so that it can revoke the devices access permissions, or revoke the device authentication credential.

B. *Integrity Sensors*

The integrity monitoring framework foresees to include a variety of integrity measurements. Depending on the specific application scenario, meaningful integrity sensors can be deployed. Depending on the evolving needs, additional sensors can be deployed as needed.

- Physical world (technical process)
- Physical world (alarm systems, access control systems, physical security as, e.g., video surveillance)
- Device world (malware, device configuration, firmware integrity)IT-based control systems (local, clod services, edge cloud)
- Infrastructure (communication networks)

Flexible extension with additional integrity sensors (even very sophisticated as, e.g., monitoring power fingerprint). The described approach is open to develop and realize sophisticated integrity measurement sensors. So the solution is design to allow evolution and innovation. Integrity sensors have to be protected against attacks so that they provide integrity measurements reliably.

C. *Integrity Verification*

The integrity monitoring events are analyzed using known data analysis tools. The system integrity can be monitored both online. In industrial environments, it is also important to have reliable information about the system integrity of a production system for the time period during which a certain production batch was performed. This allows performing the verification also afterwards to check whether during a past production batch integrity-violations occurred.

The final decision whether a certain configuration is accepted as correct is up to human operators. After reconfiguration, or for a production step, the configuration is to be approved. The approval decision can be automated according to previously accepted decisions, or preconfigured good configurations).

As integrity measurements are collected from a multitude of integrity sensors, integrity attacks can be detected reliably. Even if some integrity sensors should be disabled or manipulated to provide malicious integrity measurements, still other integrity sensors can provide integrity information that allows detecting the integrity violation. Checking integrity using measurements from independent integrity sensors and on different levels (physical level, field devices, control and supervisory systems) allows detecting integrity violations by checking for inconsistencies between independent integrity measurements.

V. Integrity Monitoring of Encrypted Communications

A specific part of monitoring the system integrity is the network communication. However, network communication is encrypted more-and-more, e.g., using the Transport Layer Security (TLS) protocol [12]. In contrast to earlier versions of the TLS protocol, the most recent version TLS1.3 [13], currently under development, supports only cipher-suites realizing authenticated encryption. Both confidentiality and integrity/authenticity of user communication is protected. No cipher suite providing integrity-only protection is supported by TLS version 1.3, anymore. So, only basic IP header data can be analyzed. This is not sufficient for integrity monitoring of TLS-protected industrial control communication.

A protocol specific solution to enable monitoring of encrypted communication channels by trusted middleboxes is provided by mcTLS [14]. With mcTLS, trusted middleboxes can be incorporated into a secure sessions established between a TLS Client and a TLS Server. Figure 4 shows the basic principle of mcTLS. A TLS authentication and key agreement is performed between a TLS client and a TLS server. As part of the handshake, the TLS client indicates those TLS middleboxes that shall be incorporated within the TLS session. After the authentication and key between client and server has been completed, both the TLS client and the TLS server send (encrypted) key material of the established TLS session to the middleboxes. This allows the middleboxes to decrypt the data exchanged between TLS client and TLS server. Note that the integrity of the data exchange is cryptographically protected by message authentication codes. The keys for integrity protection are not made available to the middleboxes, so that the middleboxes can only decrypt the data, but not interfere with the contents of the data. So, data integrity is ensured end-to-end although middleboxes can decrypt the data.

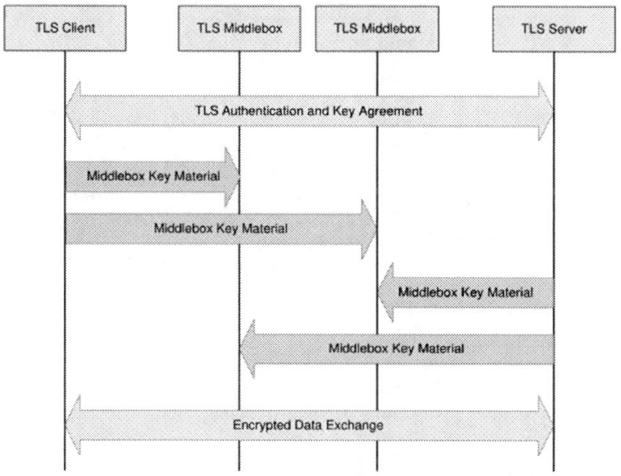

Figure 4. Multi-Context TLS

The basic principle is to perform an enhanced handshake involving middleboxes into the handshake phase of TLS, see Figure 4. Specifically, the middleboxes are authenticated during the handshake and thus known to both communicating ends. Moreover, each side is involved in the generation of the session key, which is also provided to the middlebox. There is also additional keying performed for the exchange of pure end-to-end keys. Specific key material known to the middlebox is used to decrypt the traffic and check the integrity. The end-to-end based keys are used to protect integrity end-to-end. The latter approach ensures that the middlebox can only read and analyze the content of the communication in the TLS record layer, but any change done by the middlebox is detected by an invalid end-to-end integrity check value. This approach has the advantage that it provides an option to check the associated security policy during the session setup and at the same time monitor traffic as an authorized component. The drawback is that the solution focuses solely on TLS and cannot be applied to other protocols without changes.

The TLS-variant mcTLS allows middleboxes to analyze the TLS-protected communication, e.g., to detect potential security breaches This approach enables communication checking the contents of the communication session without breaking end-to-end security. So, with mcTLS, the contents of encrypted data communication, in particular of industrial control communication, can be checked.

VI. EVALUATION

The security of a cyber system can be evaluated in practice in various approaches and stages of the system's lifecycle:

- Threat and risk analysis (TRA) of cyber system
- Checks during operation to determine key performance indicators (e.g., check for compliance of device configurations).
- Security testing (penetration testing)

During the design phase of a cyber system, the security demand is determined, and the appropriateness of a security design is validated using a threat and risk analysis. Assets to be protected and possible threats are identified, and the risk is evaluated in a qualitative way depending on probability and impact of threats. The effectiveness of the proposed enhanced device authentication means can be reflected in a system TRA.

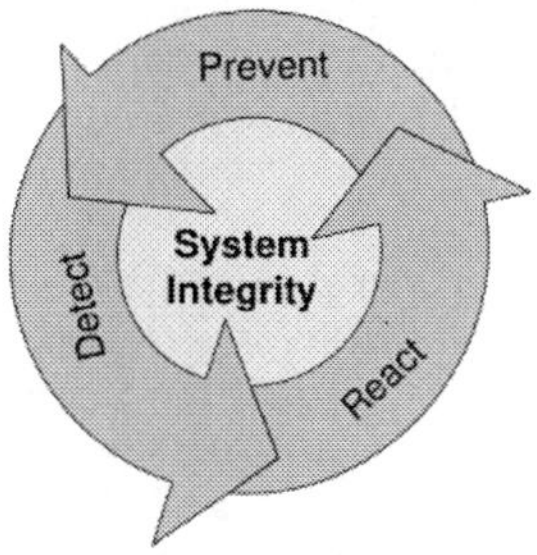

Figure 5. Prevent Detect React Cycle

So, the main evaluation of security tools is coming during security operation, when as part of an overall operational security management appropriate technologies are chose that, in combination, reduce the risk to an acceptable level.

The new approach presented in this paper provides an additional component of a security architecture that reduces the risk of integrity violations. Compared to existing solutions covering IT-related aspects only, the integrity of the control application and the physical world are included. The solution approach does not intend to have a single technology, but it realizes a system-oriented approach that can evolve as part of the security management life cycle covering prevent, detect, and response, see also Figure 5.

VII. RELATED WORK

A security operation center (SOC) is a centralized unit for detecting and handling security incidents. Main functionalities are continued security monitoring reporting, and post-incident analysis [15][16]. Security incident and Event management (SIEM) systems can be used within a SOC to analyze security monitoring data. Compliance management systems support a centralized reporting of server configuration in data centers.

Host-based intrusion detection systems (HIDS) as SAMHAIN [17] and OSSEC [18] analyze the integrity of hosts and report the results to a backend security monitoring system. Network based intrusion detection systems (NIDS) capture the network traffic, e.g., using a network tap or a mirroring port of a network switch, and analyze the traffic. Examples are SNORT [19] and Suricata [20].

Two main strategies can be followed by an intrusion detection system (IDS): Known malicious activities can be looked for (signature based detection), or any change compared to a learned reference network policy is detected (anomaly detection).

An "automotive thin profile" of the Trusted Platform Module TPM 2.0 has been specified [21]. A vehicle is composed of multiple control units that are equipped with TPMs. A rich TPM manages a set of thin TPMs, so that the vehicle can be represented by a vehicle TPM to the external world. The vehicle's rich TPM can check the integrity of the vehicle by verifying attestations provided by thin TPMs.

Approaches to utilize the context information on the CPS operation, device capabilities, device context to enhance the authentication of a single device, have been described by the authors of this paper in previous work [22]. The effect of an integrity attack on the degradation of a control system has been investigated by Mo and Sinopoli [23].

VIII. Conclusion

Ensuring system integrity is an essential security feature for cyber physical systems and the Internet of Things. The security design principle of "defense in depth" basically means that multiple layers of defenses are designed. This design principle can not only be applied at the system level, but also at the level of a single security mechanism.

This paper proposed a framework for ensuring system integrity in flexibly adaptable cyber physical systems. With new concepts for flexible automation systems coming with Industrial IoT / Industrie 4.0, the focus of system integrity has to move from preventing changes to device and system configuration in having transparency on the device and system configuration and checking it for compliance. This paper focused on integrity of devices, communication, and cyber systems. Integrity in a broader sense covers the whole life cycle, including development, secure procurement, secure manufacturing, and supply chain security.

References

[1] IEC 62443, "Industrial Automation and Control System Security" (formerly ISA99), available from: http://isa99.isa.org/Documents/Forms/AllItems.aspx 2017.09.26

[2] ISO/IEC 27001, "Information technology – Security techniques – Information security management systems – Requirements", October 2013, available from: https://www.iso.org/standard/54534.html 2017.09.26

[3] IEC62443-3-3:2013, "Industrial communication networks – Network and system security – Part 3-3: System security requirements and security levels", Edition 1.0, August 2013

[4] Trusted Computing Group: "TPM Main Specification", Version 1.2, , available from http://www.trustedcomputinggroup.org/resources/tpm_main_specification 2017.09.26

[5] Trusted Computing Group, "Trusted Platform Module Library Specification, Family 2.0", 2014, available from http://www.trustedcomputinggroup.org/resources/tpm_library_specification 2017.09.26

[6] SELinux, "Security Enhanced Linux", available online: https://selinuxproject.org/page/Main_Page 2017.09.26

[7] AppArmor, "AppArmor Security Project", available online: http://wiki.apparmor.net/index.php/Main_Page 2017.09.26

[8] SMACK, "Simplified Mandatory Access Control Kernel", available online: https://www.kernel.org/doc/html/latest/admin-guide/LSM/Smack.html 2017.09.26

[9] OPC Foundation, "OPC Unified Architecture (UA)", available online: https://opcfoundation.org/about/opc-technologies/opc-ua/ 2017.09.26

[10] J. Case, R. Mundy, et al., "Introduction and Applicability Statements for Internet Standard Management Framework", RFC3410, available online: https://tools.ietf.org/html/rfc3410 2017.09.26

[11] R. Gerhards, "The Syslog Protocol", RFC5424, March 2009, available online: https://tools.ietf.org/html/rfc5424 2017.09.26

[12] T. Dierks and E. Rescorla, "The Transport Layer Security (TLS) Protocol Version 1.2", RFC 5246, Aug. 2008, available from http://tools.ietf.org/html/rfc5246 2017.09.26

[13] E. Rescorla: "The Transport Layer Security (TLS) Protocol Version 1.3", Internet draft (work in progres), September 2017, available online: https://tlswg.github.io/tls13-spec/draft-ietf-tls-tls13.html 2017.09.26

[14] D. Naylor, K. Schomp, et al., "Multi-Context TLS (mcTLS), Enabling Secure In-Network Functionality in TLS," available from http://mctls.org/ 2017.09.26

[15] B. Rothke, "Building a Security Operations Center (SoC)", RSA Conference, 2012, available from https://www.rsaconference.com/writable/presentations/file_upload/tech-203.pdf 2017.09.26

[16] McAffee Foundstone® Professional Services, "Creating and Maintaining a SoC", Intel Security Whitepaper, available from: https://www.mcafee.com/us/resources/white-papers/foundstone/wp-creating-maintaining-soc.pdf 2017.09.26

[17] R. Wichmann, "The Samhain HIDS", fact sheet, 2011, available from http://la-samhna.de/samhain/samhain_leaf.pdf 2017.09.26

[18] OSSEC, "Open Source HIDS SECurity", web site, 2010 - 2015, available from http://ossec.github.io/ 2017.09.26

[19] "SNORT", web site, available from https://www.snort.org/ 2017.09.26

[20] "Suricata", web site, available from https://suricata-ids.org/ 2017.09.26

[21] Trusted Computing Group, "TCG TPM 2.0 Automotive Thin Profile", level 00, version 1.0, 2015, available from http://www.trustedcomputinggroup.org/resources/tcg_tpm_20_library_profile_for_automotivethin 2017.09.26

[22] R. Falk and S. Fries, "Advanced Device Authentication: Bringing Multi-Factor Authentication and Continuous Authentication to the Internet of Things", The First International Conference on Advances in Cyber-Technologies and Cyber-Systems, CYBER 2016, October 9 - 13, 2016 - Venice, Italy , available from http://www.thinkmind.org/index.php?view=article&articleid=cyber_2016_4_20_80029 2017.09.26

[23] Y. Mo and B. Sinopoli, "On the Performance Degradation of Cyber-Physical Systems Under Stealthy Integrity Attacks", IEEE Transactions on Automatic Control 61.9 (2016): 2618-2624.

Vaccine: A Block Cipher Method for Masking and Unmasking of Ciphertexts' Features

Ray R. Hashemi
Amar Rasheed
Jeffrey Young
Department of Computer Science
Armstrong State University,
Savannah, GA, USA
e-mails: {rayhashemi, amarrasheed, alanyoung7}@gmail.com

Azita A. Bahrami
IT Consultation
Savannah, GA, USA
e-mail: Azita.G.Bahrami@gmail.com

***Abstract*— A ciphertext inherits some properties of the plaintext, which is considered as a source of vulnerability and, therefore, it may be decrypted through a vigorous datamining process. Masking the ciphertext is the solution to the problem. In this paper, we have developed a new block cipher technique named *Vaccine* for which the block size is random and each block is further divided into segments of random size. Each byte within a segment is instantiated using a dynamic multi-instantiation approach, which means (i) the use of Vaccine does not produce the same masked outcome for the same given ciphertext and key and (ii) the options for masking different occurrences of a byte is extremely high. Two sets (100 members in each) of 1K long plaintexts of *natural* (borrowed from natural texts) and *synthesized* (randomly generated from 10 characters to increase the frequency of characters in the plaintext) are built. For each plaintext, two ciphertexts are generated using Advanced Encryption System (AES-128) and Data Encryption Standard (DES) algorithms. Vaccine and two well-known masking approaches of Cipher Block Chaining (CBC), and Cipher Feedback (CFB) are applied separately on each ciphertext. On average: (a) the Hamming distance between masked and unmasked occurrences of a byte using Vaccine is 0.72 bits higher than using the CBC, and CFB, and (b) Vaccine throughput is also 3.4 times and 1.8 times higher than the throughput for CBC and CFB, correspondingly, and (c) Vaccine *masking strength* is 1.5% and 1.8% higher than the masking strength for CBC and CFB, respectively.**

Keywords- Cyber Security; Masking and Unmasking Ciphertext; Variable-Block Cipher Vaccination; Masking Strength

I. INTRODUCTION

Protecting sensitive electronic documents and electronic messages from unintended eyes is a critical task. Such protections are often provided by applying encryption. However, the encrypted text (ciphertext) is often vulnerable to datamining. For example, let us consider the plaintext message of: "*The center is under an imminent attack*". The plaintext may be converted into the following ciphertext using, for instance, a simple *displacement* encryption algorithm: "xligirxvmwyrhivermqqmrirxexxego". The features of the plaintext are also inherited by the ciphertext—a point of vulnerability.

To explain it further, word "attack" is among the key words related to security. The characteristics of the word are: (i) length is six, (ii) the first and the fourth characters are the same, and (iii) the second and the third characters are the same. Using these characteristics, one can mine the given ciphertext and isolate the subtext of "exxego" that stands for "attack" which, in turn, may lead to decryption of the entire message.

More sophisticated encryption modes, such as CBC and CFB [1][2][3] are not exempt from the inherited-features problem. The Block cipher techniques that employ CBC/CFB encryption mode to produce distinct ciphertexts are vulnerable to information leakage. In the case of CBC/CFB employing the same Initial text Vector (IV) with the same encryption key for multiple encryption operations could reveal information about the first block of plaintext, and about any common prefix shared by two plaintext messages. In CBC mode, the IV must, in addition, be unpredictable at encryption time; in particular, the (previously) common practice of re-using the last ciphertext block of a message as the IV for the next message is insecure (for example, this method was used by SSL 2.0). If an attacker knows the IV (or the previous block of ciphertext) before he specifies the next plaintext, he can check his guess about plaintext of some block that was encrypted with the same key before (this is known as the TLS CBC IV attack) [4].

The logical solution for inherited-features problem is to mask the ciphertext using a masking mechanism that is *dynamic* and supports a high degree of *multi-instantiations* for each byte. A dynamic masking mechanism does not produce the same masked outcome for the same given ciphertext and the same key. The high degree of multi-instantiation masking mechanism replaces the *n* occurrences of a given byte in the ciphertext with *m* new bytes such that *m* is either equal to *n* or extremely close to *n*. The literature addresses many of these masking techniques [5][6].

Our goal is to introduce a masking mechanism named Vaccine that can mask the inherited features of a ciphertext in the eye of a data miner while providing for transformation of masked ciphertext into its original form, when needed. Vaccine will be dynamic and support a high degree of multi-instantiations for each byte of data, and has the following three unique traits, which makes it a powerful masking mechanism: It (1) divides the ciphertext into random size blocks, (2) divides each block into random size segments, and (3) every byte within each segment is randomly instantiated into another byte. All three traits are major departures from the norm of masking mechanisms.

The rest of the paper is organized as follows. The Previous Works is the subject of Section 2. The Methodology is presented in Section 3. The Empirical Results are discussed in Section 4. The Conclusions and Future Research are covered in Section 5.

II. PREVIOUS WORKS

Masking the features of a ciphertext that are either inherited from the plaintext or generated by the encryption scheme itself is the essential step in protecting a ciphertext. The block cipher and stream cipher mode of operations provides for such a step. We are specifically interested in CBC [7][8][9] and CFB [10] as samples of the block cipher and stream cipher mode of operations. They are to some degree comparable to the proposed Vaccine.

CBC divides the ciphertext into fixed–length blocks and masks each block separately. The use of fixed-length block demands padding for the last partial block of the ciphertext, if the latter exist. The CBC avoids generating the same ciphertext when the input text and key remain the same by employing an Initial text Vector (IV). CFB eliminates the need for possible padding of the last block (that is considered vulnerability for CBC [11]) by assuming the unit of transmission is 8-bits. However, CFB also uses IV for the same purpose that it was used by CBC. In contrast, Vaccine splits the ciphertext into the random size blocks and then divides each block into segments of random size. Masking each pair of segments is done by using a pair of randomly generated patterns. As a result, Vaccine needs neither padding nor IV. The randomness of the block size, segment size, and patterns used for instantiation of a given character are the major departure points of Vaccine from the other block and stream cipher approaches.

III. METHODOLOGY

We first present our methodology for instantiation of a byte, which contributes into dynamicity of Vaccine and then introduce our methodology for building Vaccine. The details of the two methodologies are the subjects of the following two subsections.

A. Instantiation

Instantiation is the replacement of a byte, c, by another one, c', such that c' is created by some modifications in c. To perform the instantiation, we present our two methods of *Self-substitution* and *Mixed-Substitution.* Through these methods, a number of parameters are introduced that are referred to as the *masking* parameters. At the end of this subsection, we present the masking parameters as a profile for the patterns suggested by the substitution methods.

1) Self-Substitution: Consider byte 10011101 and let us (i) pick two bits in positions p_1 and p_2 such that $p_1 \neq p_2$, (ii) flip the bit in position p_1, and (iii) swap its place with the bit in position p_2—Two-Bit-One-Flip-Circular-Swap technique.

It is clear that the pairs (p_1=1, p_2=7) and (p_1=7, p_2=1) create different instances for the byte. Therefore, the order of p_1 and p_2 is important. The number of possible ways selecting a pair (p_1, p_2) from the byte is 7*8=56, which means a byte may be instantiated by 56 possible different ways using Two-Bit-One-Flip-Circular Swap technique. The technique name may be generalized as *K-R-Bit-M-Flip-Circular-Swap.* For the above example K=2 and M=1, as shown in Figure 1. (We introduce the parameter R shortly.)

One may pick 3-bits (K=3) to instantiate the byte. Let us assume 3 bits randomly selected that are located in the positions p_1, p_2, and p_3. There are many ways that M-Flip-Circular-Swap technique can be applied:

a. (One-Flip-Circular-Swap) Flip one of the three bits and then make a circular swap among p_1, p_2, and p_3.
b. (Two-Flip-Circular-Swap) Flip two out of the three bits and then apply circular swapping.
c. (Three-Flip-Circular-Swap) Flip all three bits and then apply circular swapping.

The number of possible combinations grows to 5040.

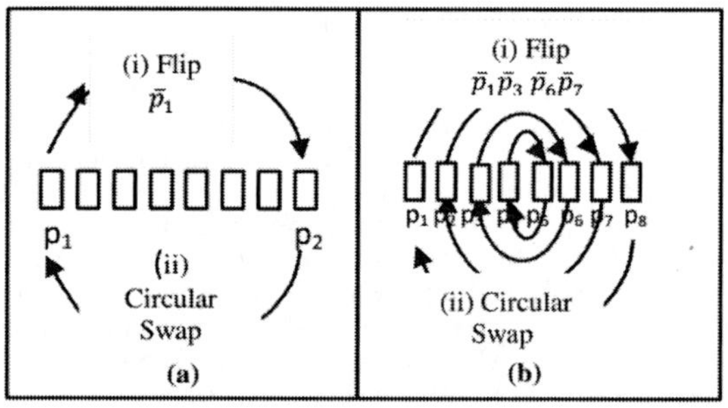

Figure 1. K-Bit-M-Flip-Circular-Swap Technique: (a) K=2 and M=1 and (b) K=8 and M=4

Using K-R-Bit-M-Flip-Circular-Swap for all possible values of K (K=2 to 8) and M (M=1 to K-1) generates the total of (X=1,643,448) possible substitutes for a given byte. If either K or M is equal to zero then, the self-substitution has not been enforced and in this case X=1 (the byte itself). Now, we explain the role of parameter, R (where, R is a byte long).

Let us refer to the case of K=2 and M=1 one more time that is able to facilitate the generation of 56 possible number of instantiations of a given byte using all the possible pairs of (p_1=•, p_2=•). That is, the two positions of p_1 and p_2 could have any value from 1 to 8 as long as $p_1 \neq p_2$. What if one is only interested in those instantiations resulting from the pairs of (p_1=3, p_2=•), which by definition also includes instantiations resulting from the pairs of (p_1=•, p_2=3). The chosen value (bit) of interest for p_1 is a value from 1 to 8 that is expressed by setting the bit of interest in R. The number of bits that are set to "1" in R is always equal to M. For our example, R="00000100".

The pairs represented by (p_1=v, p_2=•) are the set of seven pairs of {(p_1=v, p_2=1), . . ., (p_1=v, p_2=8)}. The seven pairs are named the *primary set* for the *primary signature* of (p_1=v, p_2=•). The (p_1=*, p_2=v), which is a tweaked version of (p_1=•, p_2=v) is the *Complementary signature* of (p_1=v, p_2=•) and stands for the other set of seven pairs {(p_1=8, p_2=v), . . ., (p_1=1, p_2=v)}. These seven pairs make the *complementary set* for (p_1=*, p_2=v). (Values of p_1, in the complementary set, are in reverse order of values of p_2 in the primary set.)

The primary and complementary sets also referred to as the *primary sub-pattern* and *complementary sub-pattern*, respectively. The two sub-patterns collectively make a *pattern* and (K=2, M=1, R="00000100") is the *pattern's profile*.

The profile of (K=4, M=3, R="00001011") means four bits are chosen from the byte out of which three bits (M=3) in positions 1, 2, and 4 are the positions of interest (p_1=1, p_2=2, p_3=4.) Therefore, the primary signature and the Complementary signatures are, respectively, defined as (p_1=1, p_2=2, p_3=4, p_4=•) and (p_1= *, p_2=2, p_3=4, p_4=1). It is clear that M cannot be equal to K, because, when M= K, the primary and complementary sets are the same and they have only one member.

When none of the bits in R is set to "1", it means R has not been enforced. In this case, we have one pattern. However, to apply Vaccine, we need to determine the primary and complementary sets for this pattern, which is provided by default value of R (i.e., R with its M least significant bits set to "1".)

2) Mixed-Substitution: In a nutshell, the instantiation of the given byte, c, and each key byte are done separately. One of the instantiated key bytes is selected as the *key image* and the final instance of c is generated by XORing the key image and the instantiated c. The details are cited below.

Application of self-substitution with masking parameters of (K, M, and R) on a given byte generates the primary and the complementary sub-patterns of $(u_p^1 \ldots u_p^n)$ and $(u_c^m \ldots u_c^1)$. The subscripts p and c stand for these two sub-patterns and there are *n* and *m* members in the p and c sub-patterns, respectively. The key byte B_j is instantiated into another byte using the self-substitution with masking parameters of (K_j, M_j, and R_j, for j=1 to 4). Application of self-substitution on the individual four bytes of the key (B_1 . . . B_4) generates the primary and the complementary sub-pattern for each byte as follows:

$(u_p^{1_{B1}} \ldots u_p^{n1_{B1}})$ and $(u_c^{m1_{B1}} \ldots u_c^{1_{B1}})$,
$(u_p^{1_{B2}} \ldots u_p^{n2_{B2}})$ and $(u_c^{m2_{B2}} \ldots u_c^{1_{B2}})$,
$(u_p^{1_{B3}} \ldots u_p^{n3_{B3}})$ and $(u_c^{m3_{B3}} \ldots u_c^{1_{B3}})$, and
$(u_p^{1_{B4}} \ldots u_p^{n4_{B4}})$ and $(u_c^{m4_{B4}} \ldots u_c^{1_{B4}})$.

A byte, say c_1, using the first member of the primary sub-pattern, u_p^1, is instantiated to c_1'. The first byte of key, B_1, using its first member of the primary sub-pattern, $u_p^{1_{B1}}$, is instantiated to B_1'. The other three bytes are also instantiated into B_2', B_3', and B_4' using their first member of the primary sub-patterns, $u_p^{1_{B2}}, u_p^{1_{B3}}, and\ u_p^{1_{B4}}$, respectively. The Hamming distance of *HD*(*c*', B_j'), for j=1 to 4, are measured and *B*'=Argmax[*HD*(*c*', B_j'), for j=1 to 4] is the key image. In the case that there are ties, the priority is given to the instantiated byte of B_1, B_2, B_3, and B_4 (and in that order.) The final substitution for c_1 is:

$$c_1'' = (c_1' \oplus B') \quad (1)$$

The next byte, c_2, within a given segment of ciphertext is instantiated to c_2' using u_p^2, and key bytes of B_1, B_2, B_3, and B_4 are instantiated to B_1', B_2', B_3', and B_4' using$u_p^{2_{B1}}, u_p^{2_{B2}}, u_p^{2_{B3}}, and\ u_p^{2_{B4}}$, respectively.

B'=Argmax[*HD*(*c*', B_j'), for j=1 to 4] and $c_2'' = (c_2' \oplus B')$. The process continues until the segment of the ciphertext is exhausted. The bytes of the next sub-list and the key bytes are instantiated using the complementary sub-patterns. Therefore, the sub-patterns are alternatively used for consecutive segments of the ciphertext.

Using the mixed substitution, the number of possible combinations for each key byte is equal to X and for the key of four bytes is X^4 (>$1.19*10^{31}$ combinations.) Reader needs to be reminded that the four-byte key may be expanded to the length of N bytes for which the outcome of XOR is one of the X^{N+1} possible combinations. For N=16 (128-bit key) The XOR is one of the X^{17} possible combinations (>$4.65*10^{105}$.)

3) Patterns' Profile: Considering both self and mixed substitutions, the masking parameters grow to fifteen: (K, M, and R) for the instantiation of a byte of segment and (K_j, M_j, and R_j, for j=1 to 4) for instantiation of the four bytes of the key. Therefore, a pattern profile includes the fifteen parameters, which are accommodated by a 96-bit long binary string as described below.

Since the possible values for each of the parameters K and K_j is nine (0 through 8), the value of each parameter can be accommodated by 4 bits (the total of 20 bits). The parameters M and M_j have eight possible values (1 through 8) and each parameter can be accommodated by 3 bits (the total of 15 bits). The parameters R and R_j need eight bits each (the total of 40 bits). In addition, we use sixteen bits as the *Flag bits* and another five bits as the *Preference bits*.

The flag bits represent a decimal number (Δ) in the range of (0: 65,535). Let us assume that the length of the ciphertext that is ready to be masked is L_{ct}. Three bytes of f_1, f_2, and f_3 of the ciphertext are flagged which are in locations: $\delta_1 = \delta$, $\delta_2 = \lfloor L_{ct}/2 + \delta/2 \rfloor$, and $\delta_3 = L_{ct} - \delta$, where, δ is calculated using formula (2)

$$\delta = \begin{cases} \Delta\ Mod\ L_{ct}, & \Delta > L_{ct} \\ L_{ct}\ Mod\ \Delta, & \Delta \le L_{ct} \end{cases} \quad (2)$$

The flagged bytes will not be masked during the vaccination process and they collectively make the *native byte* of $F = (f_1 \oplus f_2 \oplus f_3)$. Since the length of the ciphertext and the length of its masked version remain the same there is no need for including the length of the ciphertext in the profile. The question of why the flagged bytes are of interest will be answered shortly.

The purpose of preference bits is to build a *model* which is influenced by both the key and flagged bytes. The model is used to create variable length blocks and segments. To build the model, a desired byte number (z) of the key is identified by the four least significant bits of the preference bits. That is, one can select any byte from a a maximum of 16-byte long key. (If a longer than 16-byte key is used, the number of bits for the preference bits needs to be increased.) The key is treated as circular and the two pairs of bytes of $A_1=(z+1||z)$ and $A_2=(z+2||z-1)$ are selected from key. A new pair of bytes of $A_3=A_1 \oplus A_2 \oplus (F||F)$ is built. If the most significant bit of the preference bits is set to zero then, model is A_3; otherwise, the model is $a_1 \oplus a_2$, where, a_1 and a_2 are the pair of bytes in A_3.

Let us assume that there are two similar ciphertexts of CT_1 and CT_2 and we are using the same key and the same profile to mask the two ciphertexts, separately, using Vaccine. As long as one of the three flagged bytes in CT_1 and CT_2 is different the native bytes and, therefore, the models of the two ciphertexts are different and so their masked versions. This is one of the major advantages of Vaccine.

To summarize, the number of bits needed for the pattern profile is 96 bits (or 24 hex digits.) Dissection of a pattern profile is shown in Figure 2. The 24 hex digits representing the pattern profile along with eight hex digits representing the key may be sent to the receiver in advance or they may hide in the masked ciphertext itself:

a. In a predefined location/locations,
b. In location/locations determined by the internal representation of the key following some formula(s), or
c. A mixture of (a) and (b).

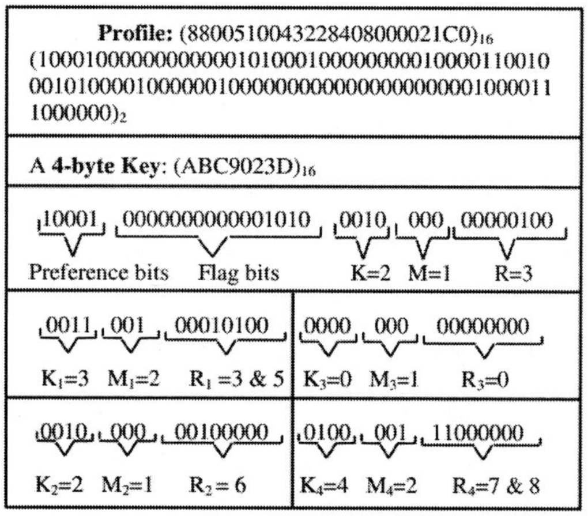

Figure 2. Dissection of the pattern's Profile of Interest

B. Vaccine

Vaccine is a variable-block cipher methodology capable of masking and unmasking a ciphertext. The details of masking and unmasking of Vaccine are presented in the following next two subsections.

1) Masking of the Ciphertext: Vaccine as a masking mechanism is able to mask the features of a ciphertext in the eye of a text miner. Vaccine: (1) divides the ciphertext into random size blocks, (2) each block, in turn, is divided into a number of segments such that the length of each segment is random, and (3) every byte within each segment is randomly instantiated to another byte using self and mixed substitutions. The masking process is presented shortly and it is encapsulated in algorithm Mask shown in Figure 3.

The algorithm is made up of four sections. In section one, (Step 1 of the algorithm) the profile is dissected to extract masking parameters and they, in turn, generate primary and complementary sub-patterns for five patterns:($Pattern_p^0$, $Pattern_c^0$), ($Pattern_p^{B1}$, $Pattern_c^{B1}$), ($Pattern_p^{B2}$, $Pattern_c^{B2}$), ($Pattern_p^{B3}$, $Pattern_c^{B3}$), and ($Pattern_p^{B4}$, $Pattern_c^{B4}$) used for masking the chosen byte of the ciphertext and the four key bytes, respectively. The array of pt with five elements keeps track of those primary and complementary sub-patterns of the five patterns that are in use. The model is also extracted in this step.

```
Algorithm Mask
Input:    A 32–bit key, a pattern's profile of 96-bit, and a
          ciphertext, CT.
Output:   Delivering IC as the masking version of CT.
Method:
 Step1- //Dissection of the profile and initializations
    Dissection delivers primary and secondary sub-patterns of
    five patterns (Pattern_p^0, Pattern_c^0), (Pattern_p^B1,
    Pattern_c^B1), (Pattern_p^B2, Pattern_c^B2), (Pattern_p^B3,
    Pattern_c^B3), and (Pattern_p^B4, Pattern_c^B4).
    κ ←Model obtained by using Preference bits, Flag bits,
         and key;
    IC ← ""; C ← CT;
    pt[5]← 0;//pt gives turn to the primary (pt[•]=0) and
         complementary (pt[•] =1) sub-patterns of the five
         patterns for initializing the CurrentP [5];
    Step 2-Repeat until C is exhausted
    |  a- Get the set of decimal numbers from κ in ascending
    |     order: D ={d_1, d_2, . . . d_y-1, d_y};
    |     Get the next random size block,
    |     β_n,=Substr(C, 0, d_y);
    |  b- CL = 0; //Current location in C
    |  c- Repeat for i =1 to y-1
    |   | //Divide β_n into y-1 segments;
    |   | s_i = Substr(β_n, CL, d_i - CL);
    |   | CL = CL+ d_i;
    |   | CurrentP[m]=Pattern_pt^m  //for m =0 to 4;
    |   | d- Repeat for each byte, c_j, in s_i
    |   |   | d_1- If (c_j is a flagged byte) Then continue;
    |   |   | d_2- If (CurrentP[0] is exhausted)
    |   |   |        Then CurrentP[0] = Pattern_pt^0;
    |   |   | d_3- c_j' = Flip c_j bits using CurrentP[0];
    |   |   | d_4- c_j' = Circularly swap proper c_j bits using
    |   |   |             CurrentP[0];
    |   |   | d_5- σ = Select(c_j', CurentP[1],
    |   |   |        CurrentP[2],CurrentP[3],CurrentP[4]);
    |   |   | d_6- a = c_j' ⊕ σ;
    |   |   | d_7- IC←IC || a;
    |   |   End;
    |   | pt[•]++; pt[•] ← pt[•] mode 2;
    |  End;
    |  e- Remove block β_n from C;
    |  f- Apply one-bit-left-rotation on κ;
   End;
End;
```

Figure 3. Algorithm Mask

The second section (Step 2.a of the algorithm) identifies a random size block prescribed by κ—the model. The identification process is done by creating y binary numbers using κ. The i-th binary number starts from the least significant bit of the κ and ends at the bit with the i-th value of "1" in κ. The binary numbers are converted into decimal numbers and sorted in ascending order, $\{d_1, d_2, \ldots d_{y-1}, d_y\}$. The block, β_n=Substr(C, 0, d_y), where C is initially a copy of the cipher text.

The third section (Step 2.c of the algorithm) divides block β_n into a number of random size segments. The size and the number of segments are dictated by κ internal representation. Block β_n has y segments: $\{ s_0 \ldots s_{y-1} \}$.

The segment s_i starts from the first byte after the segment s_{i-1} (the location is preserved in variable CL) and contains $\lambda_i = d_{i+1} - d_i$ bytes. The number of segments and their lengths are not the same for different blocks.

To get the next block of the ciphertext, the block β_n is removed from C (Step 2.e) and κ is changed by having a one-bit-left-rotation (Step 2.f). Using the above process along with new κ, the next block with a different size is identified. This process continues until C is exhausted. It is clear that the lengths of blocks are not necessarily the same. In fact, the lengths of blocks are random. It needs to be mentioned that length of the block β_i and β_{i+8} are the same when κ is one byte long. When κ is two bytes long, the length of the block β_i and β_{i+16} are the same. And a block on average is 32,768 bytes long. As a result, the ciphertext, on average, must be longer than 491,520 bytes before the blocks' lengths are repeated.

Algorithm Select
Input: A byte (c), Key, and four patterns for the four key bytes.
Output: key image, k.
Method:
a. Repeat for (w = 1 to 4)
  | If (CurrentP[w] is exhausted)
  | Then CurrentP[w] = $Pattern_{pt}^{w}$;
  End;
b. h ← -1;
c. Repeat for v= 1 to 4;
  | i. c_v ← An instantiated version of $KeyByte_v$ using related sub-pattern.
  | ii. If HD(c, c_v) >h //HD is Hamming distance function
  | Then h = HD(c, c_v); k = c_v;
  End;
End;

Figure 4. Algorithm Select

The fourth section (Step 2.d of the algorithm) delivers the masked version of the ciphertext, byte by byte, for a given segment. Flagged bytes are not masked (Step 2.d_1). If the number of bytes in the segment s_i is greater than the cardinality of the pattern then, the pattern repeats itself (Step 2.d_2). Each byte, c_j, of the segments s_i (for i=1 to y-1) are masked by applying (i) the relevant member of the current sub-pattern on byte c_j (Step 2.d_3 and 2.d_4), (ii) identifying the key image (Step 2.d_5), by invoking the Algorithm Select (Figure 4), (iii) create c_j', the masked version of the c_j, by XORing the outcome of process (i) and process (ii), (Step 2.d_6), and (iv) concatenate the masked version of the c_j, to string of IC which ultimately becomes the inoculated version of the inputted ciphertext (Step 2.d_7).

2) Unmasking of the Ciphertext: For unmasking a masked ciphertext, those steps that were taken during the masking process are applied in reverse order. Therefore, the Algorithm Mask with a minor change in step 2.d can be used for unmasking. We show only the changes to Step d of Figure 3 in Figure 5.

d- Repeat for each byte, c_j', in s_i
  d_1- If (c_j is a flagged byte) Then continue;
  d_2- If (CurrentP[0] is exhausted) Then CurrentP[0] = $Pattern_{pt}^{0}$;
  d_3- σ = Select(c_j', CurentP[1], CurrentP[2], CurrentP[3], CurrentP[4];
  d_4- $\alpha = c_j' \oplus \sigma$;
  d_5- α = Circularly swap bits of α using CurrentP[0];
  d_6- α = Flip a bits using CurrentP[0];
  d_7- UM←UM‖α; //UM is the unmasked ciphertext;

Figure 5. The modified part of the Algorithm Mask

IV. EMPIRICAL RESULTS

To measure the effectiveness of the proposed Vaccine, we compare its performance with the performance of the well-established masking algorithms of CBC and CFB. The behavior of Vaccine was observed using three separate profiles of simple, moderate, and complex. These observations are named VAC_s, VAC_m, and VAC_c.

Two plaintext templates of *natural* and *synthetic* were chosen and 100 plaintexts were generated for each template. Each plaintext following the first template was selected from a natural document made up of the lower and upper case alphabets and the 10 digits—total of 62 unique symbols. Each plaintext following the second template was randomly synthesized using the10 symbols set of {A, b, C, L, x, y, 0, 4, 6, 9}. The goal was to synthesize plaintexts with high occurrences of a small set of symbols. Each plaintext created under both templates was 1K bytes long.

For each plaintext, two ciphertexts of C_a and C_d were generated using Advanced Encryption System (AES-128) and Data Encryption Standard (DES) algorithms [12][13][14]. The masking approaches of CBC, CFB, VAC_s, VAC_m, and VAC_c were applied separately on C_a and C_d generating the masked ciphertexts of:

$\{C_a^{cbc}, C_a^{cfb}, C_a^{vac_s}, C_a^{vac_m}, C_a^{vac_c}\}$ and
$\{C_d^{cbc}, C_d^{cfb}, C_d^{vac_s}, C_d^{vac_m}, C_d^{vac_c}\}$.

When CFB applied on C_a and C_d the key lengths were 64-bit and 128-bit, respectively, and IV chosen from a natural document. (The least significant 64 bits of the 128-bit key was used as the key when CFB was applied on C_a. The key used by VAC_s, VAC_m, and VAC_c was also borrowed from the least significant 32 bits of the 128-bit key used for CFB.)

Let us consider the first set of masked ciphertexts $\{C_a^{cbc}, C_a^{cfb}, C_a^{vac_s}, C_a^{vac_m}, C_a^{vac_c}\}$ generated from C_a. The following steps are used to compare the effectiveness of the proposed Vaccine with CBC and CFB. (The same steps are also followed to compare the effectiveness of the proposed Vaccine with CBC and CFB using the masked ciphertexts of $\{C_d^{cbc}, C_d^{cfb}, C_d^{vac_s}, C_d^{vac_m}, C_d^{vac_c}\}$.)

a. Get the list of unique symbols that the plaintext is made up of, List=$\{\sigma_1 \ldots \sigma_m\}$.
b. Get the frequency of symbol σ_i, for i = 1 to m, and calculate the average frequency of the symbols.
c. Repeating the next two steps for every symbol, σ_i, in the list.
d. Identify the locations for all the occurrences of the symbol, σ_i, in the plaintext, $(\ell^i_1 \ldots \ell^i_n)$.
e. Identify the bytes in the locations of $(\ell^i_1 \ldots \ell^i_n)$ within the $C_a^\bullet$ and calculate the Hamming distance, h_j, between the two bytes in location ℓ_j, for j=1 to n, in the plaintext and $C_a^\bullet$. The overall average of Hamming distance for the symbol σ_i is $h_{\sigma i}$=Average($h_1 \ldots h_n$),
f. Concluding that the underline masking methodology with the highest average values of the Hamming distances have a superior performance.

The outcome of applying the above steps on the ciphertexts of $\{C_a^{cbc}, C_a^{cfb}, C_a^{vac_s}, C_a^{vac_m}, C_a^{vac_c}\}$ and $\{C_d^{cbc}, C_d^{cfb}, C_d^{vac_s}, C_d^{vac_m}, C_d^{vac_c}\}$ are shown in Table 1.a and Table 1.b. We have also used the system clock to calculate the average throughput (in millisecond) for the masking approaches of CBC, CFB, VAC_s, VAC_m, and VAC_c and reported in Tables 2.a and 2.b.

TABLE I. AVERAGE OF HAMMING DISTANCES BETWEEN THE TWO 100 PLAINTEXTS OF 1K BYTE LONG (GENERATED BY TWO TEMPLATES) AND THEIR RELATED MASKED CIPHERTEXTS: (A) ENCRYPTED BY AES AND (B) ENCRYPTED BY DES

Tem.	Avg. Symb. Freq.	AES-128				
		CBC	*CFB128*	*VAC_s*	*VAC_m*	*VAC_c*
		Dist.	Dist.	Dist.	Dist.	Dist.
Syn.	103	3.568	3.570	4.415	4.373	4.411
Natu.	16.5	3.569	3.561	4.423	4.361	4.411

(a)

Tem.	Avg. Symb. Freq.	DES				
		CBC	*CFB64*	*VAC_s*	*VAC_m*	*VAC_c*
		Dist.	Dist.	Dist.	Dist.	Dist.
Syn.	103	3.527	3.526	4.182	4.153	4.223
Natu.	16.5	3.513	3.515	4.176	4.141	4.221

(b)

In addition, a *masking strength* of μ ($0 < \mu < 1$), is introduced that is defined as $\mu = N_{inst} / N_{occ}$, where N_{inst} is the number of unique bytes in the masked ciphertext representing the instantiations of the N_{occ} occurrences of symbol σ_i in the underlying plaintext of the masked ciphertext. The masking strength for CBC, CFB, VAC_s, VAC_m, and VAC_c are presented in Tables 3.a and 3.b.

V. CONCLUSIONS AND FUTURE RESEARCH

The performance of the presented new cipher block approach, Vaccine, for masking and unmasking of ciphertexts seems superior to the performance of the well-known masking approaches of CBC and CFB.

TABLE II. THROUGHPUT AVERAGE IN MILISECOND FOR THE TWO 100 PLAINTEXTS OF 1K BYTE LONG (GENERATED BY TWO TEMPLATES): (A) ENCRYPTED BY AES AND (B) ENCRYPTED BY DES

Tem.	Avg Symb. Freq.	AES-128				
		CBC	*CFB128*	*VAC_s*	*VAC_m*	*VAC_c*
		TPut.	*TPut.*	*TPut.*	*TPut.*	*TPut.*
Syn.	103	4545	11111	25000	33334	20000
Natu.	16.5	12500	10000	16667	20000	12500

(a)

Tem.	Avg Symb. Freq.	DES				
		CBC	*CFB64*	*VAC_s*	*VAC_m*	*VAC_c*
		TPut.	*TPut.*	*TPut.*	*TPut.*	*TPut.*
Syn.	103	3846	11111	20000	25000	14286
Natu.	16.5	10000	10000	14286	20000	11111

(b)

TABLE III. AVERAGE MASKING STRENGTH FOR THE TWO 100 PLAINTEXTS OF 1K BYTE LONG (GENERATED BY TWO TEMPLATES): (A) ENCRYPTED BY AES AND (B) ENCRYPTED BY DES

Tem.	Avg. Symb. Freq.	AES-128				
		CBC	*CFB128*	*VAC_s*	*VAC_m*	*VAC_c*
		μ	μ	μ	μ	μ
Syn.	103	0.506	0.486	0.451	0.540	0.571
Natu.	16.5	0.882	0.878	0.845	0.890	0.889

(a)

Tem.	Avg. Symb. Freq.	DES				
		CBC	*CFB64*	*VAC_s*	*VAC_m*	*VAC_c*
		μ	μ	μ	μ	μ
Syn.	103	0.501	0.494	0.490	0.564	0.570
Natu.	16.5	0.878	0.894	0.880	0.909	0.893

(b)

The advantages of Vaccine over CBC and CFB are numerated as follows:

a. The key and patterns' profile may hide in the masked ciphertext.
b. The block size for Vaccine is not fixed and it is selected randomly.
c. Each block is divided into segments of random size.
d. The masking pattern changes from one byte to the next in a given segment.
e. Masking a ciphertext using Vaccine demands mandatory changes in the ciphertext. Therefore, the identity transformation could not be provided through the outcome of Vaccine. The simple proof is that the Hamming weight is modified.
f. The results revealed that on average:
   i. The Hamming distance between masked and unmasked occurrences of a byte using Vaccine is 0.72 bits higher than using CBC and CFB.
   ii. Vaccine throughput is 3.4 times and 1.8 times higher than throughput for CBC and CFB.
   iii. Vaccine masking strength is 1.5% and 1.8% higher than masking strength for CBC and CFB.

iv. VAC_m masking strength is 3.6% and 3.7% higher than masking strength for CBC and CFB. And VAC_c masking strength is 3.9% and 4.2% higher than masking strength for CBC and CFB.

As the future research, building a new version of Vaccine is in progress to make the throughput and the masking strength of the methodology even higher. In addition, the use of Vaccine in a parallel processing environment also will be investigated. In addition, a feasibility study for using Vaccine as an authentication method is in progress.

REFERENCES

[1] A. A. Rasheed, M. Cotter, B. Smith, D. Levan, and S. Phoha, "Dynamically Reconfigurable AES Cryptographic Core for Small, Power Limited Mobile Sensors", The 35th IEEE International Performance Computing and Communication Conference and Workshop, pp. 1-7, 2016.

[2] G. P. Saggese, A. Mazzeo, N. Mazzocca and A. G. M. Strollo, "An FPGA-based performance analysis of the unrolling, tiling, and pipelining of the AES algorithm", LNCS 2778, pp. 292-302, 2003.

[3] N. Pramstaller and J. Wolkerstorfer, "A Universal and Efficient AES Co-processor for Field Programmable Logic Arrays", Lecture Notes in Computer Science, Springer, Vol.3203, pp. 565-574, 2004.

[4] B. Moeller. *Security of CBC Cipher suites in SSL/TLS: Problems and Countermeasures. [Online].* Available from: https://www.openssl.org/~bodo/tls-cbc.txt

[5] W. Stallings, "Cryptography and Network Security: Principles and Practice", Pearson, 2014.

[6] C. A. Henk and V. Tilborg, "Fundamentals of Cryptology: "A Professional Reference and Interactive Tutorial", Springer Science & Business Media, 2006.

[7] N. Feruson, B. Schneier, and T. Kohno, "Cryptography Engineering: Design Principles and Practical Applications", Indianapolis: Wiley Publishing, Inc., pp. 63-64, 2010.

[8] W. F. Ehrsam, C. H. W. Meyer, J. L. Smith, and L. W. Tuchman, "Message Verification and Transmission Error Detection by Block Chaining", US Patent 4074066, 1976.

[9] C. Kaufman, R. Perlman, and M. Speciner, "Network Security", 2nd ed., Upper Saddle River, NJ: Prentice Hall, p. 319, 2002.

[10] National Institute of Standards and Technology (NIST), Advanced Encryption Standard (AES), Federal Information Processing Standards Publications 197 (FIPS197), Nov. 2001.

[11] S. Vaudenay, "Security Flaws Induced by CBC Padding — Applications to SSL, IPSEC, WTLS....", Lecture Notes in Computer Science, Springer, vol. 2332, pp. 534-546, 2002.

[12] H. Kuo-Tsang, C. Jung-Hui, and S. Sung-Shiou, "A Novel Structure with Dynamic Operation Mode for Symmetric-Key Block Ciphers", International Journal of Network Security & Its Applications, Vol. 5, No. 1, p. 19, 2013.

[13] H. Feistel, "Cryptography and Computer Privacy", Scientific American, Vol. 228, No. 5, pp 15–23, 1973.

[14] F. Charot, and E. Yahya, and C. Wagner, "Efficient Modular-Pipelined AES Implementation in Counter Mode on ALTERA FPGA", (FPL 2003), Lisbon, Portugal, pp. 282-291, 2003.

A Study on Introducing Cyber Security Incident Reporting Regulations for Nuclear Facilities

Chaechang Lee

Korea Institute of Nuclear Nonproliferation and Control
Daejeon, Republic of Korea
Email: chiching@kinac.re.kr

***Abstract*—Industrial control systems have recently become easy prey for cyber attacks as they expand to the Internet, beyond data communication through the network. Among industrial control systems, the systems used by nuclear facilities are especially at high risk against cyber attacks because their dangerous assets are used in managing nuclear materials. Most of the nuclear licensees have recently established cyber security response plans to protect their critical systems from cyber threats. To enable the response plans, effective incident reporting procedures should also be established and notified to personnel who has responsibilities to discover and report an undesired event in a timely manner. This study presents ongoing work, which is part of the study for establishing a cyber security incident response framework for nuclear facilities, and to introduce cyber security incident reporting regulations at nuclear facilities in the Republic of Korea.**

Keywords–Cyber Security; Incident Response; Nuclear Facilities; Reporting Regulation.

I. INTRODUCTION

Cyber security threats to industrial control environments have increased significantly because industrial control systems (ICSs) have changed from proprietary, isolated systems to PC-based open architectures and standard technologies interconnected with other networks and the Internet [1].

If a cyber attack occurs and results in damage, infrastructures such as public transportation, water, gas, as well as general IT systems incur financial losses or inconveniences to public amenities. However, cyber attacks on nuclear facilities threaten public safety and life by causing adverse effects on the safety functions of nuclear facilities. Therefore, in order to respond quickly and properly to cyber security incidents, nuclear licensees are required to have a more detailed cyber security incident response system than any other environmental licensees and to prepare incident reporting regulations to enable this. This paper, as a part of the research on building a cyber security incident response system for nuclear facilities in the Republic of Korea (ROK), presents the essential considerations of a regulatory authority in the process of developing and introducing incident reporting regulations.

It also uses practical contexts derived from consultations between regulators and nuclear licensees. In Section 1, the related works and contributions of this paper are presented. In Section 2, the paper describes the difference between incident reporting regulations for nuclear facilities compared to other critical infrastructures or general IT systems. Considerations to introduce incident reporting regulations at nuclear facilities are also presented in Section 2. Section 3 concludes the paper.

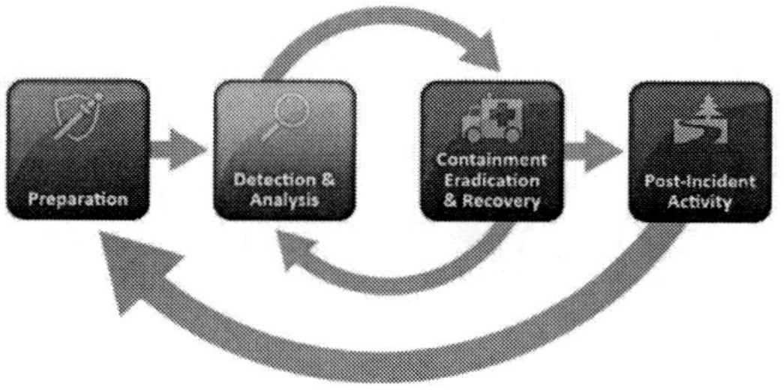

Figure 1. Incident Response Life Cycle [2]

A. *Related work*

There are several related standards and documents that guide cyber security incident response and reporting.

The National Institute of Standards and Technology (NIST) suggests the standard process to response cyber security incidents [2] and the International Atomic Energy Agency (IAEA) also cites it as the computer security incident response phases [3]. Figure 1 shows the process of incident response. NIST also demands the establishment of an incident report mechanism that permits people to report incidents anonymously [2].

The European Network and Information Security Agency (ENISA) describes good practices guide for the management of network and information security incidents on incident handling [4]. The main topic of the guideline is the incident handling process. The guide includes the formal framework for Computer Emergency Response Teams (CERTs, also known as CSIRTs), roles, workflows, basic CERT policies, cooperation, outsourcing, and reporting. However, the report guideline of the publication is presented for senior managers on how to manage incidents, and not for incident responses. ENISA also presents proposals for incident reporting to public authorities, private organizations and trust service providers, trying an introduction of a new reporting scheme or an improvement of standing procedures, under Article 19 of the electronic IDentification, Authentication and trust Services (eIDAS) regulation [5][6]. Guidelines for managing and reporting cyber security events presented by ENISA cover general IT environments. However, responding to and reporting of cyber security incidents that apply to nuclear facilities are distinct from general IT environments and other critical infrastructures. A detailed analysis is provided in Section 3.

In earlier studies, J. J. Gonzalez introduced a cyber security reporting system to share cyber security data, such as intrusion attempts, successful intrusions, and incidents of all types. He urged that it could lead to a more comprehensive and effective cyber data collection and analysis [7]. C. W. Johnson identified some of the challenges that frustrate the exchange of lessons learned from cyber security incidents in safety-related applications. He then argued for the integration of reporting mechanisms for cyber attacks on safety-critical national infrastructures [8]. R. Leszczyna and M. R. Wrobel proposed an approach to developing a data model for security information sharing platform for the smart grid [9]. All these previous research were focused on information sharing of security data. They however did not introduce reporting regulations for instant incident responses.

Especially at nuclear facilities, the IAEA states the goal and challenges of reporting during the computer security incident response process [3]. Additionally, the IAEA states that the goal of reporting is to ensure that everyone who needs to know about a computer security incident is informed in a timely manner. The IAEA further presents that the determination of the frequency of reporting and the level of detail required is a challenge to organizations [3]. However, it focuses on phases of incident response at nuclear facilities and analysis of the incident, and reporting is only briefly mentioned as one of the phases.

The United States (US) and Nuclear Regulatory Commission (NRC) have already introduced and applied cyber security event notification in the form of Code of Federal Regulations (CFR). [10] and [11] classify the cyber security events and set a time limit for reporting according to its severity. They also describe the process and method to notify the events in detail. However, they are based on the incident response infrastructure and systems in the US, and it is difficult to apply it in a country where the well-organized environment is not prepared.

This paper presents the essential items, based on experience of practical regulation and policy introduction, to be considered by the countries and regulatory agencies that intend to introduce reporting rules of responding to cyber incidents at nuclear facilities.

II. CONSIDERATIONS TO INTRODUCING THE POLICY

Cyber security incident response and reporting at nuclear facilities are different from the ordinary IT environments and other critical infrastructure.

- Unlike a typical IT environment, when a cyber security incident occurs at a nuclear facility, the personnel who discover and respond to the incident must consider the radiation effects. The activities that need to be done between report and response depend on the nature of the radiation effects, the content to report, and the status of the person or extent of the organization receiving the report. Hence, subsequent reporting of the situation is required whenever circumstances change.
- Systems at nuclear facilities, such as PLC, DCS, and HMI have a variety of accessible users: operators, maintenance personnel, security personnel, auditors, and contractors. Therefore, if anyone with access to the system discovers an undesired event, a standardized reporting form is required to accurately communicate the situation. Additionally, because the physical space of the facility is large, compared to an IT environment and, additionally, because there are dangerous areas where CERTs have restrict access, it may be difficult to directly assess the situation and notify the appropriate authorities or experts. Therefore, it is necessary to establish a clear reporting method for all accessible users to report the situation to the experts, and periodical training should be carried out.
- Some systems at a nuclear facility may be out of date, need to be updated, or run security programs such as an antivirus software. In such a case, it may be difficult for the user to notice a malicious access to the systems. If no security programs are run and no security policies are set, it may be difficult to detect a malicious intrusion. The operator may suspect the possibility of a compromise of the system only after finding an abnormality in the operation of the facility. Therefore, in order to confirm a cyber attack, it is necessary to consider not only notifications of cyber threats but also notifications of an abnormal situation related to the operation of the facility, such as rapid pressure or temperature change.
- In IT systems, data confidentiality and integrity are typically the primary concerns. For an ICS, human safety and fault tolerance in preventing loss of life or endangerment of public health or confidence, regulatory compliance, loss of equipment, loss of intellectual property, or lost or damaged products, are the primary concerns. Therefore, incidents that should be reported in the IT environment may not be necessary to report because of their low severity at a nuclear facility. Conversely, incidents that are overlooked in an IT environment may be a serious incident that must be reported at a nuclear facility.

Depending on the mission and nature of the organization that is responsible for introducing cyber security incident reporting policy, the purpose of creating the reporting requirements is different. Accordingly, the considerations in developing and introducing reporting regulations may vary. This section presents the considerations that the organizations should address to establish cyber security incident reporting regulations.

A. *Scope of cyber security incident*

First, the scope of cyber security incidents that may arise at a nuclear facility should be defined to apply incident reporting and incident response procedures. This means that assets, in the same manner as systems and network at nuclear facilities, should be identified to protect from cyber attacks by carrying out planned response activities.

Nuclear facilities have various services from enterprise business networks, including e-mail service, web server, and the Internet, to process control instrumentation bus network connected to sensors, actuators, and instrumentation. In addition, there are various systems, such as not only office PCs but also PLCs, DCSs, and HMIs located in the operations zone of nuclear facilities. Licensees should identify and select the essential assets among them to apply the established reporting regulation. For example, the NRC defined systems that perform safety, security, and emergency preparedness functions as critical digital assets that should be thoroughly protected from cyber attacks [12].

B. Subject of report

The person or entity to be responsible for the decision to report an incidence should be taken into consideration. If a reporting entity is not specified, it may result in unnecessary time loss from the time of incidence report to an appropriate response. As a reporting entity, the following persons may be considered: Operators of the nuclear facilities who first discover an undesired event; the team manager of the operators; and cyber security experts at the nuclear facilities who can determine whether the event was caused by digital threats. Because the reporting entity affects the immediacy and the concreteness of the reporting, it may vary according to the mission and nature of the organization.

NIST requires at least one reporting mechanism that allows for anonymous reporting [2].

C. Reportable incidents

It is not easy to damage nuclear facilities and disrupt normal operation with cyber attacks. The control networks of the nuclear facilities are usually separated from the external network such as the Internet. The control systems of the nuclear facilities have different platforms from the ordinary personal computer and requires specialized skills to implement malicious codes with the intent of compromising the control system. Nonetheless, nuclear facilities are an attractive prey to cyber terrorists because of their impact and influence. Attackers would gather the necessary information to carry out cyber attacks and infiltrate the control network based on the collected information. Thereafter, they would attempt to control the targeted systems and damage the nuclear facilities. All these processes are referred to as Advanced Persistent Threats (APT) attack.

When defining the reportable events, the nuclear facilities can categorize the cyber security events possible in the nuclear facility and present them as reportable events according to each stage of the APT attack: Preparation, Access, Resident, Harvest [13].

However, it is difficult for an on-site operator to determine immediately if the undesired events on the systems and networks are caused by the harvest stage of an APT attack, or by other causes such as mechanical or electrical faults, malfunctions due to the lifetime of the device, and human error. Therefore, when creating cyber security reporting regulations, it is necessary to provide a criterion for judging an incident that cannot be clearly determined as a cyber threat as a reportable event.

The most representative event, detectable and reportable at the stage of access or resident in an APT attack process, is a discovery of malicious software, also known as a malware, by an antivirus program. Even if the malicious effect of the malware on the systems and networks of nuclear facilities is difficult to establish immediately upon discovery, it must be reported because of the potential to adversely impact them. Additionally, the malware need to be analyzed to ascertain their infiltration routes and take preventive measures. Any unauthorized activities including creation, deletion, and modification of an account ID/PW, programs, and processes, and the alteration to configurations are also reportable events, which can be discovered at the stage of access or resident stage.

The events that can be discovered and reported during the preparation stage of the cyber attack include the collection of information indicating a planned cyber attack against nuclear facilities, such as a threatening message on SNS or a website posting. Although these events may not yet have been initiated and their severity and immediacy of response are relatively low, they must be reported and a proactive approach should be taken thereafter.

NRC has classified the reportable events into three cases and presents example events for each case [11].

D. Report flow

In cyber security reporting regulations, the organization or agency to which report must be made after the discovery of a cyber security incident should be defined. The IAEA suggests, as part of its goal of reporting, that everyone who needs to know about a computer security incident should be informed in a timely manner [3]. First, if the person who discovers an undesired event cannot determine whether incident responses are required with cyber security approaches, he or she should notify a cyber security team who can determine whether it is a result of cyber threats. The cyber security team should determine whether a professional technical support is needed, and report it to the incident handler or CSIRT. In addition, because similar cyber attacks at other nuclear sites such as cyber terrorism can occur simultaneously, it should be reported to a regulatory authority and the relevant authorities that manage and supervise nuclear facilities. The authorities related to nuclear facilities should collect information about the situation at other facilities and determine whether a national cyber terrorism crisis is ongoing, then report it to a national control center for the cyber crisis response.

The scope of the people who need to know about a computer security incident can be extended as much as possible according to the determinant of the situation being reported. In particular, if it is deemed that there are possibilities of a radiological damage due to a discovered incident, a radiological emergency must be promptly declared and appropriate the radiological disaster prevention organization, which implements appropriate protective measures, must be notified of the situation.

E. Means and contents of reporting

Various means can be used to report, such as by means of a phone, fax, or e-mail. Telecommunications is a useful reporting tool to deliver the fastest in-the-field situation. However, because of the nature of the information being disseminated verbally, untrained reporters may omit the important information that must be included in the report or may deliver ambiguous semantics. In the case of faxes or e-mails, because the recipients may not be reached in time or be aware of the reporting, they are unsuitable for the initial reporting of incidents. In particular, e-mails that require access to the Internet can be an inappropriate reporting tool in some cases. This is because the location of nuclear facilities where a cyber security incident occurs may be situated far away from the office where the Internet service is available. Additionally, the cyber attacks may have compromised the Internet connection or the e-mail system. The contacts used for reporting should always be kept up-to-date and multiple methods should be prepared in advance [2].

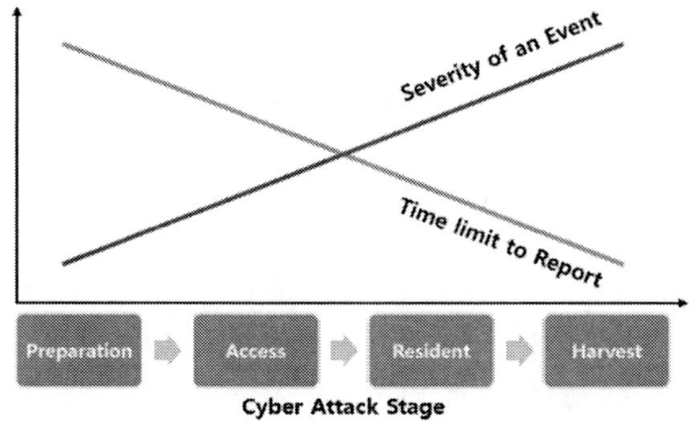

Figure 2. The correlations of the severity of the incident and the time limit to report by the stage of an APT attack

A form of written reports should be prepared in a pre-defined form so that senders know in advance what kind of information needs to be written and reported. The written reports must include the name and contact number of the reporter, the date and time when the event occurred or was discovered, the affected systems and networks of the nuclear facility, the actions that were taken, and the current status of the facility [2][11].

F. Report process

Most reports do not get finalized on the first attempt. After the initial reporting of a discovered situation, follow-up reporting is continuously required, based on changes in circumstances or gathered information. When a cyber security incident reporting regulation is enacted, a 2-step or 3-step reporting procedure can be presented in conjunction with the reporting method. Both processes take verbal reports as the first step in event reporting. When the event is initially discovered, it is important to promptly report through the available telephonic systems, such as by means of a telephone, hotline, or mobile phone.

Thereafter, the 2-step reporting procedure, such as the one implemented by the regulation of NRC, requires a detailed description of the discovered incident and the corresponding response activities in a single written report.

The 3-step reporting procedure requires, additionally, an analysis of the incident, which may take a long time after the licensee's second report. It also includes a description of corrective plans to take as preventive measures against similar types of incidents. This method is useful for the regulatory authority responsible for assessing and determining whether the incident response activities and their corrective plans are appropriate for the nuclear facilities.

The discovered cyber security incidents should be reported in a timely manner, depending on the severity of the incident to the nuclear facility. Time loss in collecting accurate information can cause delays to a timely response. The more likely an impactful incident on the safety of a nuclear facility, the more desirable a fast report and quick response.

Figure 2 shows the correlations of the severity of the incident and the time limit to report by the stage of the APT attack.

G. Report on classified information

Cyber security incident reporting regulation should contain the reporting method for sensitive information classified as confidential such as [11]. During the ongoing cyber attack, reporting the incident through an open network, which is an unprotected channel, can result in additional cyber security damage such as information leakage. It is therefore best to prepare a channel for secure communication that uses asymmetric key encryption with a certification for public key verification. However, if the dedicated systems are not prepared for transmission and reception of sensitive information, a guideline should be prepared to indicate the temporary measures for reporting the classified information, such as using a symmetric key to encrypt the file containing the information, and transmitting the key via another channel.

H. Response and follow-up action

When introducing cyber security reporting regulations, it should include the response and follow-up actions that each team and organization received the report should perform.

Because the operator in charge of a system at the nuclear facility always operates and manages the on-site system, he or she has the primary responsibility to find out the cause of the abnormal situation when the undesired event was discovered. The system operator should determine whether there are radiological effects and evaluate the event according to the International Nuclear and Radiological Event Scale (INES) standards, based on the severity of the event, by checking the status of the nuclear facility [14]. If there is no radiological effect, the operator should check whether the undesired event is the result of a simple mechanical or electrical fault, or whether the guaranteed days of the system has expired.

A cyber security team at a nuclear facility has the responsibility of determining whether the abnormal situation of the reported system is the result of cyber threats. Various system logs can be used by the team as reasonable evidence for cyber threats, such as the event log, the status of the executed process, network configuration, antivirus log, and register values. The cyber security team also should determine whether it is possible to deal with the cyber threats using their own response capabilities. In the case of planned cyber attacks, ongoing incidents, or incidents requiring the services of a professional cyber security response team for an initial incident investigation, the situation should be notified to CSIRT.

CSIRT, the special team for cyber security incident responses, protects nuclear facilities by preventing ongoing cyber security attacks and analyzing the incidents. In the case of an intended cyber attack, they find possible suspects and hand over the case to the appropriate law enforcement agencies. The cyber security team and CSIRT should identify the cause of the incident and establish corrective actions to take as preventive measures against similar types of incidents in the future.

Figure 3 shows the report flow with responses and follow-up actions.

III. Conclusion

This paper presented the issues that a regulatory body should consider when introducing reporting regulations for cyber security incidents at nuclear facilities. The regulator should ensure that nuclear facilities not only establish cyber security

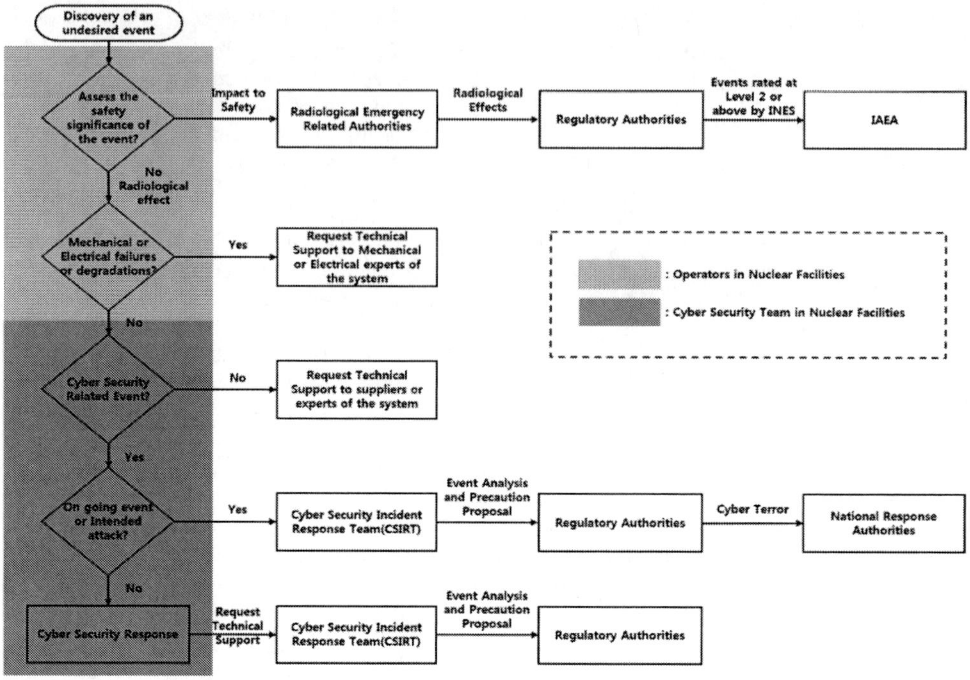

Figure 3. The report flow with responses and follow-up actions

incident response plans or procedures as preparatory measures against increasing terrorism threats, but also pay attention to prepare reporting regulations so that the prepared response systems can be activated in a timely manner. The reporting regulations should be created through thorough discussions by the relevant personnel and authorities on the presented considerations according to the role and nature of the organization introducing the reporting regulation. In addition, established regulations should be a practical guideline with continuous cyber security education and incident response training. For this, the subsequent study will discuss how incident reporting regulations can be implemented effectively and how regulators can identify unforeseen loopholes in the reporting system.

REFERENCES

[1] "Cyber Risks for Industrial Control Systems," 2015, URL: https://www.if-insurance.com/ [accessed: 2017-06-08].

[2] P. Cichonski, T. Mllar, T. Grance, and K. Scarfone, Computer Security Incident Handling Guide: NIST Special Publication 800-61, Revision 2, National Institute of Standards and Technology, Ed. USA, 2012.

[3] International Atomic Energy Agency(IAEA), Ed., Computer Security Incident Response Planning at Nuclear Facilities. IAEA, 2016.

[4] M. Maj, R. Reijers, and D. Stikvoort, Good practice guide for incident management. ENISA, 2010.

[5] D. V. Ouzounis, Good practice on Reporting Security Incidents. ENISA, 2009.

[6] C. K. Dr. Konstantinos Moulinos, Dr. Marnix Dekker, Proposal for Article 19 Incident reporting. ENISA, 2015.

[7] J. Gonzalez, "Towards a cyber security reporting system–a quality improvement process," Computer Safety, Reliability, and Security, 2005, pp. 368–380.

[8] C. Johnson, "Tools and techniques for reporting and analysing the causes of cyber-security incidents in safety-critical systems," 2014.

[9] R. Leszczyna and M. R. Wrobel, "Security information sharing for smart grids," network, vol. 1, 2014, p. 3.

[10] U.S Code of Federal Regulations, Ed., Physical Protection of Plants and Materials, part 73, chapter 1, title 10. USA, 2015.

[11] U.S Nuclear Regulatory Commission(NRC), Ed., Regulatory Guides 5.83, Cyber Security Event Notifications. USA, 2015.

[12] NRC, Ed., Regulatory Guides 5.71, Cyber Security Programs for Nuclear Facilities. USA, 2010.

[13] M. Li, W. Huang, Y. Wang, W. Fan, and J. Li, "The study of APT attack stage model," in 2016 IEEE/ACIS 15th International Conference on Computer and Information Science (ICIS). IEEE Computer Society, June 2016, pp. 1–5.

[14] IAEA, Ed., The International Nuclear and Radiological Event Scale User's Manual. IAEA, 2008.

Improving the Effectiveness of CSIRTs

Maria Bada*[1] Sadie Creese* Michael Goldsmith* and Chris J. Mitchell[†]

* University of Oxford, Global Cyber Security Capacity Centre, Oxford, UK
[†] University of London, Royal Holloway, London, UK
E-mail: {maria.bada | sadie.creese | michael.goldsmith}@cs.ox.ac.uk | C.Mitchell@rhul.ac.uk

Abstract-**This paper reports on research designed to measure the effectiveness of national Computer Security Incident Response Teams (CSIRTs). Specifically, our aim is to identify: 1) the ways in which a CSIRT might be considered to be effective; 2) the issues which may limit the performance of a CSIRT; and 3) approaches towards developing CSIRT effectiveness metrics. A primary motive for doing so is to enable more effective CSIRTs to be implemented, focusing on activities with the maximum impact on threat mitigation. The research was conducted using both online survey and interviews, in two phases. The study participants were experts within the existing CSIRT community. In total, 46 participants responded to the survey, from 27 countries in Europe, Africa, South and North America, and Asia. Three experts working for CSIRTs in the UK and USA were also interviewed. Questions asked during the interviews and the online survey queried the personal knowledge and experience of participants regarding CSIRTs. In our analysis, issues such as cooperation, data-sharing and trust are discussed as crucial components of an effective CSIRT. Existing measurement approaches for computer security incident response are presented, before a set of suggested direct and indirect measures of the effectiveness of a CSIRT is defined.**

Keywords-Cybersecurity; CSIRT; Metrics; Effectiveness.

I. INTRODUCTION

This paper considers the problem of assessing the effectiveness of Computer Security Incident Response Teams (CSIRTs). In order to be able to tackle any kind of cybersecurity incident, it is imperative for an incident response capacity to be available at least in some organisational form, in particular as a CSIRT.

The name Computer Emergency Response Team is the historic designation for the first such response team (CERT/CC) [1], established at Carnegie Mellon University (CMU). The term CERT is now a registered service mark of Carnegie Mellon University that is licensed to other teams around the world. Some teams have taken on the more generic name of CSIRT, in particular to clarify that they are involved with the task of handling computer security incidents rather than other technical support work. CSIRTs [2] have as their main responsibility detecting and informing a wider public about vulnerabilities, making patches available to organisations and to the general public, providing technical assistance in dealing with computer incidents, and coordinating responses in emergencies. CSIRTs can operate on a nationwide basis, either inside or outside of the governmental sector. Apart from their main mission, CSIRTs need to be able to adapt to a continuous changing environment and have the flexibility to deal with unexpected incidents. Today's challenges have an impact on the effectiveness of CSIRTs. CSIRTs need effective methods to collaborate and share information, efficient mechanisms to triage incoming information, and policies and procedures that are well-established and understood. Their effectiveness can be affected by a variety of factors [3].

Before considering ways of improving the effectiveness of a CSIRT, it is vital to understand how to assess its effectiveness. Issues such as cooperation, data-sharing and trust are crucial in order for a CSIRT to accomplish high levels of performance. In this paper, we will try to describe the factors which can enhance the capacity of a national CSIRT and improve its processes.

In Section II, we describe existing measurement approaches for computer security incident response before defining a set of measures. Following more information on issues such as cooperation, data-sharing and trust is provided, which are crucial in order a CSIRT to accomplish high levels of performance. In Section III, related work internationally is presented while section IV describes the methodology. Section V presents our results and finally section VI describes our conclusions.

The results presented in this paper are intended to be particularly valuable for CSIRT experts, Chief Information Officers (CIOs), Chief Information Security officers (CISOs), Senior Agency Information Security Officers (SAISOs), Information System Security Officers (ISSOs), and Community Support Officers (CSOs) and (CISOs).

The measures presented can be used both within government and industry contexts.

II. METRICS TO ASSESS THE EFFECTIVENESS OF A CSIRT

Well-defined metrics are essential to determine which security practices are worth investing in. Every CSIRT will need to develop mechanisms to evaluate the effectiveness of its practice. This should be done in conjunction with its management and its constituency [4]. Effectiveness, as well as efficiency measures address two aspects of security control implementation results: the robustness of the result itself (effectiveness) and the timeliness of the result (efficiency). These measures can provide important information for security decision makers in order to improve the performance of CSIRTs, and they help in determining the effectiveness of security controls.

By measuring the effectiveness of information security, there can be [5]:

a) Increases in accountability: Measuring effectiveness can help in identifying specific security controls that are implemented incorrectly or are ineffective.

b) Improvements in Information Security Effectiveness: Measuring information security can determine the effectiveness of implemented information security processes and procedures by interrelating the results of various activities and events to security controls and investments.

c) Demonstration of Compliance: Organisations can demonstrate compliance with applicable laws and regulations by maintaining an information security measurement program.

The International Telecommunication Union (ITU) [6], is helping countries to establish National Computer Incident Response Teams (CIRTs), which serve as a national focus point for coordinating cybersecurity incident response to cyber-attacks in the country. The objective of the Assessment of a CSIRT is to define the readiness to implement a national CSIRT. Part of this assessment includes the incident response capabilities of a country and the existence of an intrusion detection service offered to the constituents.

In order to improve the effectiveness of a CSIRT, it is vital to understand how to assess its effectiveness. Following we will be providing more information on issues such as cooperation, data-sharing and trust which are crucial in order a CSIRT to accomplish high levels of performance [3], [4], [7], [8].

A. *Cooperation*

The OECD report (2005) [9], describes the importance of international cooperation for fostering a culture of security and the role of regional facilitating interactions and exchanges. Moreover, national CSIRTs can help foster a cybersecurity culture by providing activities for awareness and education to the public, educating national stakeholders on the impact of virtual activities to their organisations, and the implications of their activities for cyber and information security. International cooperation is considered an integral part of the activities of a national CSIRT, and a number of countries have already established operational networks through which they exchange information and good practice. Most countries cooperate at the regional (European TF-CSIRT and EGC, APCERT) or global level (FIRST).

ENISA [10] while discussing the subject of the effectiveness of CSIRTs, has focused on possible barriers that can inhibit it. Specifically, four areas of benefit from a possible cooperation were identified: Incident Handling; Project establishment; Resource and information sharing; Social networking.

B. *Information sharing*

ENISA [10] has dealt with the issue of threat and incident information exchange and sharing practices used among CSIRTs in Europe, especially, but not limited to, national/governmental CSIRTs. ENISA identified the functional and technical gaps that limit threat intelligence exchanges between national/governmental CSIRTs and their counterparts in Europe, as well as other CSIRTs within their respective countries.

Interactions between CSIRTs can include asking other teams for advice, disseminating knowledge of problems, and working cooperatively to resolve an incident affecting one or more of CSIRT constituencies. Response teams have to decide what kinds of agreements can exist between them in order to share but still safeguard information, as well as which information can be disclosed and to whom. A peer agreement refers to simple cooperation between CSIRTs, where a team contacts another and asks for help and advice [11].

ENISA [7] presented a variety of issues which can hinder information sharing. The main barriers to cooperation between CSIRTs are: a) poor quality of information; b) poor management of information sharing; c) misaligned incentives stemming from reputational risks; d) uncertainty about senior level awareness of cybersecurity; and e) the disincentive for private sector organisations to disclose information because of possible reputational damage. ENISA defines basic requirements for improved communications interoperable with existing solutions in order to improve information sharing. Better utilization of current communication tools and practices is needed. Local detection of incidents accompanied by trusted forms of information exchange, can ultimately lead to improved prevention of cyber incidents on a global scale.

The Information Sharing Framework (ISF, MACCSA, 2013) [8] provides guidance on establishing the capability to increase an organisation's cyber Situational Awareness, enabled by sharing information across a trusted community of interest to achieve Collaborative Cyber Situational Awareness (CCSA).

C. *Trust*

CSIRT cooperation is based on trust. Without trust, national/governmental CSIRTs will be less willing to share information and less open to work together on incident response and handling when needed. Measuring trust and defining criteria by which to measure a CSIRT trustworthiness is an ongoing challenge, particularly when the aim of the cooperation is to exchange and share sensitive information. Key criteria that national CSIRTs look for include: technical expertise with a proven track record; membership in CERT initiatives; ability to respond quickly and act on security threats; and a stable team [3].

Trust can be one of the biggest obstacles to enhanced and effective communication between CSIRTs but also between CSIRTs and other stakeholders. Lack of trust between stakeholders can lead to a lack of sharing of security incident information. This component is of vital importance for cooperation and information sharing, as discussed above.

According to Messenger (2005) [12], trust in public/private partnerships has a very significant role which can be enhanced through frequency of contact between counterpart individuals, identification and sharing of common intentions and objectives, or technical credibility of technical staff.

According to the Information Sharing Framework [8], Trust depends on an AAA Model: Authentication (Are you who you claim you are?), Authorisation (Do you have permission to undertake the activities?) and Accountability (Can you evidence compliance in any court of law?).

D. Resources

The effectiveness of CSIRTs can be limited as a result of growing work load and limited resources [13], [14]. It seems obvious, but a national incident response team without a steady source of funding will not be able to function beyond the short term [15]. The typical work overload situation in a CSIRT, limits its effectiveness [14]. A CSIRT that has over-stretched its resources over a long time period must be prepared to go through a worse-before-better scenario to escape the "Capability Trap". Such a transition process can be quite painful to the CSIRT and its surrounding environment, for example, through adjustments to scope of service to release resources for improvement [13].

III. RELATED WORK

The key to security metrics is obtaining measurements that have the following ideal characteristics: they should measure organisationally meaningful things; they should be reproducible; they should be objective and unbiased; they should be able to measure some type of progression towards a goal.

There are existing publications which refer to how we can measure the performance and create accountability for the capabilities of a CSIRT. The NIST Special Publication 800-55 Revision 1 (2008) [16] defined measurement types for information security such as implementation, effectiveness/efficiency, and impact. The authors established that these are not just measurement types but they are actually purposes or the drive for measuring information security. In another NIST publication, NIST Special Publication 800-61 Revision 1 [17] possible metrics were proposed: a) the number of incidents handled; b) time per incident; c) objective assessment of each incident; and d) subjective assessment of each incident. These metrics are very practical but suggest only a small portion of possible metrics and measurement types for measuring CSIRT.

A technical report from Carnegie Mellon's Software Engineering Institute [18] measured incident management based on common functions and processes within CSIRT work flow. Sritapan, et al. [19] developed a metrics framework for incident response to serve as an internal analysis, in order to support the incident reporting improvement and strengthen the security posture for an organisation' s mission.

The OECD report on Improving the Evidence Base for Information Security and Privacy Policies [20] indicates that many CSIRTs already generate statistics based on their daily activities, including statistics on the number of alerts and warnings issued or incidents handled.

The OECD report [21] presents the ability of CSIRTs to report data about their constituencies, the size of the networks and users under their responsibility, organisational capacity and incidents, as well as information on the quality of these responses.

ENISA [22] also released a report which, "*builds upon the current practice of CERTs with responsibilities for ICS networks, and also on the earlier work of ENISA on a baseline capabilities scheme for national/ governmental (n/g) CERTs*," without prescribing which entity should provide these services for the EU. The good practice guide divides ICS-CERC provisions into four categories: mandate capabilities; technical operational capabilities; organisational operational capabilities and co-operational capabilities.

IV. METHODOLOGY

A focus group was conducted, with participation of 15 experts working in both academia and industry. The research itself was conducted using an online survey and interviews, in two phases, a pilot phase and the main survey phase.

Questions asked during the interviews and online survey, solicit the personal knowledge and experience of participants regarding CSIRTs. Prior to taking part in the study, participants were required to read and sign a consent form that informed them of the project, its goals and how their information and feedback would be treated and used. All data were anonymised immediately following its collection, and information was treated as confidential. This project has been reviewed by, and received ethics clearance through, the University of Oxford Central University Research Ethics Committee (Ref No: SSD/CUREC1A/14-127, Annex C).

A. Pilot Phase

An online tool-survey was developed using Qualtrics [23]. During the pilot phase, the online survey consisted of 51 questions on various factors determining the effectiveness of CSIRTs, and participants were required to answer the questionnaire through a web link.

B. Main Research Phase

After the pilot phase, feedback from participants was collected, which resulted in the survey consisting of 19 questions. Furthermore, during this phase three interviews were conducted in order to gain a deeper insight on the experience of experts working for CSIRTs, and on the level of cybersecurity capacity of a nation, region or organisation.

C. Participants

The participants who took part in the study are experts within the existing CSIRT community, currently working in a CSIRT environment or who have done so in the past, or have been involved in the creation of a CSIRT. In total, 46 participants responded to the survey, from 27 different countries in Europe, Africa, the Americas, and Asia. Also, three experts working for CSIRTs in the UK and USA were interviewed.

V. RESULTS

This section presents the results from the research described above.

Regarding the type of the constituency the participants have worked for, the majority stated that their constituency was a government or a commercial organisation. Some participants stated that they have worked for the Internet Society, a non-governmental organisation, a research group, an academic organisation or a coordination centre.

A. Training

A very important aspect of measuring the effectiveness of a CSIRT is the training provided to its members. Our findings indicated that the training is provided for most experts working for a CSIRT. When considering the types of training provided to employees working for a CSIRT, the responses referred to training on operational, technical issues as well as on forensics and conducting CSIRT exercises.

Training on communication and legal issues is less commonly provided. Moreover, some participants mentioned other areas of training provided, such as tools for operationalising a CSIRT, threat intelligence resources, policies and procedures as well as TRANSITS courses. Usually, CSIRT programs are made up of qualified experts, but lack full-time staff. Most of the training provided focuses on operational, technical issues as well as on forensics and conducting CSIRT exercises [3]. Consistent training of CSIRT staff, as well as the continuous building of a network of experts who can provide advice and help, is necessary.

B. Type of services provided

Our findings indicate that most of the services provided are reactive, including incident handling, alerts and warnings, and vulnerability handing; although proactive services, such as security audit/assessments and dissemination, are also provided. Lastly, a significant volume of security quality management services are provided, such as awareness, education and training. Other noteworthy services provided, as indicated by the participants, include monitoring; the applicability of Audit Law and the protection of the critical infrastructure and situational awareness services.

C. Security incidents

According to our results, most frequent classes of security incident are: malicious code; unauthorised access; and spam. Less frequent incident types include: denial of service attacks; improper usage; scans/probes/attempted access; data breach; ransomware and destructive malware. Some other security incidents referred to by participants are website defacement; computers in botnet; phishing; and fraud attempts.

Although security experts claim that they can identify security incidents within hours, it typically takes about a month to work through the entire process of incident investigation, service restoration and verification. The identification of a security incident is only a small part of the overall process of handling that incident. Investment is critical for effective cyber incident response programs. Also, a crucial aspect is that usually management is largely unaware of cybersecurity threats [24].

D. Cooperation and Trust

International cooperation is widely regarded as an integral part of the activities of national CSIRTs, and several countries have already established operational networks through which they exchange information and good practice. Most countries cooperate at the regional (e.g., European TF-CSIRT and EGC, APCERT) or global level (e.g., FIRST). ENISA [22], while discussing the subject of the effectiveness of CSIRTs, addressed the topic of multi various cooperation between CSIRTs. From our research, we found that cooperation is strongest at a national level, less evident in the context of cooperation between EU member States, and at its lowest level for cooperation at an international level.

As trust is not inherent, CSIRTs can go about establishing a first bond of trust in three ways: necessity, opportunity [25] and through trusted introducers. As indicated at the latest paper of the Global Public Policy Institute (GPPi) [24], *'Necessity drives cooperation, and if cooperation leads to a positive outcome it builds trust'*.

E. Metrics

In this section, we present results of our findings regarding possible ways of measuring the effectiveness of CSIRTs. The metrics identified from our research and suggested by stakeholders could be categorised in six categories: a) impact measures; b) incident response quality; c) incident prevention; d) situational awareness capability; e) measures on general capability of CSIRTs; f) outreach mission.

a) Impact measures: These measures are used in order to assess the impact of a CSIRT's mission. Examples of these measures are: 1) the volume of information output by the CSIRT (advisories, bulletins, reports) or 2) the amount of information reported to constituency about computer security issues or ongoing activity.

b) Incident Response Quality: Examples of measuring incident response quality are: 1) digital forensics capability; 2) well-defined processes with identified steps, stakeholders and escalation lists; 3) the number of high impact incidents measured in dollars or damage; 4) re-occurring incidents that were already handled; 5) the speed of initial response to an event; 6) the speed of identification of incident nature / attack characteristics (estimated time); ability to achieve normal work flow through attack status in face of incidents (indication of skills/adequate capabilities); 7) stakeholder level of awareness (communications ability); 8) percentage of security incidents that were managed in accordance with established policies, procedures, and processes (Incident Management Procedures) [26], [27]; 9) percentage of incidents reported within required time frame per applicable incident category [15]; 10) percentage of successful attacks handled in accordance with policy, defined procedures, and in-place processes in a disciplined repeatable, predictable manner (this assumes that well-defined processes for incident management exist) [24]; 11) ability to cooperate with other CSIRT teams in support of investigations and prosecutions (the latter requiring the evidence capability) [3], [4].

c) Incident prevention: Examples of measuring incident prevention quality are metrics such as: 1) the number of vulnerability exploits for organisations and/or individuals in the target audience for the CSIRT; 2) the percentage of security incidents that exploited existing vulnerabilities with known solutions, patches, or workarounds and 3) the mean times between incidents (high performers have long mean times).

d) Situational Awareness Capability: This capability can me measured by looking at: 1) access to threat and attack data feeds; 2) the synthesis of data feeds into single data model (indicator of fusion capability); 3) the support for threat and attack intelligence capability; 4) the translation into information for distribution to stakeholder community; 5) the translation into actionable information for incident response; 6) the integration of feedback into refinement of architectures and best practices; 7) the involvement in disaster recovery planning [28].

e) Measures on general capability of CSIRTs: As mentioned above there are other capabilities which define the effectiveness of a CSIRT. These are: 1) the existence of enough funding [29]; 2) the existence or possible access to specialised legal and PR experts among staff members [14]; 3) the existence or possible access to specialised personnel in reverse engineering or digital forensics; 4) the security posture of the organisation; 5) the effectiveness of a Government to support a CSIRT policy; 6) the existence of a portal on CSIRTs; 7) the number of staff members with [X] years of incident handling experience.

f) Outreach Mission: Metrics such as: 1) the promotion of stakeholder awareness on existing national CSIRTs and their responsibilities and 2) training in specialised technical aspects [3] are also identified as crucial factors regarding the effectiveness of CSIRTs.

g) Other Measures: The current research has also identified other essential qualities that could reinforce the effectiveness of a CSIRT. These are: a) the collaboration with law enforcement agencies; b) capacity-building programmes; c) public-private partnerships; d) career tracks for all staff members; e) establishment of national regional and international centres for a coordinated response in real time and training CSIRT; and f) the presence of pre-established channels of communication prior to actual incident responses.

Awareness and education is also a central and ongoing process for a CSIRT. Therefore, the improvement of awareness of CSIRTs in target audience is crucial. This might be done by various ways, such as via web sites, conferences and white papers.

Also, better communication, information sharing and cooperation between CSIRTs can lead to better performance. Therefore, by improving the means of communication to target audience through multiple communication channels can improve the effectiveness of CSIRTs [9], [30].

In order to enhance the flow of vulnerability information to CSIRTs and improve the use of information provided by CSIRTs trust is of vital importance. Improving trust in and between CSIRTs can ensure that (a) as much information is provided to CSIRTs as possible, and (b) take-up (action on) of information provided by a CSIRT is maximised.

Moreover, having a good legal framework and establishing collaboration with law enforcement agencies can enhance sharing of data. A possible approach might be to draft regulation and/or legislation to make organisations take action on CSIRT warnings and/or increase their liability so they feel obliged to take warnings seriously. Better enforcement of existing legislation (including data privacy legislation) could also enforce organisations to take privacy and security into consideration.

VI. CONCLUSION

Further research in this field would be highly desirable. Improving the effectiveness of CSIRTs is likely to be a long-term process. Experts working in CSIRTs need to share their knowledge and experience with a wider network of experts in order to enhance their capabilities.

As shown in this study, better communication, information sharing and cooperation between CSIRTs can lead to better performance. The suggested steps in order to improve the effectiveness of CSIRTs include, improvement of awareness of CSIRTs in target audience, improvement of the flow of vulnerability information to CSIRTs, improving use of information provided by CSIRTs, improving trust in CSIRTs to ensure that as much information is provided as possible, better enforcement of existing legislation and of course existence of enough resources.

Limitations and future research

Our research was subject to a number of limitations. First, our sample involved 46 participants, from 27 countries in Europe, Africa, the Americas and Asia. Although we tried to cover a broad range of countries at various levels of development, a larger sample would provide more accurate data. Second, the majority of participants have current or previous experience in national CSIRTs and less in organisational CSIRTs. This can partly be explained by the nature of the experts that were contacted. Future research might usefully explore the effectiveness of CSIRTs in the private sector.

REFERENCES

[1] Computer Emergency Response Team, CERT. [Online]. Available: http://www.cert.org/ [Accessed 5 June 2017].

[2] Organisation for Economic Co-operation and Development (OECD): "Studies in Risk Management, Norway Information Security", 2006. [Online]. Available from: http://www.oecd.org/norway/36100106.pdf [Accessed 24 June 2017].

[3] European Network and Information Security Agency (ENISA): "Deployment of Baseline Capabilities of National/ Governmental CERTs", 2012. [Online]. Available: https://www.sbs.ox.ac.uk/cybersecurity-capacity/content/deployment-baseline-capabilities-nationalgovernmental-certs [Accessed 10 June 2017].

[4] S. Bradshaw, "Combatting Cyber Threats: CSIRTs and Fostering International Cooperation on Cybersecurity", Centre for International Governance Innovation and Chatham House, Paper Series: No. 23 – December 2015. [Online]. Available: https://www.cigionline.org/sites/default/files/gcig_no23web_0.pdf [Accessed 9 June 2017].

[5] National Institute of Standards and Technology (NIST): "Special Publication 800-55 Revision 1, Performance Measurement Guide for Information Security", E. Chew, M. Swanson, K. Stine, N. Bartol, A. Brown, and W. Robinson, July 2008. Available: http://csrc.nist.gov/publications/nistpubs/800-55-Rev1/SP800-55-rev1.pdf [Accessed 10 June 2017].

[6] F. Wamala, "National Cybersecurity Strategy Guide", International Telecommunication Union (ITU), September 2011. [Online]. Available: http://www.itu.int/ITU-D/cyb/cybersecurity/docs/ITUNationalCybersecurityStrategyGuide.pdf [Accessed 30 May 2017].

[7] European Network and Information Security Agency (ENISA): "Incentives and Barriers to Information Sharing", 2010. [Online]. Available: https://www.enisa.europa.eu/publications/incentives-and-barriers-to-information-sharing/ [Accessed 15 June 2017].

[8] Multinational Alliance for Collaborative Cyber Situational Awareness (MACCSA): "Information Sharing Framework (ISF), version 2.4", 20 November 2013. [Online]. Available: https://www.terena.org/mail-archives/refeds/pdfjJz1CRtYC4.pdf [Accessed 10 May 2017].

[9] Organisation for Economic Co-operation and Development (OECD): "The Promotion of a Culture of Security for Information Systems and Networks in OECD Countries, Working Party on Information Security and Privacy", December 2005. [Online]. Available: http://www.oecd.org/internet/ieconomy/35884541.pdf [Accessed 2 May 2017].

[10] European Network and Information Security Agency (ENISA): "Detect, SHARE, Protect - Solutions for Improving Threat Data Exchange among CERTs", 2013. [Online]. Available: https://www.enisa.europa.eu/activities/cert/support/data-sharing [Accessed 4 May 2017].

[11] N. Brownlee and E. Guttman, "Expectations for Computer Security Incident Response. Best Current Practice", ISF, Network Working Group RFC 2350, June 1998. [Online]. Available: http://tools.ietf.org/html/draft-ietf-grip-framework-irt-04 [Accessed 24 June 2017].

[12] M. Messenger, "Why would I tell you? Perceived influences for disclosure decisions by senior professionals in inter organisation sharing forums", Unpublished Masters dissertation, University of London Birkbeck School of Management and Organisational Psychology, 2005.

[13] W. Johannes, J. Gonzalez, and K. P. Kossakowski, "Limits to Effectiveness in Computer Security Incident Response Teams", In 23rd International Conference of the System Dynamics Society, V. 11, Oxford, pp. 55-74, 2004. Available: http://scholarworks.lib.csusb.edu/ciima/vol11/iss3/5 [Accessed 24 May 2017].

[14] M. Nurul, Y. Zahri, A. Aswami, and N. Azlan, "CSIRT Management Workflow: Practical Guide for Critical Infrastructure Organizations", Proceedings of the 10th European Conference on Information Systems Management: ECISM 2016, Portugal September, pp.138-146, 2016.

[15] Organization of American States (OAS): "Best Practices for Establishing a National CSIRT", 2016. [Online]. Available: https://www.sites.oas.org/cyber/Documents/2016%20-%20Best%20Practices%20CSIRT.pdf [Accessed 2 May 2017].

[16] National Institute of Standards and Technology (NIST): "Special Publication 800-55 Revision 1", 2008. [Online]. Available: http://csrc.nist.gov/publications/nistpubs/800-55-Rev1/SP800-55-rev1.pdf [Accessed 17 June 2017].

[17] National Institute of Standards and Technology (NIST): "Special Publication 800-61 Revision 2, Computer Security Incident Handling Guide", Recommendations of the National Institute of Standards and Technology, P., Cichonski, T., Millar, and T.G.K., Scarfone, August 2012. [Online]. Available: http://csrc.nist.gov/publications/nistpubs/800-61rev2/SP800-61rev2.pdf [Accessed 24 June 2017].

[18] Software Engineering Institute (SEI): "Incident Management Capability Metrics Version 0.1", 2007. [Online]. Available: http://resources.sei.cmu.edu/library/asset-view.cfm?AssetID=8379 [Accessed 12 May 2017].

[19] V. Sritapan, S.W. Zhu, and C. E. Tapie Rohm Jr., "Developing a Metrics Framework for the Federal Government in Computer Security Incident Response", 2011. [Online]. Available: http://scholarworks.lib.csusb.edu/cgi/viewcontent.cgi?article=1170&context=ciima [Accessed 16 June 2017].

[20] Organisation for Economic Co-operation and Development (OECD): "Improving the Evidence Base for Information Security and Privacy Policies: Understanding the Opportunities and Challenges related to Measuring Information Security, Privacy and the Protection of Children Online", OECD Digital Economy Papers, no. 214, OECD, 2012, Paris.

[21] Organisation for Economic Co-operation and Development (OECD): "Directorate for Science, Technology and Industry, Committee for Information, Computer and Communications Policy. Improving the International Comparability of Statistics Produced by Computer Security Incident Response Teams", 18 June 2014.

[22] European Network and Information Security Agency (ENISA): "Good practice guide for CERTs in the area of Industrial Control Systems - Computer Emergency Response Capabilities considerations for ICS", December 2013. [Online]. Available: http://www.enisa.europa.eu/activities/cert/support/baseline-capabilities/ics-cerc/good-practice-guide-for-certs-in-the-area-of-industrial-control-systems/at_download/fullReport [Accessed 5 June 2017].

[23] Qualtrics, http://www.qualtrics.com/

[24] I. Skierka, M. Hohmann, R. Morgus, and T. Maurer, "CSIRT Basics for Policy-Makers: The History, Types & Culture of Computer Security Incident Response Teams", Global Public Policy Institute (GPPi), April 29, 2015. [Online]. Available: http://www.digitaldebates.org/fileadmin/media/cyber/CSIRT_Basics_for_Policy-Makers_May_2015_WEB_09-15.pdf [Accessed 18 May 2017].

[25] K. Silicki and M. Maj, "Barriers to CSIRTs cooperation. Challenge in practice", the CLOSER Project, 20th FIRST Annual Conference, Vancouver, Canada, 2008.

[26] Carnegie Mellon University, "CERT's Podcasts: Security for Business Leaders", Show Notes, 2008. [Online]. Available: http://resources.sei.cmu.edu/asset_files/Podcast/2008_016_102_67465.pdf [Accessed 19 June 2017].

[27] CC. Chiu and KS. Lin, "Importance-Performance Analysis Based Evaluation Method for Security Incident Management Capability", In: Nguyen N., Tojo S., Nguyen L., Trawiński B. (eds) Intelligent Information and Database Systems, ACIIDS, pp. 180-194, 2017. Lecture Notes in Computer Science, vol 10192. Springer.

[28] T. Pahi, M. Leitner, and F. Skopik, "Analysis and Assessment of Situational Awareness Models for National Cyber Security Centers," In Proceedings of the 3rd International Conference on Information Systems Security and Privacy (ICISSP), SCITEPRESS, pp. 334-345, 2017. ISBN 978-989-758-209-7. DOI: 10.5220/0006149703340345

[29] Ponemon Institute LLC, "Cyber Security Incident Response – Are we as prepared as we think?", January 2014. [Online]. Available: http://www.lancope.com/ponemon-incident-response/ [Accessed 19 June 2017].

[30] European Network and Information Security Agency (ENISA): "CERT cooperation and its further facilitation by relevant stakeholders", 2006. [Online]. Available: CERT_cooperation_ENISA.pdf [Accessed 11 June 2017]

On the Alignment of Safety and Security for Autonomous Vehicles

Jin Cui, Giedre Sabaliauskaite
Centre for Research in Cyber Security (iTrust)
Singapore University of Technology and Design, SUTD
Email:{jin_cui, giedre}@sutd.edu.sg

***Abstract*—Safety is the primary requirement and the key challenge in autonomous vehicles. Any accidental failures (safety issue) and/or intentional attacks (security issue) may result in severe injury or loss of life. Thus, any missing consideration on either failures or attacks may lead to terrible consequence. Safety and security are inter-related and, therefore, have to be aligned early in the development process. International standards, International Organization for Standardization (ISO 26262), and Society of Automotive Engineers (SAE J3061), have been proposed for vehicle safety and security. However, they do not address all the aspects of autonomous vehicles as they rely on a human driver controlling the vehicle. In high automation vehicles (level 3 or above, as defined by the international standard SAE J3016), the autonomous driving system is fully responsible for driving the vehicle. Thus, different driving automation levels have to be taken into consideration when designing autonomous vehicle safety and security. We propose an approach for aligning safety and security lifecycles, based on SAE J3061, SAE J3016, and ISO 26262 standards at an early development phase. The proposed approach uses the Failure, Attack and Countermeasure (FACT) graph to connect safety failures, security attacks, and the associated countermeasures. The proposed approach is helpful for designing or tailoring the safety and security processes, and selecting appropriate countermeasures for autonomous vehicles taking into consideration the driving automation levels.**

Keywords–Autonomous vehicle; Safety; Security; FACT graph; SAE J3016; SAE J3061; ISO 26262.

I. INTRODUCTION

Autonomous Vehicle (AV) is a vehicle capable of fulfilling the main transportation capabilities of a traditional car. The main difference to a traditional car is a *Driving Automation System (DAS)* designed for AV. DAS provides driving automation to the vehicle platform, thereby offering the possibility of fundamentally changing transportation in order to reduce crashes, energy consumption, pollution, and cost of congestion [1]. Such vehicle attracts lots of attention from academia, industry and government.

AV is a safety critical system. Any failure of AV may result in severe human injuries or even death. Meanwhile, as a cyber physical system, an autonomous vehicle consists of a myriad of heterogeneous components, both cyber and physical, which pose additional security challenges. The complex interactions between these components inside the AV make it difficult to model the system, and to align the safety and security in an autonomous vehicle.

For a cyber physical system, safety aims at protecting the system from accidental failures in order to avoid hazards, while security focuses on protecting the system from intentional attacks [2]. AV's safety and security is shown in Figure 1. Safety of AV includes mechanical system safety and Electrical and Electronic (E/E) system safety. While considering E/E safety, it is composed of DAS safety and vehicle platform safety. Standard ISO 26262 [3] defines the E/E safety for vehicle platform. Similarity, AV security includes physical security and cyber security. For the latter one, DAS security and vehicle security have to be considered. Standard SAE J3061 [4] defines the cyber security for conventional vehicle. Accidental failures may trigger safety losses, such as harm to life, property and environment, and intentional attacks can result in privacy, financial, operational and safety losses. In this paper, we focus on the alignment between E/E system safety and security.

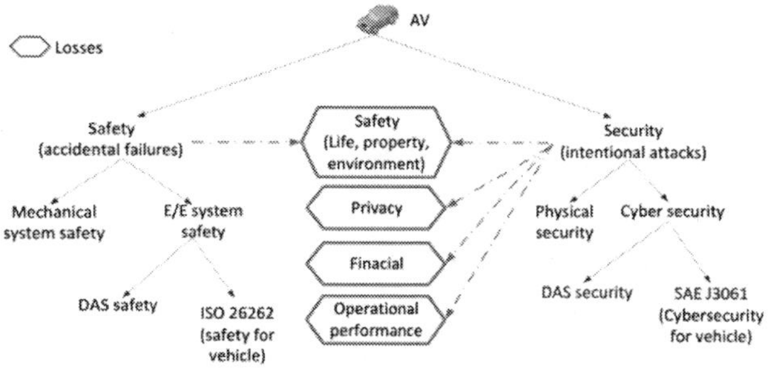

Figure 1. Safety and security in Autonomous Vehicles.

Aligning safety and security is crucial for autonomous vehicles, since any of failures or attacks may lead to safety losses (as seen in Figure 1). The alignment issues for cyber physical system have been discussed in literature [5] [6] [7]. However, such alignment for AVs has not been addressed yet. In SAE J3016 [8], six *levels of driving automation* have been defined. The recent advanced driver assistance systems are only listed around level 1 and 2 (as described in [9]). This will not satisfy the growing demand on driving automation systems. Different level of DAS is corresponding to different driving functions and safety requirements. In addition, different levels will face more potential hazards, threats, and challenges. Thus, it is necessary to consider DAS when we analyse safety and security for AV system, because the selection of safety and security countermeasures for an AV with the same driving function differs depending on its automation level. However, ISO 26262 does not take into consideration driving automation levels and assumes that a human driver is always present [10].

In this paper, we propose an approach for aligning AV's safety and security at early development phases by synchronizing safety and security lifecycles based on SAE J3061, SAE J3016 and ISO 26262 standards. We use Failure Attack and Countermeasure (FACT) graph [2] to list safety failures, security attacks and the associated countermeasures together, which will avoid the safety losses incurred by either failures or attacks, thereby guaranteeing the safety of autonomous vehicles. Moreover, this alignment is helpful to design or tailor the safety and security processes for autonomous vehicle considering the driving automation levels, and to support safety and security analysis.

The rest of the paper is organized as follow: we introduce the preliminary information in Section II, and explore AV's safety and security alignment in Section III. Finally, we conclude our work in Section IV.

II. PRELIMINARY

To demonstrate our alignment method, we give some preliminary information in this section.

A. Dynamic Driving Task

The driving task is the function required to operate a vehicle in on-road traffic and includes operational functions (basic vehicle motion control), tactical functions (planning and execution for event/object avoidance and expedited route following) and strategic functions (route and destination timing and selection) [8]. The *Dynamic Driving Task (DDT)* [8] includes the operational and tactical functions, such as (without limitation):

1. Lateral vehicle motion control via steering (operational);
2. Longitudinal vehicle motion control via acceleration and deceleration (operational);
3. Monitoring the driving environment via object and event detection, recognition, classification, and response preparation (operational and tactical);
4. Object and event response execution (operational and tactical);
5. Maneuver planning (tactical);
6. Enhancing conspicuity via lighting, signaling and gesturing, etc. (tactical).

Because the subtasks 3 and 4 are all related to **o**bject and **e**vent **d**etection and **r**esponse, they are collectively referred to as *OEDR*.

When a DDT fails, the response to either re-perform the DDT or reduce the risk of crash is considered as *DDT-fallback*. An example of this is when the adaptive cruise control on a car experiences a system failure that causes the feature to stop performing its intended function. The driver will perform the DDT-fallback by resuming performance of the complete DDT.

B. Levels of driving automation

Driving Automation System, DAS, is the hardware and software that are collectively capable of performing the entire DDT on a sustained basis, which is the key property that can replace a human driver for AV. The levels of driving automation are also classified by the requirements on DAS, which include [8]:

- Level 1, the DAS performs either the longitudinal or the lateral vehicle motion control (subtask 1 **or** 2 of the DDT).
- Level 2, the DAS performs both the longitudinal and the lateral vehicle motion control (subtasks 1 **and** 2 of the DDT simultaneously).
- Level 3, the DAS also performs the OEDR (subtask 3 and 4 of the DDT).
- Level 4, the DAS also performs DDT-fallback.
- Level 5, the DAS is unlimited by **O**perational **D**esign **D**omain (ODD).

Here, the ODD is a specific operating domain in which an automated function or system is designed to properly operate, including but not limited to roadway types, speed range, geography, traffic, environmental conditions (e.g., weather, daytime/nighttime), and other domain constraints [11]. For example, we can design a ODD like this: road way is fixed as express way, the vehicle can hold a speed lower than $35km/h$ driving in the daytime only.

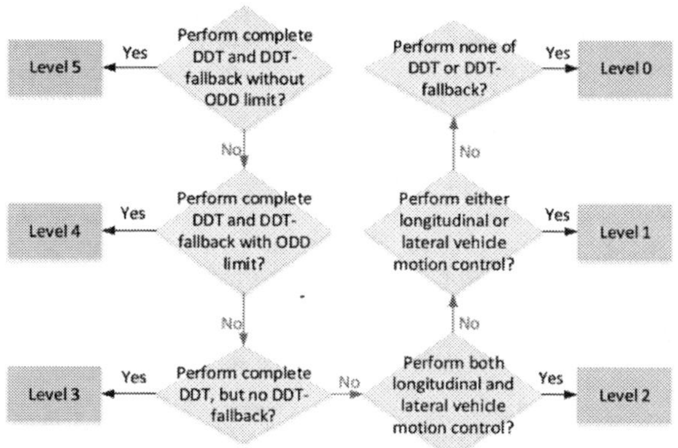

Figure 2. Levels of driving automation.

Figure 2 shows the levels of driving automation and the corresponding features. For the low driving automation (level 0 to level 2), a driver is needed to perform part or all driving task; while for high automation (level 3 to level 5), DAS can replace the driver to perform the complete DDT. The conventional cars in our daily life are at level 0, *No Driving Automation*. The human driver is necessary to perform the driving task and to respond to all the fallback. Level 1 is *Driver Assistance*, which means a DAS can perform **either** lateral **or** longitudinal control for the car. When the DAS performs **both** lateral **and** longitudinal control, such automation is in level 2, i.e., *Partial Driving Automation*.

For the level 3, i.e., *Conditional Driving Automation*, DAS can perform the whole DDT. But a user of the vehicle who is able to operate the vehicle is expected to be able to resume DDT performance when a DDT system failure occurs or when the DAS is about to leave its ODD. If the DAS also can perform DDT-fallback but with limited ODD, this division of role corresponds to level 4, i.e., *High Driving Automation*. The *Full Driving Automation* (level 5) is the situation when DAS can perform complete DDT and DDT-fallback, and meanwhile, the corresponding ODD is unlimited.

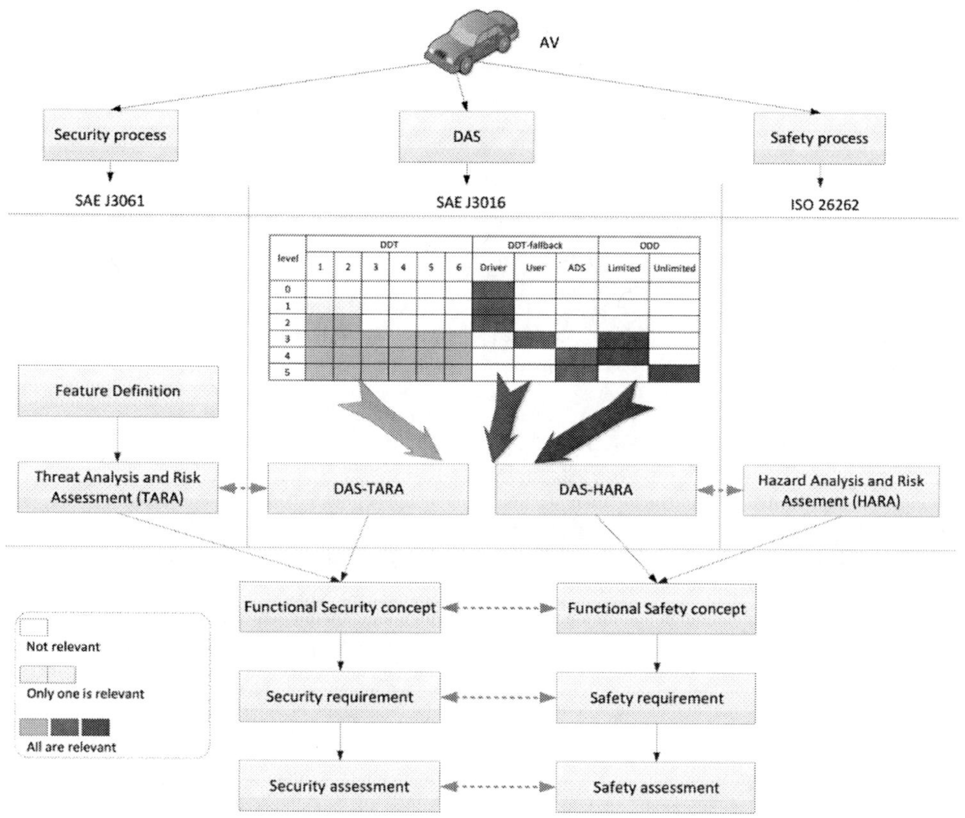

Figure 3. Aligning the safety and security concept phase based on standards SAE J3016, SAE J3061 and ISO 26262.

C. Related safety and security standards

SAE J3061 [4] is a cyber security guidebook for vehicle systems, which defines the lifecycle process framework, and provides guiding principles etc. In SAE J3061, the cyber security lifecycle can be divided into several phases: concept phase, product development phase (system level, hardware level and software level), production and operation phase. The concept phase is the first step for the whole lifecycle, which includes the following activities: feature definition, threat analysis and risk assessment, functional security concept, security requirements, and security assessment. The feature definition defines the system being developed to which the cyber security process will be applied, i.e., it defines the boundary of the features. *Threat Analysis and Risk Assessment* (TARA) identifies threats and assesses the risk, and the result of TARA drives all downstream activates. Security concept describes the high-level strategy for obtaining security from TARA phase, and once the concept is determined for satisfying the feature, the security requirement can be determined. Security assessment is performed to identify the current security posture of the cyber physical vehicle, and it is developed in stages throughout the security lifecycle.

ISO 26262 [3] is an international standard for functional safety of E/E systems in production automobiles defined by the International Organization for Standardization, which provides an automotive safety lifecycle (management, development, production, operation, service, decommissioning) and supports tailoring the necessary activities during these phases. In the development part, similarly to SAE J3061, the safety process is composed of *Hazard Analysis and Risk Assessment* (HARA), functional safety concept, safety requirement and safety assessment.

III. ALIGNING SAFETY AND SECURITY FOR AVs

In this section, we introduce an approach to align safety and security for autonomous vehicles.

A. Concept phase of safety and security

Standard SAE J3061 [4] proposes a way to integrate vehicle safety (ISO 26262) and security (SAE J3061) processes by establishing communication paths between safety and cybersecurity concept phase activities, e.g., cybersecurity TARA activity and safety HARA activities, cybersecurity requirement and safety requirement activities. We propose to extend this approach by adding the AV-specific information from SAE J3016 standard, as shown in Figure 3. Additional activities, DAS-TARA and DAS-HARA are added to the integrated safety and security analysis process. Furthermore, communication links are established between DAS-TARA, DAS-HARA, TARA, and HARA activities, as shown in Figure 3.

Figure 3 shows the merged safety and security concept phases, which consists of the phases from different standards. There is no successive order between the activities of safety and security, but for each stage, we need to consider them simultaneously. We use dotted line with double arrows to depict the simultaneous activities in Figure 3. Because of the automation levels of DAS, TARA and HARA should correspond to each level. A colorful table is used to demonstrate the levels and their properties: yellow denotes the DDT, red represents executor of DDT-fallback, and blue shows ODD constraints. After completion of TARA and DAS-TARA, an activity security concept is performed, which integrates the results of TARA and DAS-TARA, followed by security requirement, and security assessment. In parallel, a functional safety concept activity is performed by DAS-HARA and HARA, followed by safety requirement and safety assessment.

B. Threat analysis and risk assessment for AVs

As mentioned in Section II-C, TARA defines the threats and assesses risks, and derives all the following activities in the security lifecycle. Thus, it is important for the whole security design and development. Most methods for TARA are designed for the automotive domain and are not specific for AVs. In this section, we study automotive TARA cases, and provide a general TARA method, which can also be used for AVs.

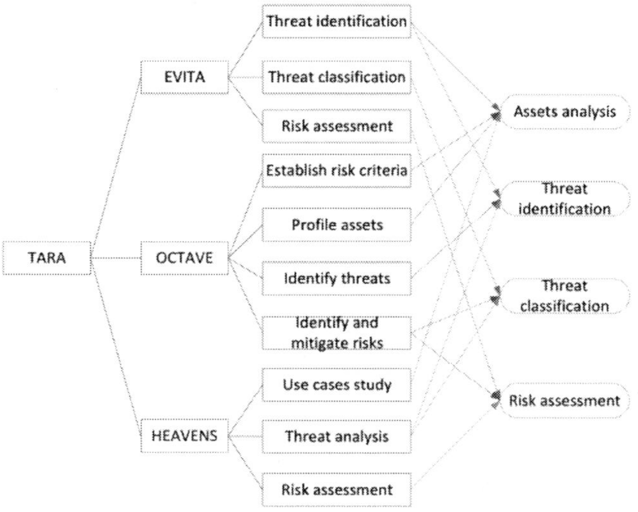

Figure 4. Methods for threat analysis and risk assessment.

EVITA method [12] comes from an European research project EVITA (E-Safety Vehicle Intrusion Protected Applications), which deals with on-board network protection. In EVITA method, TARA phase includes mainly three activities: threat identification, threat classification and risk analysis. Thread identification uses attack trees [13] to identify generic threats; threat classification means classify the threat risk; and risk assessment recommends actions based on the resulting risk classification of the threats.

OCTAVE [14] stands for Operationally Critical Threat, Asset, and Vulnerability Evaluation, which is a process-driven threat/risk assessment methodology. In OCTAVE, TARA phase can be done by such processes: establish risk criteria, profile assets, identify threats, and identify and mitigate risks.

HEAVENS Security Model [15] focuses on methods, processes and tool support for security analysis. In HEAVENS, the main workflow for TARA includes: use case study, threat analysis and risk assessment.

The TARA methods of EVITA, OCTAVE and HEAVENS have different processes (as shown in Figure 4), but these processes have similar functions or similar effects. We classify them into our general method (denoted by arrows in Figure 4). The proposed method has four activities: assets analysis, threat identification, threat classification and risk assessment (rounded rectangles in Figure 4). Assets analysis includes studying use cases, establishing risk criteria, and identifying the assets. Threat identification uses attack trees to identify threats (similar to EVITA). Threat classification classifies the threat risks, and analyzes the mains risks considering use cases. Risk assessment assesses the risks and generates security requirements.

For AVs, the four processes have broader definitions. For assets, besides the visible and information assets on a vehicle, the functional assets (e.g., DDT function) should also be considered. The threats for DAS should be treated as key threats to mitigate, because any functional error of DAS may incur terrible injuries for humans. Thus, the threats which effect DAS should assessed to be of higher risk.

Attack tree [13] is a popular methodology for TARA, which is a graph that describes the steps of the attack process. It uses some basic symbols to demonstrate an attack, e.g., nodes (represent attack events), gates (AND and OR gates) and edges (path of attacks through the system).

C. Hazard Analysis and Risk Assessment for AVs

Following ISO 26262 standard, a HARA is performed to determine the possible hazards, and criticality of the system under consideration. Similar to TARA, the results of HARAs strongly influence the effort to be undertaken in the following activities of ensuring functional safety.

SAHARA [16] is a security-aware HARA method, which expands the inductive analysis of HARA, and encompasses threats from STRIDE model [17], which describes the main security threat categories. SAHARA proposes a security level determination method, and uses it in combination with Automotive Safety Integrity Levels (ASILs) to assess the possible threat.

In [18], the authors propose a HARA method for AV at level 4, i.e., the vehicle is operated on the emergency stopping lane of highway with speed lower than $12km/h$. In this work, ASILs are iteratively refined to achieve specific safety goals for such vehicle.

In summary, conventional HARA is of limited suitability for AVs. But the ASIL is key point that can be used for AVs, because it can be used to assess the threats or hazards impacting DDT or related components of AVs. Fault tree [19] is often used for HARA. Fault trees are similar to attack trees, where the tree nodes represent failure events.

D. Alignment of safety and security

We use FACT graph [2] to combine the safety and security lifecycles. FACT graph is a tree-shaped graph to show system failures, attacks and the associated countermeasures together,

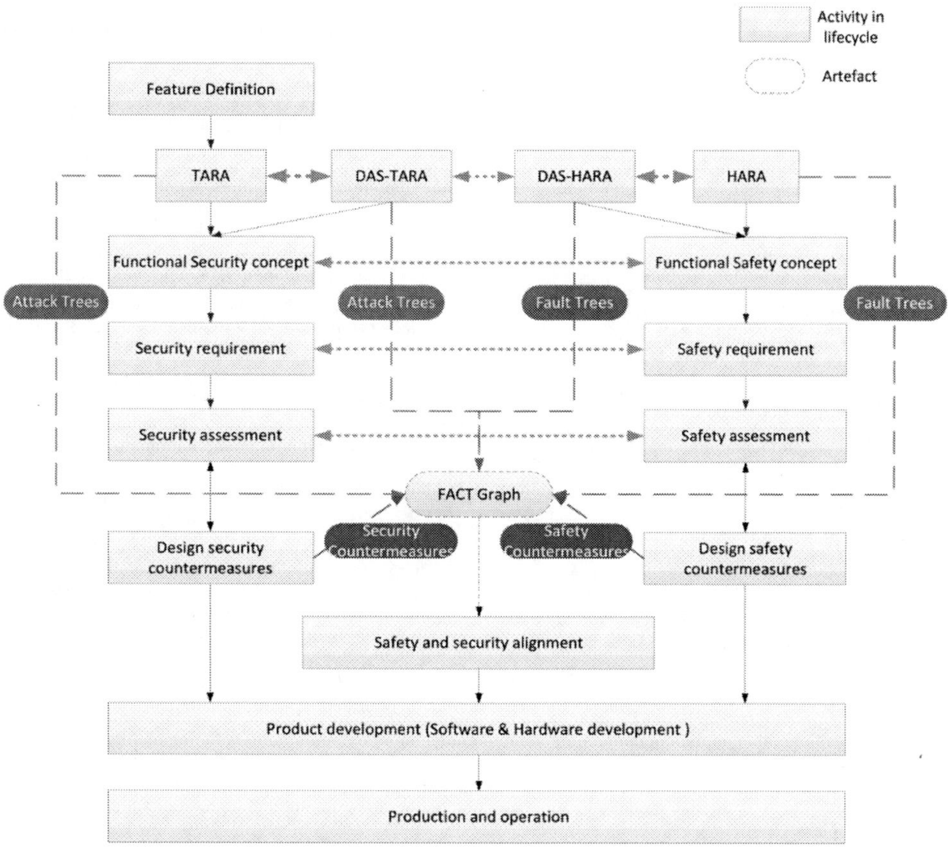

Figure 5. Safety and security alignment for autonomous vehicles.

which is formed throughout several activities of the merged safety and security lifecycle.

The alignment approach is shown in Figure 5, where we use rectangles to denote the activity in lifecycle, and rounded rectangles to present the artefact (i.e., the methodology used for activity). The concept phase comes from Figure 3. We can see that DAS-TARA and TARA constitute the threat analysis and risk assessment part for autonomous vehicles. This is followed by the security concept, the security requirement and the security assessment. Simultaneously, DAS-HARA and HARA should be achieved from a safety view, followed by functional safety concept, safety requirement and safety assessment. After the concept phase part, design of safety and security countermeasures is added to provide mitigation approaches. This activity is not only served for alignment purpose (proposing countermeasure to FACT graph), but also served for the next phases, such as production development, and production and operation as defined in standard SAE J3061.

Figure 6 depicts a simple example of AV FACT graph, which includes Global Positioning System (GPS) failures. GPS data is very important for autonomous vehicles, which is used for localizing the car. If this data is wrong, the consequences could be disastrous. For example, wrong GPS data may lead to traffic disturbance or crash hazard [20]. Here, we consider GPS data on AVs to be the target of an attacker. The associated FACT graph is formed using the following steps (as shown in Figure 6):

- 1. Add safety failures as a subtree of the attack goal (e.g., GPS error). In this situation, a functional fail is considered as a type of safety failure.
- 2. Add security attack as a subtree of GPS error. We consider two types of intentional attacks: spoofing and jamming. Spoofing attacks will modify GPS data, while jamming attacks will prevent AV from receiving GPS data.
- 3. Add safety countermeasures (if any) to associated safety failure. For functional failures, we can consider periodic inspection as one of mitigation technique.
- 4. Add security countermeasures (if any) to corresponding security attack. To avoid spoofing GPS data, we can consider to set the authentication before reading the GPS data. To mitigate jamming GPS data, we can use anti-jam GPS techniques [20]. They are marked as SEC_1 and SEC_2 in Figure 6 respectively.

With the use of FACT graph, any misalignment between safety and security countermeasures can be identified, as well as countermeasure duplicates and missing means of protection. Furthermore, safety and security countermeasures are associated to the relevant faults and attacks, thus, it is easy to analyze

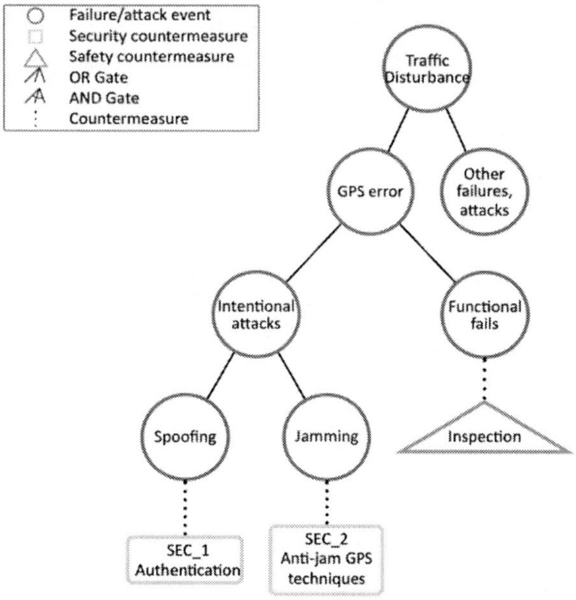

Figure 6. Forming an FACT graph considering GPS error.

the potential failure and attack, and then analyze safety and security requirements.

IV. CONCLUSION

Safety is the primary target when designing autonomous vehicles. Any accidental failures (safety issues) and/or intentional attacks (security issues) for such vehicle may result in severe safety losses, e.g., human injuries or even death. Thus, the effective alignment of safety and security for AVs is of great importance.

The main difference between AV and conventional vehicle is that there are different levels of driving automation in AV that define which operational and tactical functions are performed by a human driver and by the driving automation system. Thus, the selection of safety and security countermeasures for an AV with the same functions differs depending on its automation level. In this paper, we have proposed an approach for aligning autonomous vehicle safety and security at early development phases considering the levels of driving automation. The proposed approach suggests a way to integrate safety and security lifecycle process phases, defined by SAE J3016, SAE J3061 and ISO 26262 standards. Using this approach, practitioners may align AV's safety and security activities, by following the merged safety and security lifecycle process.

Our proposal can be used for analyzing safety and security of existing AVs, as well on designing new AVs. In the future, we will extend our alignment framework to enable more comprehensive AV safety-security analysis.

REFERENCES

[1] J. M. Anderson, K. Nidhi, K. D. Stanley, P. Sorensen, C. Samaras, and O. A. Oluwatola, Autonomous vehicle technology: A guide for policymakers. Rand Corporation, 2014, ISBN:978-08-33-08-39-82.

[2] G. Sabaliauskaite and A. P. Mathur, "Aligning cyber-physical system safety and security," Complex Systems Design & Management Asia, 2015, pp. 41–53, ISBN:978-33-19-12-54-42.

[3] International Organization for Standardization (ISO), ISO-26262: Road Vehicles - Functional safety, Dec 2016.

[4] Society of Automotive Engineers (SAE), SAE-J3061: Cybersecurity Guidebook for Cyber-Physical Vehicle Systems, Jan 2016.

[5] A. Banerjee, K. K. Venkatasubramanian, T. Mukherjee, and S. K. S. Gupta, "Ensuring safety, security, and sustainability of mission-critical cyber–physical systems," Proceedings of the IEEE, vol. 100, 2012, pp. 283–299, ISSN:0018-9219.

[6] L. Piètre-Cambacédès and M. Bouissou, "Cross-fertilization between safety and security engineering," Reliability Engineering & System Safety, vol. 110, 2013, pp. 110–126, ISSN: 0951-8320.

[7] T. Novak and A. Treytl, "Functional safety and system security in automation systems-a life cycle model," in IEEE International Conference on Emerging Technologies and Factory Automation (ETFA) Sept. 15-18, 2008, Hamburg, Germany, Sep. 2008, pp. 311–318, ISSN:1946-0740, URL: http://ieeexplore.ieee.org/document/4638412/ [accessed: 2017-09-20].

[8] Society of Automotive Engineers (SAE), SAE-J3016: Taxonomy and Definitions for terms Related to Driving Automation Systems for On-ROad Motor Vehicles, Sep 2016.

[9] H. Martin, K. Tschabuschnig, O. Bridal, and D. Watzenig, Functional Safety of Automated Driving Systems: Does ISO 26262 Meet the Challenges? Springer International Publishing, Sep 2017, chapter 16, pp. 387–416, in Automated Driving, ISBN:978-33-19-31-89-50.

[10] F. Warg, M. Gassilewski, J. Tryggvesson, V. Izosimov, A. Werneman, and R. Johansson, "Defining autonomous functions using iterative hazard analysis and requirements refinement," in International Conference on Computer Safety, Reliability, and Security September 20-23, 2016, Trondheim, Norway, September 2016, pp. 286–297, ISBN:978-33-19-45-48-01, URL: https://doi.org/10.1007/978-3-319-45480-1_23 [accessed: 2017-09-20].

[11] NHTSA, "Federal automated vehicles policy," 2016, URL: https://www.transportation.gov/AV [accessed: 2017-09-20].

[12] R. A. et al., "Deliverable d2.3: Security requirements for automotive on-board networks based on dark-side scenarios," Tech. Rep., 2008, URL: https://rieke.link/EVITAD2.3v1.1.pdf [accessed: 2017-09-20].

[13] B. Schneier, Attack trees. Wiley Publishing, Inc., Oct 2015, chapter 21, pp. 318–333, in Secrets and Lies, ISBN:978-11-19-18-36-31.

[14] C. J. Alberts, S. G. Behrens, R. D. Pethia, and W. R. Wilson, "Operationally critical threat, asset, and vulnerability evaluation (octave) framework, version 1.0," DTIC Document, Tech. Rep., 1999, URL:https://resources.sei.cmu.edu/asset_files/TechnicalReport/1999_005_001_16769.pdf [accessed: 2017-09-20].

[15] M. I. et al., "Deliverable d2 security models," Tech. Rep., 2014, URL:https://research.chalmers.se/en/project/5809 [accessed: 2017-09-20].

[16] G. Macher, H. Sporer, R. Berlach, E. Armengaud, and C. Kreiner, "Sahara: a security-aware hazard and risk analysis method," in Design, Automation Test in Europe Conference Exhibition (DATE) March 09-13, 2015, Grenoble, France, Mar 2015, pp. 621–624, ISSN:1530-1591, URL: http://ieeexplore.ieee.org/document/7092463/ [accessed: 2017-09-20].

[17] M. Corporation, "The stride threat model," 2005, URL: https://msdn.microsoft.com/en-us/library/ee823878(v=cs.20).aspx [accessed: 2017-09-20].

[18] T. Stolte, G. Bagschik, A. Reschka et al., "Hazard analysis and risk assessment for an automated unmanned protective vehicle," in IEEE Intelligent Vehicles Symposium (IV) June 11-14, 2017, Los Angeles, CA, USA, June 2017, pp. 1848–1855, ISBN:978-15-09-04-80-45, URL: http://ieeexplore.ieee.org/document/7995974/ [accessed: 2017-09-20].

[19] E. Ruijters and M. Stoelinga, "Fault tree analysis: A survey of the state-of-the-art in modeling, analysis and tools," Computer science review, vol. 15, 2015, pp. 29–62, ISSN:1574-0137.

[20] J. Petit and S. E. Shladover, "Potential cyberattacks on automated vehicles," IEEE Transactions on Intelligent Transportation Systems, vol. 16, no. 2, 2015, pp. 546–556, ISSN:1524-9050.

Trends in Building Hardware and Software for Smart Things in Internet of Things

Xing Liu
Dept. of Computer Science and Information Technology
Kwantlen Polytechnic University
Surrey, Canada
Email: xing.liu@kpu.ca

Abstract—**Internet of Things (IoT) is considered to be another revolution in information technology. Previous revolutions built a global network of computers for people to communicate digitally. IoT aims to connect the things globally and these things are frequently physical objects. In order to realize the full potential of IoT, the things need to be smart. Hardware and software resources are required to instantiate the smartness. This paper examines the essential smartness attributes for IoT things and the hardware and software for implementing the attributes. Industrial trends in IoT hardware and software design are reviewed.**

Keywords - Internet of Things; IoT; smart things; smartness; implementation; hardware; software.

I. INTRODUCTION

Internet of Things (IoT) is one of the most important revolutions in technology in decades. IoT strives to connect the physical objects (things) globally. In an IoT system, the things communicate with each other and with human beings and act autonomously. In this sense, the things have smartness in addition to their common daily functionalities. For example, the common functionality of a door lock is "lock the door with a latch". The smartness part of an IoT-enabled door lock would be "remotely controllable over the Internet" and "able to recognize the owner and unlock the door" [1].

In order to equip the things with smartness, specific hardware and software are required. Most of the hardware can be built into a single integrated electronic circuit chip called System-on-Chip (SoC). These SoCs are named IoT processors. Special software has to run on IoT processors in order to empower the things with real smartness. In the case it is not feasible for a single IoT processor to carry all the needed hardware, a so-called IoT hardware platform (board) can be developed instead.

Although the attributes that define smartness vary greatly with the types of things, many attributes are commonly shared. Ideally, these attributes should be provided by IoT processors or IoT hardware platforms. However, no up-to-date systematic research has been conducted on what smartness really means for IoT things and what hardware and software are needed to realize such smartness. Results of smartness research can be useful for guiding the design and evaluation of smart products.

This paper gives a brief overview of Internet of Things in Section II. Then the paper identifies the general smartness attributes expected for IoT smart things in Section III. Hardware and software for implementing the smartness attributes are discussed in Section IV. Section V reviews the current industrial trends in hardware and software design for IoT processors and hardware platforms. Conclusions are given in Section VI.

II. INTERNET OF THINGS

A. *Physical Objects and IoT Things*

IoT is essentially a network of connected physical objects or things. The things exist with reasons. For example, a microwave is for heating up food. An air-conditioner is for cooling down a room. Traditionally, most things operate locally and are standalone. People need to be in close proximity in order to operate the objects.

B. *The Internet*

The Internet connects the things together. It provides the communication medium for the things. The things communicate and collaborate with each other via the Internet. Human beings can remotely access and control the things through the Internet. Wired or wireless links can be used to connect to the things. Wired links can be Ethernet, cable or telephone lines. Wireless links can be satellite, cellular, Wi-Fi, Bluetooth, or other new technologies being developed.

C. *The Cloud*

The Cloud is where IoT data is stored, visualized and analyzed. The Cloud also works like a "control center" which relays messages and commands between things and between things and humans. The Cloud is also used to manage things, create control policies, and call upon other Cloud services. The "elasticity" of the cloud makes it a highly suitable candidate for hosting IoT platforms [2].

D. *Smart Homes and Smart Cities*

Smart homes and smart cities [3] are two main application domains of IoT. In a smart home, connected things can be lamps, microwaves, fridges, ovens, heaters, ventilation systems, TVs and motion sensors. A smart city has many more connected things, such as cars, utility meters, parking meters, traffic cameras, power sources, waste collectors, street lights, just to name a few.

E. *Smart Things*

Connected things in an IoT system need to be smart [1][4]. For example, lights should turn on automatically when people are present and should turn off when people move away. Doors should open automatically when the right person wants to get in. Alerts should be sent to home owners when there is a home invasion. Ventilation fans should change speed based on room occupancy to maintain air quality. Traffic cameras should work together to route street traffic and provide parking availability information. Traffic lights should inform car drivers or even directly interact with cars regarding upcoming color changes to avoid unnecessary braking. All these observations lead to the concept of smartness.

III. Smartness Attributes

Under what condition is an IoT thing smart? What are the attributes that make a thing smart? This section derives these attributes from common sense. Smart things should have some or all of these smartness attributes built-in based on the specific applications. These attributes will determine what hardware and software are required to make things smart and the feasibility of doing so in a practical design.

A. Aware of Environment

In an IoT system, the things should be aware of its surroundings. They should monitor what is going on around them. Parameters to monitor can be temperature, humidity, radiation, presence, proximity and darkness. Other awareness includes what other physical objects are doing and their impacts to the IoT system.

B. Able to Memorize

The things should have memory. They should memorize what has happened to themselves and to other related things. Information should be saved somewhere and can be recalled when needed. The things should decide what to memorize, how much to memorize and for how long. For example, should temperature be stored? How frequently should temperature be sampled? How many data points should be stored in memory?

C. Able to Communicate

The things should be able to communicate. They should be able to interact with each other and with human beings. They should be able to report their status when requested and accept commands whenever required and respond in proper "language" and "manners". For example, a thing should be able to tell other things if it is switched on or off when asked, and start taking an action when it is asked to.

D. Able to Make Decisions

The things should be able to decide what they should do and how to do it. For example, should a door lock grant access to someone? If in doubt for any reason, the door lock should initiate an inquiry to the right party; and based on the responses received, it then decides the correct operations to take.

E. Able to Act

The things should be able to take actions. Examples may be start moving, turning off a switch, opening a door, playing music, turning on a heater, starting a fan, sending a message, or sounding an alarm.

F. Able to Perform Many Tasks at the Same Time

The things should be able to perform many tasks at the same time. These tasks may run concurrently. They should know which tasks are more important and have priority, and prioritize the tasks given to them. They should be able to switch between tasks based on operating conditions without losing information.

G. Able to Work Autonomously

The things should be able to work without supervision. They should know when to start, to interact, to adjust, to pause, or to stop. They should know how to protect themselves and protect others in the system.

H. Able to Learn from Experience

The things should be able to improve themselves based on what happened to them in the past, perhaps based on the data stored in local memory. They should learn from mistakes. They should be able to optimize and negotiate. An example of this is a smart robotic vacuum controller. Based on the impact it had against the wall in the past when it returned to the base charging station, it will work out the best moment to start slowing down. The robotic vacuum will find the new location of the charging station if the owner has moved it and use the new location next time. Another example is the smart heating controller which will work with the motion sensor to learn what times the owner usually goes to work. It will develop a flexible schedule to turn off the heating in advance (e.g. 30 minutes) to reduce energy consumption, instead of a pre-set fixed time.

I. Able to Predict into the Future

The things should be able to foresee what is going to happen to themselves and assist in predicting what will happen in the overall IoT system. They should also help human beings in predicting what will happen in the environment. An example of this case is predicting the breakdown of a smart device. If a smart device learns what happened inside a sister device before breaking down, for example, the sister device temperature pattern, then the smart device can predict its own breakdown time and notify maintenance personnel to replace it ahead of time.

J. Protection of Self and the Whole System

The things should know how to fight against physical or virtual attacks to themselves. They should not create security holes and propagate viruses. They should not do anything to damage the credibility of the overall IoT system.

K. Energy Consciousness

The things should be able to manage power consumption themselves. They should be power conscious. They should know when to do the work, when to sleep and do nothing. They should try to harvest energy from the surroundings whenever and wherever possible.

L. *Self-Imaging and Twinning*

A thing should establish and store a model of itself. This includes storing necessary parameters that can fully describe its own static and dynamic status and behavior. This may include mathematical models and statistical tools which assists in establishing the models. The model together with status information works as an image (twin) of the real thing and can be used to conduct simulations locally or can be uploaded into the Cloud for further simulation, visualization and examination. The twin image can be sent to whoever needs it. An example of this is a smart engine which stores its design model and running states. These states and the model will enable users to conduct simulations and potentially help create maintenance schedules and diagnose the causes of problems.

There can be more smartness attributes than listed above depending on the applications in the real world. The list can grow as time goes on as well.

IV. Implementing the Smartness Attributes

In order to equip the IoT things with the above smartness attributes, electronic components, computing hardware and software are required [5].

A. *Sensors*

Sensors power the things with awareness. Typically, sensors measure temperature, humidity, speed, motion, acceleration, height, position, distance, PH values, flow rate, brightness, color, radiation, sound, images, or a combination of these variables. Sensors can be chemical, mechanical, electrical, optical, or some other forms. They can be standalone components or can be integrated into electronic chips or into circuit boards. Sensors can be cameras when inputs are images or videos. Sensors are microphones when inputs are audio signals.

B. *Local Memory*

Memorization is achieved using digital storage such as Read Only Memory (ROM), Random Access Memory (RAM), flash memory, Secure Digital (SD) cards, or magnetic tapes. Memorization also includes proper organization of data for easy storage and retrieval, such as appropriate file systems and databases.

C. *Communication Interfaces*

Interfaces for communications among IoT things can be “traditional”, such as analog/digital converter, serial/parallel communication ports, such as General-Purpose Input/Output (GPIO) [6], Universal Asynchronous Receiver-Transmitter (UART) [7], Inter-Integrated Circuit (I^2C) [8], Universal Serial Bus (USB) [9] and Serial Peripheral Interface (SPI) [10]. Interfaces can also be computer networks, such as Ethernet for wired communications. Wireless communication interfaces are more important for IoT things. Wireless interfaces can be satellite, cellular, Wi-Fi, Bluetooth, and ZigBee etc.

D. *Local Control Logic*

Local control logic enables thing autonomy. This can be algorithms for automatic control systems, adaptive control algorithms, optimal control algorithms, path planning algorithms, pattern recognition algorithms, and decision making algorithms.

E. *Actuators*

Actuators generate motion, movements, and initiate signal transmission. Actuators can be electrical motors, pneumatic devices, hydraulic devices and signal transmitters.

F. *Analytics and Machine Learning Software*

Such software is located locally inside the things, or remotely in the Cloud. These are typically mathematical tools for data analytics which can be descriptive, prescriptive or predictive. They can also be artificial intelligence and machine learning algorithms.

G. *Multitasking or Multithreading*

This is typically software that enables task concurrency locally inside the things, frequently implemented as part of the functionalities found inside an operating system.

H. *Security Software*

Security is extremely important for IoT things. There is need to have access control to the electronics and mechanical components of the things. Software in the things need to be immune to viruses. Communication information needs to be encrypted. Security algorithms can be embedded at different levels of the IoT system, such as in the electronics and in communication protocols.

I. *Energy Management and Harvesting*

Circuit modules are used for power management and energy harvesting. Power management modules optimize the use of power in power sources. Circuit modules are used to harvest energy from lights, heat sources, motion, and electromagnetic signals etc.

J. *Digital Twinning and Device Shadows*

Parameters, mathematical or statistical models, and status information of physical objects are used to build the twin image of a device. The image is also called a device shadow. The image can be stored in local memory. It can be used to diagnose problems, answer queries, perform simulations and provide predictions. Twin images can be loaded to the Cloud for further analysis or can be shared among devices.

V. Industrial Trends in IoT Hardware and Software Implementation

The actual hardware and software implementation of IoT things with the above smartness attributes depend on the technologies available and the cost allowed. The ideal solution is that all attributes are implemented on a single SoC module. This will minimize interference, power consumption, and thing sizes. The implementation can also be several electronic chips installed on a circuit board. In this case, the implementation is called an IoT hardware platform. Some attributes may not be feasible to be integrated and therefore have to remain separate. Software also has to be carefully designed and implemented to realize the smartness attributes. A thing essentially makes an embedded system.

A. *IoT Processors*

An IoT processor is a SoC device designed for IoT applications. It is very much like a microcontroller and has most functionalities that a microcontroller has, plus many other functionalities.

Components of IoT processors generally include computing power, memory, on-chip sensors, input/output interfaces, wired and wireless networking interfaces, security measures, IoT operating systems (OSes), and power management modules. Companies that are making IoT processors include ARM (Cortex-M23 and Cortex– M33) [11], Qualcomm (Snapdragon processors and LTE modems) [12], Texas Instruments (CC3320) [13], and Cypress (PSoC 6) [14].

B. *IoT Boards or "IoT Hardware Platforms"*

IoT boards, also called IoT hardware platforms, usually have more functionalities than what IoT processors have. An example is the mangOH Red [15] jointly developed by Sierra Wireless and its partners. The mangOH Red is smaller than a credit card. It has built-in Wi-Fi b/g/n and Bluetooth 4.2 BLE (Bluetooth Low Energy) and built-in light, accelerometer, gyroscope, temperature and pressure sensors. However, it has only sockets for 2G to 4G and LTE-M (Long Term Evolution Category M1) and NB-IoT (NarrowBand IoT) wireless modules. It can connect to the AirVantage IoT cloud Platform. Legato is the Linux based open source development tool.

Raspberry Pi is another popular IoT hardware platform [16]. A Raspberry Pi has memory (RAM and a SD memory card), networking interface (Ethernet, Wi-Fi, and Bluetooth), Input/Output ports (USB, Camera interface, video interface, audio interface, GPIO pins which can be used as UART, I^2C, and SPI). By default, a Raspberry Pi runs a Linux-type OS called Raspbian [17]. Numerous smartness attributes can be readily implemented locally using the C, JavaScript, Java, or Python programming languages. Other OSes, such as the Windows 10 IoT Core [18], can also run on a Raspberry Pi.

C. *IoT OSes*

An OS is usually multithreading, has a task scheduler, and can frequently run real-time. For example, the ARM mbed OS [19] is an open-source embedded operating system designed to run in the things of an IoT system, specifically, on IoT processors. It is modular and configurable to reduce memory usage. The ARM mbed OS provides drivers for sensors, I/O devices and networking. It also provides cloud management services and security services. The ARM mbed OS is designed for ARM Cortex-M microcontrollers. Other IoT OSes include Contiki [20], Google Brillo (now called Android Things) [21], RIOT OS [22], and Windows 10 IoT [18]. Common features of IoT OSes include support for network communications, sensor interface, security, multi-tasking, and real-time.

D. *Other Software*

Signal processing software processes data from sensors, such as software for digital filters. System identification and modelling software build models for the things. Automatic control system algorithms and control software control the things. There are software that process audio and video signals and for pattern recognition. Web software now enables the Web interface for the things. Most such IoT software are based traditional software, with customization to support contemporary hardware, novel programming languages, and real-time applications. An example is OpenCV [23].

E. *IoT Software Platforms*

IoT software platforms are frequently called IoT platforms. They are the upper-level software in an IoT system. An IoT platform is a cloud-based software service that connects the things, collects data, manages the things, visualizes data, and performs data analytics. Additional smartness for the things is provided by IoT platforms. IoT platforms are also called middleware. Example commercial platforms are Amazon IoT [24], Microsoft Azure [25], and Xively [26].

F. *Other Emerging Technologies*

As the communication medium between IoT things and the Cloud, wireless communication networks are critically important. For this reason, tremendous efforts have been placed on developing new wireless communication networks that are suitable for IoT applications. Numerous new wireless technologies are on the horizon. These include NB-IoT [27], LTE-M [28], 6LoWPAN [29], Sigfox [30], BLE [31], and Bluetooth mesh networking (BLE-Mesh) [32]. Characteristics of these new technologies are low power consumption, small data packets and low data transmission overheads. However, IoT involves almost every aspect of the IoT ecosystem. Therefore, other technologies are also being developed. These include new sensor technologies, new software technologies, and new security technologies, as well as new applications.

VI. CONCLUSIONS

This paper has discussed the attributes that can make the IoT things smart, as well as hardware and software resources essential for implementing these attributes. Current industrial efforts in building powerful hardware and software for implementing smart things are also reviewed. Major technologies and products are identified.

REFERENCES

[1] G. Kortuem, F. Kawsar, D. Fitton, and V. Sundramoorthy, "Smart objects as building blocks for the Internet of Things", IEEE Internet Computing, vol.14, no.1, pp. 44-51, 2010.

[2] Y. Karam et al., "Security Support for Intention Driven Elastic Cloud Computing", The Sixth UKSim/AMSS

European Symposium on Computer Modeling and Simulation (EMS), 14-16 Nov., 2012.

[3] A. Zanella, N. Bui, A. Castellani, L. Vangelista, and M. Zorzi, Internet of Things for Smart Cities, IEEE Internet of Things Journal, vol.1, no.1, pp.22-32, 2014.

[4] G. Fortino, A. Rovella, W. Russo, and C. Savaglio, "On the classication of cyberphysical smart objects in the Internet of Things, Proceedings of the 5th International Workshop on Networks of Cooperating Objects for Smart Cities (UBICITEC 2014), pp.86-94, Berlin, Germany, Apr 14, 2014.

[5] M. Beigl and H. Gellersen, "Smart-Its: An Embedded Platform for Smart Objects", Smart Objects Conference (sOc), Grenoble, France. May 15-17, 2003.

[6] Adafruit, The GPIO Connector. [Online]. Available from: https://learn.adafruit.com/adafruits-raspberry-pi-lesson-4-gpio-setup/the-gpio-connector. 2017.11.02.

[7] Cypress, Universal Asynchronous Receiver Transmitter (UART). [Online]. Available from: http://www.cypress.com/file/132486/download. 2017.11.02.

[8] I2C-bus.org, I2C – What's That? [Online]. Available from: https://www.i2c-bus.org/. 2017.11.02.

[9] usb.org, USB 3.2 Specification. [Online]. Available from: http://www.usb.org/developers/docs/. 2017.11.02.

[10] Texas Instruments, Serial Peripheral Interface (SPI). [Online]. Available from: http://www.ti.com/lit/ug/sprugp2a/sprugp2a.pdf/. 2017.11.02.

[11] ZigBee Allaince, ARM Accelerates Secure IoT from Chip to Cloud. [Online]. Available from: http://www.zigbee.org/arm-accelerates-secure-iot-from-chip-to-cloud/. 2017.09.29.

[12] Qualcomm, Internet of Things. Available from: https://www.qualcomm.com/solutions/internet-of-things. [Online]. Available from: http://www.zigbee.org/arm-accelerates-secure-iot-from-chip-to-cloud/. 2017.0.9.29.

[13] J. Wyatt and B. Fankem, SimpleLink Wi-Fi CC3220 and CC3120 Product Overview. [Online]. Available from: https://training.ti.com/simplelink-wi-fi-cc3220-and-cc3120-product-overview. 2017.09.29.

[14] Cypress, Welcome to the PSOC 6 Community. [Online]. Available from: https://community.cypress.com/community/psoc-6. 2017.11.02.

[15] Wavefront, Sierra Wireless launches mangOH Red open source platform for industrial IoT devices. [Online]. Available from: http://wavefront.ca/sierra-wireless-launches-mangoh-red-open-source-platform-industrial-iot-devices/. 2017.11.02.

[16] Raspberry Pi Foundation, Raspberrry Pi Hardware Guide, [Online]. Available from: https://www.raspberrypi.org/learning/hardware-guide/. 2017.11.02.

[17] Raspberry Pi Foundation, Raspbian, [Online]. Available from: https://www.raspberrypi.org/downloads/raspbian/. 2017.11.02.

[18] Microsoft, Windows 10 IoT Core - The operating system built for your Internet of Things. [Online]. Available from: https://developer.microsoft.com/en-us/windows/iot. 2017.11.02.

[19] ARM, mBed OS. [Online]. Available from: https://www.mbed.com/en/platform/mbed-os/. 2017.09.27.

[20] Contiki-os.org, Contiki: The Open Source OS for the Internet of Things. [Online]. Available from: http://www.contiki-os.org/. 2017.09.27.

[21] developer.android.com, Android Things, [Online]. Available from: https://developer.android.com/things/index.html. 2017.11.02.

[22] riot-os.org, RIOT: The friendly Operating System for the Internet of Things. [Online]. Available from: https://riot-os.org/. 2017.11.02.

[23] opencv.org, OpenCV. [Online]. Available from: https://opencv.org/. 2017.11.02.

[24] Amazon, AWS IoT. [Online]. Available from: https://aws.amazon.com/iot-platform/. 2017.11.02.

[25] Microsoft, Azure IoT Suite. [Online]. Available from: https://www.microsoft.com/en-us/internet-of-things/azure-iot-suite. 2017.11.02.

[26] LogMeIn, Profit from the Connected Product Conversation with the Xively IoT Platform. [Online]. Available from: https://www.xively.com/xively-iot-platform. 2017.11.02.

[27] 3GPP, Standardization of NB-IOT completed. [Online]. Available from: http://www.3gpp.org/news-events/3gpp-news/1785-nb_iot_complete. 2017.11.02.

[28] GSMA, Long Term Evolution for Machines: LTE-M. [Online]. Available from: https://www.gsma.com/iot/mobile-iot-technology-lte-m/. 2017.11.02.

[29] IETF, 6lowpan Status Pages. [Online]. Available from: https://tools.ietf.org/wg/6lowpan/charters. 2017.11.02.

[30] Sigfox, the world's leading Internet of things (IoT) connectivity service. [Online]. Available from: https://www.sigfox.com/en. 2017.11.02.

[31] Cypress, Bluetooth® Low Energy (BLE) Profiles and Services. [Online]. Available from: http://www.cypress.com/documentation/software-and-drivers/bluetooth-low-energy-ble-profiles-and-services. 2017.11.02.

[32] Bluetooth SIG, Inc, Bluetooth LE: mesh. [Online]. Available from: https://www.bluetooth.com/what-is-bluetooth-technology/how-it-works/le-mesh. 2017.11.02.

RF Fingerprinting for 802.15.4 Devices: Combining Convolutional Neural Networks and RF-DNA

Bernard Lebel

Thales Canada Inc. - TRT
Québec, Québec, Canada
Email: bernard.lebel[at]ca.thalesgroup.com

Louis N. Bélanger,
M. A. Haji Bagheri Fard,
and Jean-Yves Chouinard

Université Laval
Québec, Québec, Canada
Emails: louis.belanger[at]gel.ulaval.ca
mohammad-amin.haji-bagheri-fard.1@ulaval.ca
jean-yves.chouinard[at]gel.ulaval.ca

***Abstract*—Wireless communications have traditionally relied on the content of the message for authenticating the sender. In protocols relying on the IEEE 802.15.4 standard, such as Zigbee, it is possible for an attacker with the right knowledge and tools to emit crafted packets that will be interpreted by the receiver as being properly identified and thus, inject arbitrary data. One way of protecting oneself from this type of attack is the use of radio frequency fingerprinting through a technique called Radio Frequency Distinct Native Attribute (RF-DNA). This approach has been demonstrated to be efficient for wireless devices of different models but still lacks accuracy when trying to identify a rogue device of the same model as the lawful emitter. This is even more of a challenge when attempting to conduct the fingerprinting using a low-cost yet flexible software defined radio. To address this challenge, the current work-in-progress attempts to train a convolutional neural network in order to be able to discriminate a legitimate device from a rogue device. Initial results show promising performance but a larger dataset of devices is required to be conclusive, which will be the focus of future work.**

Keywords–RF-DNA; Wireless Security; Physical Layer; Neural Networks; Machine Learning.

I. Introduction

A tide of electronic devices traditionally used in isolated small-scale hard-lined networks were augmented with full networking capabilities in the recent years. This mass of newly connected devices comprises industrial controllers, Internet Protocol (IP) cameras, sensors, actuators, and many others collectively forming what is called the Internet of Things (IoT). It is known for some of those devices to rely on wireless communications to operate. Protocols using the standards IEEE 802.15.4 [1] and IEEE 802.11 [2] are popular choices in the IoT [3].

Wireless communications can be used as an entry point to a private and/or restricted network where a malicious actor may interfere with the proper functioning of a system from a distant location. Moreover, attacks have been demonstrated (e.g., [4], [5]) with potential impacts including denial-of-service (DoS), impersonation attacks and Man-in-the-Middle (MitM) amongst others. Implementations of security measures (e.g., Wired Equivalent Privacy (WEP), Wireless Protected Access (WPA) and WPA2 [6]) usually rely on network layers at or above the data-link (MAC) layer of the open systems interconnection (OSI) model [7]. Those layers have been known to be susceptible to manipulations coming from an attacker, sometimes requiring only open-source tools (e.g., Aircrack-ng [8] or KillerBee [9] for IEEE 802.11 and IEEE 802.15.4 respectively) with commercial-off-the-shelf (COTS) wireless adapters that behave as rogue devices. A rogue device can be defined as an illegitimate device that behaves outside of what the communication protocol normally states in order to inject arbitrary traffic into a wireless network and forge data packets to contain misleading data intended to interfere with other devices or the communication itself.

A countermeasure to this problem is to implement security, and more pointedly, authentication at the physical (PHY) layer itself of the OSI model. It has been demonstrated that devices generating radio-signals involuntarily alter the desired theoretical signal due to the physical limitations of the device characteristics that are not part of the communication protocol but rather are due to the electronics of the device itself [10]. Those imperfections are usually within the normal threshold tolerated by a given protocol and do not interfere with the communication itself and constitute the RF fingerprints of a device. The RF fingerprints can be used to authenticate the emitter of a message as they differ across devices.

Also, forging the RF fingerprints of a victim is a challenge in itself for an attacker. Indeed, it requires identifying and mimicking those fingerprints. This in itself is not a trivial problem as the attacking device would also need to prevent its own RF fingerprints from leaking into the resulting signal. This adds a layer of protection that relies on an intrinsic property of the emitter itself (what it is) rather than a preshared secret key (what is known) or an authentication token (what is possessed). As those informations have been known to be stolen, cracked or guessed, they may come short for critical infrastructure protection. Thus, the approach is complementary to the other methods and can strengthen the confidence in the authenticity of the identity of an emitter.

Ramsey et al. [11] used an approach called the Radio Frequency Distinct Native Attribute (RF-DNA) to the Zigbee protocol which uses the IEEE 802.15.4 standard. This approach relies on calculating statistics (i.e., variance (σ^2), skewness (γ) and kurtosis (κ) on physical characteristics (instantaneous phase (ϕ_i), frequency (f_i) and amplitude (a_i))

of subregions of an incoming signal.

Additionally, Ramsey et al. [11] demonstrated that it is possible to use a COTS software-defined radio (SDR) to obtain satisfactory results for discriminating an impersonator from a legitimate device. A SDR is a device capable of acquiring a radio-signal in a wide range of frequencies and which delegates the processing of this signal to a software implementation rather than using specialized hardware to do so. This allows a user to have access to a wide range of protocols and frequencies using a single device. It requires a software implementation of the protocol stack and that the communication occurs within the SDR frequency range and bandwidth. SDR vary greatly in terms of price range but some solutions, such as the USRP B200mini from Ettus Research [12] are fairly low-cost when compared to high-end lab equipment and have a smaller size factor. One concern of using a SDR for acquiring the signal to extract its RF-DNA is to ensure sufficient bandwidth can be achieved to capture the hardware-specific variations. The results obtained in [11] supported that a low-cost SDR, such as the B200mini, was enough to discriminate devices based on the comparison of their RF-DNA. The true verification rate (TVR) (i.e., how often a packet was accepted when it came from a legitimate device) neared 100% while the rogue acceptance rate (RAR) (i.e., how often the spoofing devices were accepted as legitimate ones) dropped to 0% for devices that were of different models. To maintain a TVR of >90% in the case where the devices were of the same model, the RAR ranged between 32% and 54%.

The current work seeks to lower the RAR while maintaining or increasing the TVR in the event of a rogue device using the same model as a legitimate one to communicate with another station using the IEEE 802.15.4 standard. The proposed approach seeks to improve the performance of the decision model from [11] that combined a multiple discriminant analysis/maximum likelihood (MDA/ML) process for dimensionality reduction and Bayesian decision criteria for classification. Instead, it is proposed to train a convolutional neural network (CNN) [13], [14] to recognize the devices without requiring that the dimensionality be reduced.

A CNN is a machine learning model that works by attempting to train a set of filters used for convolutions on the input signal to highlight the most discriminant features that can be spatially distributed in that signal. The response to the input signal of each filter at each location across the signal is the output of a convolutional layer (CL). This output is then passed to a subsampling layer which is responsible of reducing the number of outputs by pooling a given region together using a given function (e.g., maximum value or the average of values). One or more fully-connected layer make for the last layers of network and are responsible for the classification itself.

CNNs have been demonstrated to be robust to data translation and are able to take into account a level of spatial distribution of a dataset [15], [16], [17], [18]. This may constitute an advantage in the context of RF fingerprinting as signals are distributed in time and slight spatial translations may occur in the captured data. The ongoing work and preliminary results aim at validating the use of CNN in that context.

The next section presents the methodology used for acquiring RF signals for analysis and the extraction of features following the RF-DNA methodology and the structure of the CNN used for analysis. Section III describes preliminary results obtained in the ongoing work. Section IV summarizes the preliminary results, discuss implications and research concerns. Finally, section V presents future work and next steps.

II. Methodology

The emitting devices were 4 Atmel RZUSBStick, or RZ for short. This device is capable of sending Zigbee packets containing arbitrary data and is also able to communicate through the Zigbee protocol [9]. Arbitrary data was sent periodically at a frequency of 40 packets/sec on channel 26 (i.e., 2.480 GHz). The acquisition was conducted through a USRP B200mini from Ettus Research at a center frequency of 2.480 GHz with a bandwidth of 20 MHz. The data collection was conducted in a RF shielded box to prevent outside interferences with the measurements. Each device was placed at the exact same location for each data collection.

The raw signal from the IEEE 802.15.4 preambles of each communication was extracted. Following the work done by Ramsey et al. [11], the preambles were split into 32 equal regions, each comprising 80 samples per region plus the full preamble itself of 2560 samples, for a total of 33 subregions per preamble captured. For each sample, the instantaneous phase (ϕ_i), instantaneous frequency (f_i) and instantaneous amplitude (a_i) were evaluated. Their variance (σ^2), skewness (γ) and kurtosis (κ) were calculated for each subregion. This amounted to a total of 297 features per preamble composed of 33 subregions $\times$ 3 RF characteristics $\times$ 3 statistics. The number of preambles collected is presented in Table I.

TABLE I. Samples per device.

	RZUSBStick1	RZUSBStick2	RZUSBStick3	RZUSBStick4
Preambles	7148	7094	6832	7086

Extracted features were standardized following (1). Standardization is required to constrain values of features within a comparable range.

$$z_i = \frac{x_i - \overline{x}}{s^2} \tag{1}$$

z_i is the standardized score, x_i the input value, $\overline{x}$ the mean and s^2 the variance. To apply the standardization, the features are structured along a $3 \times 33 \times 3$ matrix as presented in (2) for each collected preamble.

$$\begin{bmatrix} [\sigma^2_{1_\phi} & \sigma^2_{1_f} & \sigma^2_{1_a}] & \dots & [\sigma^2_{33_\phi} & \sigma^2_{33_f} & \sigma^2_{33_a}] \\ [\gamma_{1_\phi} & \gamma_{1_f} & \gamma_{1_a}] & \dots & [\gamma_{33_\phi} & \gamma_{33_f} & \gamma_{33_a}] \\ [\kappa_{1_\phi} & \kappa_{1_f} & \kappa_{1_a}] & \dots & [\kappa_{33_\phi} & \kappa_{33_f} & \kappa_{33_a}] \end{bmatrix} \tag{2}$$

The values s^2 and $\overline{x}$ are calculated along all collected preambles for the 33 subregions. The result is two matrices containing the s^2 and $\overline{x}$ values for the 33 subregions across all collected preambles. The resulting matrix is shown in (3) for $\overline{x}$. s^2 follows the same structure.

$$\begin{bmatrix} \overline{\sigma^2_\phi} & \overline{\sigma^2_f} & \overline{\sigma^2_a} \\ \overline{\gamma_\phi} & \overline{\gamma_f} & \overline{\gamma_a} \\ \overline{\kappa_\phi} & \overline{\kappa_f} & \overline{\kappa_a} \end{bmatrix} \tag{3}$$

The set of features for each of the 33 subregions per preamble was standardized according to its RF characteristics and statistics.

A. Convolutional Neural Network

The 297 standardized features were passed on to a CNN constituted of 2 CL with 32 3×1 filters and 64 3×1 filters. Each CL output was connected to a subsampling layer (3×1 average pooling function with 2-step strides). The last subsampling layer was followed by a fully connected layer of 1024 neurons trained with a 0.75 dropout chance before connecting to the output layer. Optimization was conducted using the adaptive moment estimation (ADAM) optimizer with a learning rate of 0.01. Batch size was set at 128 preambles per mini-batch. The implemented model is presented in Figure 1.

III. Preliminary Results

Collected results were analyzed according to two scenarios. Scenario 1 explored training a CNN to discriminate between the 4 known devices. This scenario is meant to demonstrate the general performance of a CNN in the context of RF-DNA. Scenario 2 seeks to replicate the case where an algorithm is trained to be specialized in recognizing if a given preamble belongs to a specific device.

A. Scenario 1: Differentiation

The collected preambles were randomized. The full dataset was divided with 80% used for training, 10% for validation and 10% for testing. The output layer has 4 classes, one for each known device. The resulting confusion matrix is reported in Table II. The calculated accuracy is 95.86%.

TABLE II. Confusion Matrix for Interdevice Classification.

		Input Labels			
		RZ1	RZ2	RZ3	RZ4
Predicted	RZ1	0.947	0.006	0.002	0.037
	RZ2	0.013	0.951	0.018	0.007
	RZ3	0.002	0.031	0.975	0.004
	RZ4	0.038	0.012	0.006	0.953

The high accuracy obtained for this task demonstrates that CNNs are especially well adapted for ingesting RF-DNA inputs for device classification. Work is still in progress to establish a baseline based on current literature to achieve a comparison between the proposed approach and the one described in [11]. However, the represented case in Scenario 1 is valid only if an algorithm can be trained on all known devices and is expected to find the correct match in a pool of devices that was used during training. In practice, this method is ineffective in the context of rogue device identification as the attacking device is usually not known before the attack occurs. This nullifies the chances that the model can be trained with all expected devices in a certain area. This problem is addressed in the next scenario.

B. Scenario 2: One vs All

This scenario aims at filling the gap from the previous one where a model was trained to identify if a preamble originates from one unique device or not. 80% of the dataset was used for training, 10% for validation and 10% for testing. In the first phase, all preambles from one device were considered as being "Good" (approx. 25% of the total dataset) and preambles from the remaining devices were considered as "Bad" (approx. 75% of the total dataset), generating an output layer of 2 classes. During training, labels were balanced according to the proportion of the dataset they represented to compensate for the unbalanced dataset. Results are reported in Table III.

TABLE III. Confusion Matrix for One-vs-Others Classification.

	Others	RZ1
Others	0.986	0.063
RZ1	0.013	0.937

$Acc = 0.973$

	Others	RZ2
Others	0.991	0.080
RZ2	0.009	0.920

$Acc = 0.972$

	Others	RZ3
Others	0.994	0.046
RZ3	0.006	0.954

$Acc = 0.984$

	Others	RZ4
Others	0.977	0.046
RZ4	0.023	0.954

$Acc = 0.987$

As the training set contained samples from each device, it has been postulated that the predictor would be confused if a new device was introduced and requested predictive measures, showing proof of overfitting. To test this hypothesis, a test was conducted by training the expert systems on the dataset but withholding all data from RZ4. The test dataset was evaluated using inputs only from RZ4. If the system did not overfit, attribution would show nearly only *others* attribution. During a subsequent phase of the ongoing work, the results will be compiled for test cases where RZ1, RZ2 or RZ3 is excluded instead of RZ4. Results are presented in Table IV.

TABLE IV. Confusion Matrix for One-vs-Others with a new device (RZ4) excluded from training set.

	RZ4
RZ4	0.168
RZ1	0.832

$Acc = 0.168$

	RZ4
RZ4	0.878
RZ2	0.122

$Acc = 0.878$

	RZ4
RZ4	0.955
RZ3	0.045

$Acc = 0.955$

As the results show, the trained model is achieving an accuracy of 95.5% for RZ3 but lower than 87.8% for RZ2 and is very poor (16.8%) for RZ1. The results from introducing a new device during the test phase demonstrate that the model has trouble differentiating devices that may have a more similar

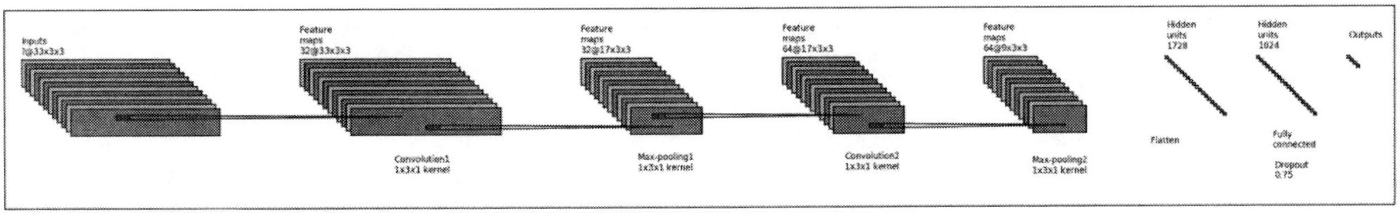

Figure 1. CNN structure.

RF-DNA such as RZ1 and RZ4. At this stage, more data from more devices is required before a conclusion can be achieved.

IV. Discussion

Firstly, when it comes to differentiating between known devices onto which data exists and can be used for training, results show that CNN with standardization from features presented in [11] are effective, achieving a 95% accuracy. Moreover, results have shown that an approach of training a system to recognize itself from other systems performs well in the case where all other systems are known.

However, when exposed to devices which were never part of the learning process, results become unreliable. It is likely that to perform better, the model would need to train on a dataset with more devices. Also, the problem defined in this research specifically targets devices of the same model and manufacturer. It is possible that it is sufficient for categorizing devices from different manufacturers and future work will investigate this.

Also, Table IV shows that some devices may be more alike than others. For instance, it is possible that RZ1 may be more alike to RZ4 and thus, is harder to discriminate when the latter is excluded from the learning process but used only for testing. This supports the hypothesis that more devices are needed for a better predictive model.

Also, when attempting to conduct the learning process on different combinations of RF characteristics, it was noted that statistics on the amplitude lead to better predictive results. This differs from Ramsey et al. [11] whom instead pointed to phase and frequency as being the most useful for categorization. More data collection is required to determine if this could be due to *environmental conditions* that might have altered the transmissions in-between acquisition campaigns.

V. Conclusion

This work-in-progress has demonstrated the potential of using CNN in the context of RF fingerprinting while using affordable and flexible SDRs. Also, RF-DNA provides promising results when used to provide features to a CNN. More work will be carried on to tweak the hyperparameters of the model to achieve better results and collect more preambles from new devices. Also, baseline measures based on the state-of-the-art are being generated and will be used for assessing the success of the current approach. New features based on the scientific literature need to be identified and extracted from the RF signal. This would allow to have more elements on which devices from the same manufacturer and of the same model could be discriminated. Finally, ongoing work focuses on trying to compute the RF-DNA in real time on an embedded system in order to optimize the signal processing component. This would ensure a real-time computation and minimize the impact of the implementation of this method on a wireless communication itself.

Acknowledgments

This research was supported by a Mitacs internship awarded to Mohammad Amin Haji Bagheri Fard and jointly funded by NSERC and Thales Canada Inc./TRT. The authors would also like to thank Mathieu Lvesque and Guillaume Godbout for their participation in data collection and Frederic Audet for his support.

References

[1] IEEE Std 802.15.4, IEEE Standard for Low-Rate Wireless Networks, IEEE Computer Society Std., 2015, accessed on 2017-09-27. [Online]. Available: http://ieeexplore.ieee.org/iel7/6677511/6677512/06677513.pdf

[2] IEEE Std 802.11, Wireless LAN Medium Access Control (MAC) and Physical Layer (PHY) Specifications, IEEE Computer Society Std., 2016, accessed on 2017-09-27. [Online]. Available: http://ieeexplore.ieee.org/iel7/6837412/6837413/06837414.pdf

[3] A. Al-Fuqaha, M. Guizani, M. Mohammadi, M. Aledhari, and M. Ayyash, "Internet of Things: A Survey on Enabling Technologies, Protocols, and Applications," IEEE Communications Surveys & Tutorials, vol. 17, no. 4, 2015, pp. 2347–2376.

[4] T. Zillner and S. Strobl, "ZigBee exploited: The good the bad and the ugly," version, Tech. Rep., 2015, accessed on 2017-09-29. [Online]. Available: http://www.sicherheitsforschung-magdeburg.de/uploads/journal/MJS_045_Zillner_ZigBee.pdf

[5] R. Sankar, "mdk3," Sep. 2015, accessed on 2017-09-29. [Online]. Available: http://kalilinuxtutorials.com/mdk3/

[6] A. H. Lashkari, M. M. S. Danesh, and B. Samadi, "A survey on wireless security protocols (WEP, WPA and WPA2/802.11i)," in 2009 2nd IEEE International Conference on Computer Science and Information Technology, Aug. 2009, pp. 48–52.

[7] J. D. Day and H. Zimmermann, "The OSI reference model," Proceedings of the IEEE, vol. 71, no. 12, Dec. 1983, pp. 1334–1340.

[8] Mister X, "aircrack-ng: WiFi security auditing tools suite," Jul. 2017, accessed on 2017-09-27. [Online]. Available: https://github.com/aircrack-ng/aircrack-ng

[9] River Loop Security, "killerbee: IEEE 802.15.4/ZigBee Security Research Toolkit," Jul. 2017, accessed on 2017-09-27. [Online]. Available: https://github.com/riverloopsec/killerbee

[10] W. C. Suski II, M. A. Temple, M. J. Mendenhall, and R. F. Mills, "Using spectral fingerprints to improve wireless network security," in Global Telecommunications Conference, 2008. IEEE, 2008, pp. 1–5.

[11] B. W. Ramsey, T. D. Stubbs, B. E. Mullins, M. A. Temple, and M. A. Buckner, "Wireless infrastructure protection using low-cost radio frequency fingerprinting receivers," International Journal of Critical Infrastructure Protection, vol. 8, Jan. 2015, pp. 27–39.

[12] Ettus Research, "USRP B200mini-i," accessed on 2017-09-27. [Online]. Available: https://www.ettus.com/product/details/USRP-B200mini-i

[13] Y. LeCun, B. Boser, J. S. Denker, D. Henderson, R. E. Howard, W. Hubbard, and L. D. Jackel, "Backpropagation Applied to Handwritten Zip Code Recognition," Neural Computation, vol. 1, no. 4, Dec. 1989, pp. 541–551.

[14] Y. LeCun and Y. Bengio, "The handbook of brain theory and neural networks," M. A. Arbib, Ed. Cambridge, MA, USA: MIT Press, 1998, ch. Convolutional Networks for Images, Speech, and Time Series, pp. 255–258.

[15] P. Y. Simard, D. Steinkraus, and J. C. Platt, "Best practices for convolutional neural networks applied to visual document analysis," in 7th International Conference on Document Analysis and Recognition. Proceedings, vol. 2. Washington, DC, USA: IEEE Computer Society, 2003, pp. 958–963.

[16] D. C. Ciresan, U. Meier, L. M. Gambardella, and J. Schmidhuber, "Convolutional Neural Network Committees for Handwritten Character Classification," in 2011 International Conference on Document Analysis and Recognition, Sep. 2011, pp. 1135–1139.

[17] S. Lawrence, C. L. Giles, A. C. Tsoi, and A. D. Back, "Face recognition: a convolutional neural-network approach," IEEE Transactions on Neural Networks, vol. 8, no. 1, Jan. 1997, pp. 98–113.

[18] A. Krizhevsky, I. Sutskever, and G. E. Hinton, "ImageNet Classification with Deep Convolutional Neural Networks," in Advances in Neural Information Processing Systems 25, F. Pereira, C. J. C. Burges, L. Bottou, and K. Q. Weinberger, Eds. Curran Associates, Inc., 2012, pp. 1097–1105.

Integrating Autonomous Vehicle Safety and Security

Giedre Sabaliauskaite

Centre for Research in Cyber Security (iTrust)
Singapore University of Technology and Design
Singapore 487372
Email: giedre@sutd.edu.sg

Jin Cui

Centre for Research in Cyber Security (iTrust)
Singapore University of Technology and Design
Singapore 487372
Email: jin_cui@sutd.edu.sg

***Abstract*—Safety and security are two inter-dependent key properties of autonomous vehicles. They are aimed at protecting the vehicles from accidental failures and intentional attacks, which could lead to injuries and loss of lives. The selection of safety and security countermeasures for autonomous vehicles depends on the driving automation levels, defined by the international standard SAE J3016. However, current vehicle safety standards ISO 26262 do not take the driving automation levels into consideration. We propose an approach for integrating autonomous vehicle safety and security processes, which is compliant with the international standards SAE J3016, SAE J3061, and ISO 26262, and which considers driving automation levels. It uses the Six-Step Model as a backbone for achieving integration and alignment among safety and security processes and artefacts. The Six-Step Model incorporates six hierarchies of autonomous vehicles, namely, functions, structure, failures, attack, safety countermeasures, and security countermeasures. It ensures the consistency among these hierarchies throughout the entire autonomous vehicle's life-cycle.**

Keywords–Autonomous vehicle; safety; security; ISO 26262; SAE J3016; SAE J3061; Six-Step Model; attack tree; fault tree.

I. INTRODUCTION

Autonomous Vehicles (AVs), the self-driving vehicles, are safety-critical Cyber-Physical Systems (CPS) – complex engineering systems, which integrate embedded computing technology into physical phenomena. Safety and security are two key properties of CPSs, which share the same goal – protecting the system from undesirable events: failures (safety) and intentional attacks (security) [1].

Ensuring the safety of autonomous vehicles, i.e., reducing the number of traffic crashes to prevent injuries and save lives, is a top priority in autonomous vehicle development. Safety and security are interdependent (e.g., security attacks can cause safety failures, or security countermeasures may weaken CPS safety and vice versa), therefore they have to be aligned in the early system development phases to ensure the required level of protection [1][2].

Although AVs could be considered to be smaller and/or less complex systems as compared to other CPSs, such as, e.g., power plants or water treatment systems, they face some unique challenges, which have to be taken into consideration when analyzing their safety and security.

Firstly, there are six different levels of driving automation ranging from no driving automation (level 0) to full driving automation (level 5), as described by the international standard SAE J3016 [3]. The levels describe who (human driver or automated system) performs the driving tasks and monitors the driving environments under certain environmental conditions. Thus, AV safety and security depend on the driving automation levels and the environmental conditions.

Secondly, the AV domain is relatively new, and therefore, there are no international standards for AV safety and security yet. Currently, the ISO 26262 standard, which describes functional safety of road vehicles, is being used for AV safety analysis [4]. However, it is not sufficient for AVs, as argued in [5][6]. ISO 26262 addresses the safety of each function, or item, of the vehicle separately, since the driver is responsible for everything what falls outside the item. However, in AV, it is necessary to ensure safety at all times, especially at the high automation levels, when there is no driver in the vehicle [5]. Thus, hazard analysis of AVs should have the broader scope and should analyze AVs functions together. Warg et al. proposed an approach to extend ISO 26262 and to add generic operational situation and hazard trees for comprehensive AV safety analysis [5].

To address vehicle security needs, the SAE J3061 standard has been developed [7]. It defines cyber-security lifecycle of cyber-physical vehicle systems. However, the security lifecycle, defined in SAE J3061, is analogous to the vehicle safety lifecycle described in ISO 26262, and therefore, it is not sufficient for AV cyber-security analysis.

How can we analyze AV safety and security throughout its entire life-cycle in a consistent way, and provide required level of protection?

In our previous work, we proposed a Six-Step Model for modeling and analysis of CPS safety and security [8][9]. It incorporates six dimensions (hierarchies) of CPS, namely, functions, structure, failures, safety countermeasures, cyber-attacks, and security countermeasures. Furthermore, it uses relationship matrices to model inter-dependencies between these dimensions. The Six-Step Model enables comprehensive analysis of CPS safety and security, as it utilizes system functions and structure as a knowledge base for understanding the effect of failures and attacks on the system.

In this paper, we propose an approach for AV safety and security analysis, which uses the Six-Step Model as a backbone for integrating and maintaining consistency among safety and security processes and artefacts. The Six-Step Model consolidated safety and security artefacts, developed throughout the entire AV life-cycle. The proposed approach is compliant with the international standards SAE J3016, SAE J3061, and ISO 26262.

The remainder of this paper is structured as follows. Section II describes preliminaries. The proposed approach is explained in Section III, and a Six-Step Model example is included in Section IV. Finally, Section V concludes the paper and describes our future work.

II. PRELIMINARIES

A. *Autonomous Vehicles' Main Terms and Definitions*

The real-time operational and tactical functions required to operate the vehicle in on-road traffic include lateral and longitudinal vehicle motion control, monitoring the driving environment, object and event response execution, maneuver planning, and enhancing conspicuity via lighting, signaling, etc. [3]. These functions are collectively called the Dynamic Driving Task (DDT) [3]. AVs perform entire or part of DDT depending of their automation level.

SAE International (SAE) has developed an international standard, SAE J3016 [3], to describe various levels of vehicle automation. The standard has been widely adopted by international organizations, such as the National Highway Traffic Safety Administration (NHTSA) [10].

There are six driving automation levels [3][10]:

- Level 0 – the human driver performs entire DDT.
- Level 1 – an automated system on the vehicle can assist the human driver to perform either the lateral or the longitudinal vehicle motion, while driver monitors the driving environment and performs the rest of DDT.
- Level 2 – an automated system performs the lateral and the longitudinal vehicle motion, while driver monitors the driving environment and performs the rest of DDT.
- Level 3 – an automated system can perform entire DDT, but the human driver must be ready to take back control when the automated system requests.
- Level 4 – there is no human driver; an automated system conducts the entire DDT, but it can operate only in certain environments and under certain conditions.
- Level 5 – there is no human driver; an automated system performs entire DDT in all environments and under all conditions that a human driver could perform them.

Level 3-5 vehicles are called the highly automated vehicles, since their automated systems (not a human driver) are responsible for monitoring the driving environment [10]. Furthermore, level 1-4 vehicles are designed to operate only in certain environments and under certain conditions, while level 5 vehicles - in all environments and under all conditions.

AV functions can be grouped into three main categories: perception (perception of the external environment/context in which vehicle operates), decision & control (decisions and control of vehicle motion, with respect to the external environment/context that is perceived), and vehicle platform manipulation (sensing, control and actuation of the vehicle, with the intention of achieving desired motion) [11][12]. A standard for describing AV functions and functional interfaces, SAE J3131, is currently under development.

AV structural architecture consists of two main systems: a) cognitive driving intelligence, which implements perception and decision & control functions, and b) vehicle platform, which is responsible for vehicle platform manipulation [11]. Each system consists of components, which belong to four major groups: hardware, software, communication, and human-machine interface [12][13].

B. *A Six-Step Model*

In our earlier work [8][9], we proposed a Six-Step Model to enable comprehensive CPS safety and security analysis (see Figure 1) . The model is constructed using the following six steps:

1) The first step is aimed at modeling the functional hierarchy of the system. The functions are defined using the Goal Tree (GT), which is constructed starting with the goal (functional objective) and then defining functions and sub-functions, needed for achieving this goal. A relationship matrix, F-F, is used to define the relationships between functions, which can be high, medium, low, or very low.
2) In the second step, system's structural hierarchy is defined using the Success Tree (ST) to describe system's structure as a collection of sub-systems and units. Furthermore, the relationships between structure and functions are defined using a relationship matrix S-F, as shown in Figure 1.
3) The third step is focused on safety hazard analysis. In this step, system's failures are identified and added to the model. In addition, the relationships between failures, system structure and functions are identified, and the corresponding relationship matrices – B-B, B-S, and B-F – are added to the model.
4) The fourth step focuses on security threat analysis. In this step, attacks are identified and added to the model along with the relationship matrices to describe relationships between attacks, failures, structure and functions. Relationship matrix A-B (attacks – failures) is used to determine which failures could be triggered by a successful attack. In the original version of the Six-Step Model [9], safety countermeasures have been identified in step 4, while attacks - in step 5. However, we decided to switch the places of these two steps in order to tackle system vulnerability (hazard and threat) analysis first, before moving to the countermeasure selection, as safety countermeasures can be used to detect and mitigate both the failures and the attacks. Thus, it is convenient to have attack identified before designing safety countermeasures.
5) In the fifth step, safety countermeasures are added to the model and their relationships are identified. Matrices X-A and X-B show the coverage of attacks and failures by safety countermeasures, where white rhombus indicates that the countermeasure provides low protection from attack/failure; gray rhombus - medium protection; black rhombus - full protection (see Figure 1).
6) Finally, in the last step, security countermeasures are added to the model and their relationships are established. Similarly to matrices X-A and X-B from the previous step, two new matrices Z-A and Z-B are added to define the coverage of attacks and failures by security countermeasures. The security

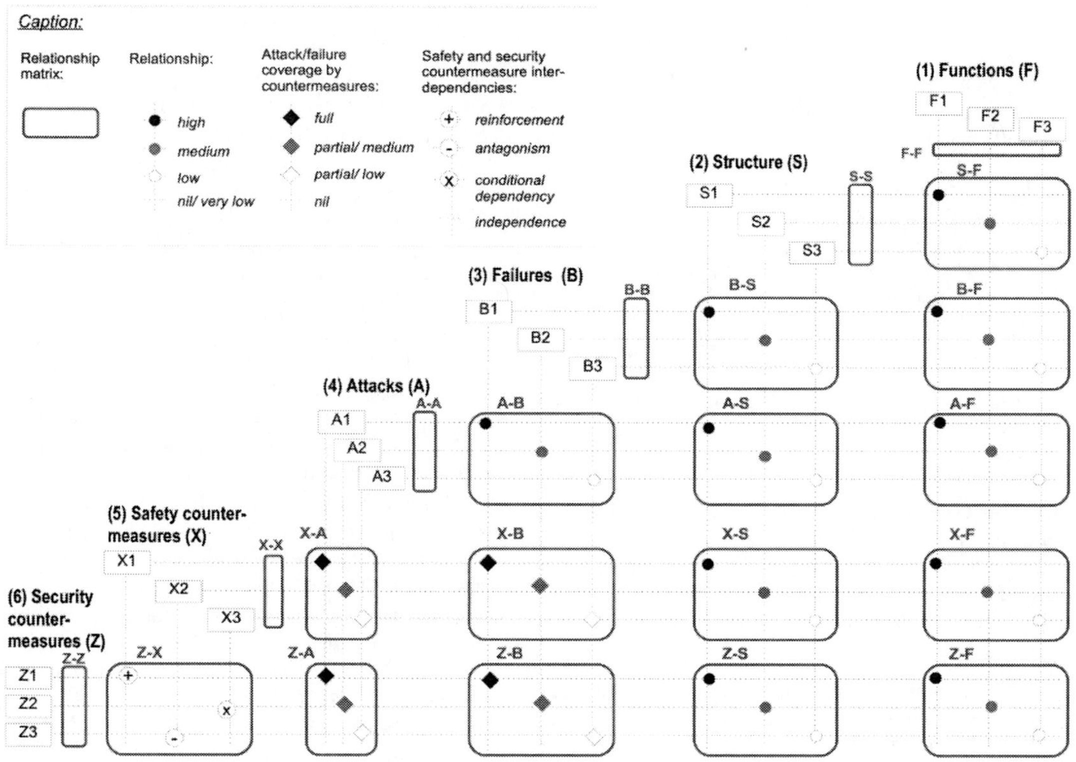

Figure 1. The Six-Step Model.

countermeasures, added in this step, could be used to protect the system from attacks and failures, not covered by the safety countermeasures. Furthermore, matrix Z-X is used to capture the inter-dependencies between safety and security countermeasures, such as reinforcement, antagonism, conditional dependency, and independence, as defined in [14].

After completion of steps 5 and 6, it is important to analyze if there were any changes made to system's structure, as some countermeasures might require the use of additional components, e.g., sensors or controllers. If the changes occur, it is necessary to return to the step 2 to add the new components, and then repeat steps 3-6.

The Six-Step Model, constructed throughout steps 1-6, interconnects six hierarchies of the systems (functions, structure, failures, attacks, and safety and security countermeasures) by forming a hexagon-shaped structure of their relationships, as shown in Figure 2. The relationships help to ensure alignment between these hierarchies. The hierarchies and relationships have to be maintained throughout the entire system's life-cycle to sustain their consistency and completeness.

C. AV Safety Analysis

The ISO 26262 standard [4] defines functional safety for automotive equipment applicable throughout the life-cycle of all automotive Electronic and Electrical (E/E) safety-related systems. It aims to address possible hazards caused by the malfunctioning behavior E/E systems. The safety process consists of several phases, such as concept, product development, and

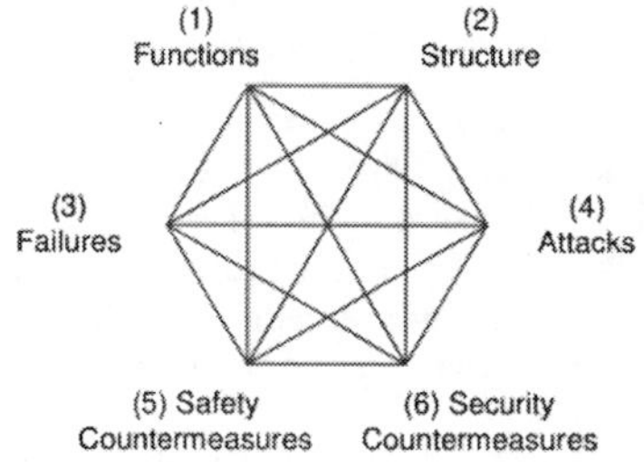

Figure 2. Relationships among hierarchies of the Six-Step Model.

production, operation, service and decommissioning. Hazard Analysis and Risk Assessment (HARA) is performed during the concept phase, where hazardous events, safety risks and goals are identified. These goals are further refined into the safety requirements during the product development phase, and the safety countermeasures are designed and implemented.

ISO 26262 requires the presence of the human driver inside the vehicle to deal with the unexpected environments and conditions [5]. In high automation AVs, where no human driver is present, it is important to consider all driving environments and conditions. In [5], Warg et al. proposed a AV hazard analysis method, which extends vehicle safety analysis process defined by ISO 26262 [4]. It uses operational situation and hazard trees as a knowledge base of potential situations and hazards to investigate.

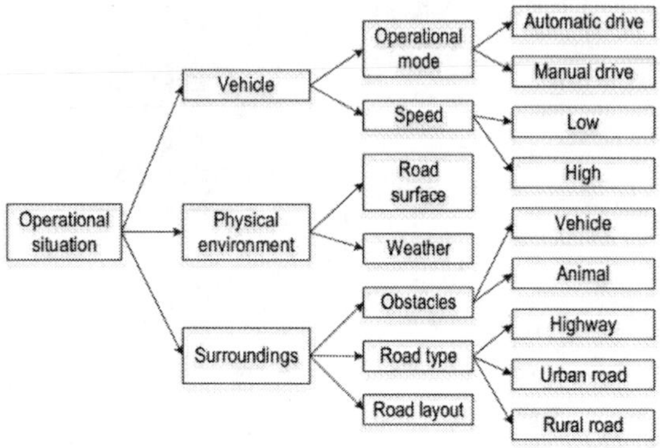

Figure 3. Generic situation tree example [5].

Figure 3 shows an example of an AV operational situation tree, borrowed from [5]. Three main aspects (tree leaves) are identified, namely, vehicle, physical environment, and surroundings, which a further refined into properties, e.g., speed is decomposed into high and low speed (see Figure 3).

Operational situations for use in the hazard analysis are composed by selecting and combining leaves from the tree. If no leaf is selected from a particular aspect, the situation is considered to be valid for all properties of that aspect. For level 5 vehicle, all operational situations have to be analyzed, while for level 1-4 vehicle – only a subset of operational situations, which includes the environment and driving conditions the AV is designed to operate in. Figure 3 shows an example of a high-level situation tree, which is further refined throughout safety lifecycle, as the new situations are identified.

The hazard tree is constructed similarly to the situation tree. Two main levels of hazards are identified: tactical and operative. Tactical hazard include foreseeable tactical mistakes, while operative hazards - hazard related to situation awareness, vehicle control, and environment. Each leaf of the tree represents a possible hazard that can be included in hazard analysis [5].

Once the situation and the hazard trees are completed, each hazard from the hazard tree is combined with each operational situation from the situation tree to form hazardous events. Subsequently, the risk assessment of these events is performed and an Automotive Safety Integrity Level (ASIL) is assigned. The risk assessment has to be updated any time a new or modified situations/hazards are added to the situation/hazard trees [5].

Hazardous events can be further refined using the Fault Tree analysis [13] in order to identify the conditions and events that could lead to these events. Fault tree refines top level hazardous event into intermediate events and basic events, which are interconnected by AND and OR logical operators. Bhavsar et al. [13] describe two fault trees for AVs: fault tree of failures related to vehicular components, and fault tree considering failures related to transportation infrastructure components. Safety risks are defined based on the results of the hazard and failure analysis, which are then used for defining AV safety requirements and, subsequently, developing safety countermeasures.

D. AV Security Analysis

SAE J3061 is a vehicle cyber-security standard, which was developed using the ISO 26262 standard as a base. Thus, both standards consist of similar phases. Security process, defined by SAE J3061, includes concept, product development, and production & operation phases. Threat Analysis and Risk Assessment (TARA) is performed during the concept phase, where threats, security risks, and security goals are defined. In the product development phase, security requirements are defined based on the security goals, and the security countermeasures are developed.

Attack tree analysis [7][15] is often used for performing TARA. It helps to determine the potential paths that an attacker could take to lead to the top level threat [7]. An attack tree is a graph, where the nodes represent attack events, and the edges - attack paths through system, which could be connected using AND and OR gates.

Behavior diagrams, such as Data-Flow Diagrams (DFD) [16] and Information-Flow Diagrams (IFD) [9] could be used for identifying the attacks to be included in attack trees analysis. DFDs include elements, such as processes, data flows, and data store, and are used to model data flows between software components. IFDs include units and information flows between them, and could be used to model information flows between software and hardware components, such as actuators, controllers, sensors, etc. In [9], we proposed a method for generating IFDs using the Six-Step model in order to identify possible attacks on CPSs.

III. INTEGRATED AUTONOMOUS VEHICLE SAFETY AND SECURITY ANALYSIS APPROACH

This section proposes an approach for integrating AV development with safety safety and security engineering, which is compliant with the international standards SAE J3016, SAE J3061 and ISO 26262. The integration is achieved by the use of the Six-Step Model, which incorporates AV functions, structure, safety failures, security attack, and safety & security countermeasures. The Six-Step Model is the backbone for achieving integration and alignment among safety and security artefacts.

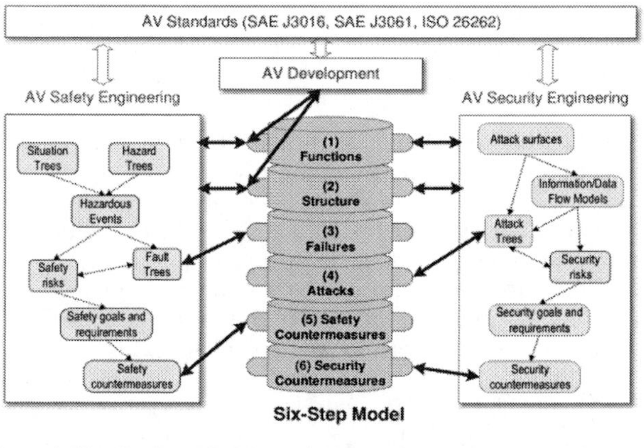

Figure 4. The Six-Step Model as a backbone for integrated AV safety and security analysis.

Figure 4 describes the proposed approach and shows the relationships between steps of the Six-Step Model and various artefacts from AV development, safety engineering, and security engineering processes.

The steps of the AV Six-Step Model are performed in the following order:

- Steps (1) and (2). Autonomous driving functions and the systems (structure), which implement these functions, are defined during AV development process. As the result, AV functional and structural hierarchies are defined and added to the Six-Step Model, along with their relationships.
- Steps (3) and (4). These steps correspond to AV vulnerability (hazard and threat) analysis. On the safety side, HARA (as defined by ISO 26262) is performed in order to identify and evaluate hazardous events, and define AV functional safety requirements. Additional models, such as situation, hazard, and fault trees, are used to ensure that all autonomous driving related hazards are considered, as described in Section II-C. At the end of the hazard analysis phase, failures, which are considered in security requirements, are extracted from the fault trees and added to the the Six-Step Model (Step (3)). On the security side, TARA (as defined by SAE J3061) is performed in order to evaluate security threats and derive AV functional security requirements. The AV structural hierarchy, defined in step (2), could be used to define attack surfaces and construct information-flow models (see [9]), which helps to identify possible attacks and construct attack trees, as described in Section II-D. The risks associated with each attack are then evaluated and security requirements are defined. Similarly to failures, the attack, included in security requirements, are extracted from the attack trees and added to the Six-Step Model (Step (4)). The relationships between attacks, failures, functions, and structures, are also added to the Six-Step model.
- Steps (5) and (6). During these steps, safety and security countermeasures are selected and added to the model along with their relationships to remaining elements of the model. On the safety side, functional safety requirements are refined into technical requirements and corresponding countermeasures are designed for satisfying these requirements. Similarly, on the security side, functional security requirements are decomposed into technical requirements for security countermeasures. The countermeasures from both sides are added to the Six-Step Model to analyze their relationships to the remaining elements of the model. In particular, the matrices are useful to make sure that each countermeasure is really needed (addresses attacks/failures not completely covered by any other countermeasures, shown in matrices X-A, X-B, Z-A, and A-B), and that there are no contradictions among countermeasures (matrix Z-X).

The AV Six-Step Model, constructed during steps (1)-(6), is a backbone of AV vulnerability analysis. It supports three AV processes, namely, AV development, AV safety engineering, and AV security engineering, as shown in Figure 4. It enables integration of safety and security artefacts, developed throughout the entire AV life-cycle (such as failures, attacks, safety and security countermeasures) into AV function and structure hierarchies to assure their consistency and completeness.

The AV Six-Step Model has to be maintained throughout the entire AV life-cycle. This is particularly important for security, as new threats are continually identified and analyzed.

The following section shows a Six-Step Model example of an AV.

IV. SIX-STEP MODEL EXAMPLE OF AN AV

The AV, described in this example, performs three main autonomous driving functions, i.e., perception, decision & control, and vehicle platform manipulation, as described in Section II-A. The perception function can be further decomposed into sensing, sensor fusion, localization, semantic understanding, and world model (see [11]). These functions are added at the top of to Six-Step Model and their inter-relationships are identified, as shown in Figure 5.

Due to space limitations, only an excerpt of the Six-Step Model is included in Figure 5. Furthermore, only the high degree relationships between elements are shown.

The main systems of AV, which implement driving automation functions, are: cognitive driving intelligence, vehicle platform, and communication system [11][12]. The cognitive driving intelligence includes on-board computer and external sensors for perception of environment, such as LIDAR, Radar, cameras, and ultrasound sensors [17]. No sensor type works well for all tasks and in all conditions, thus it is necessary to provide sensor redundancy and perform sensor fusion. A combination of LIDAR, Radar, and camera provides good coverage of AV tasks in most of the environmental conditions [17]. The vehicle platform includes controllers (ECUs), actuators, which implement the desired motion. The communication system includes in-vehicle and V2X (vehicle to vehicle, infrastructure, and humans) communication networks. In this example, only in-vehicle communication is considered. All these structural elements are added to model in step (2).

In steps (3) and (4), we included LIDAR failure and LIDAR attack. LIDAR is a laser sensor used in AVs for object detection. As we can see from Figure 5, the main function affected by either the LIDAR failure or attack is the sensing function. Furthermore, there is a strong relationship between LIDAR attack and failure, LIDAR attack is strongly related to Ethernet (i.e., an attacker can attack LIDAR through Ethernet).

Attacks on LIDAR and security countermeasures are summarized in [18]. An attacker could perform a relay attack (relaying the original signal sent from target vehicle LIDAR from another position to create fake echoes) or a spoofing attack (replaying objects and controlling their position) on LIDAR.

Radar is added to the model in step (5) as a safety countermeasure. In case of of LIDAR failure, Radar and camera will still be able to perform sensing of the driving environment.

Security countermeasures could include redundancy: multiple LIDARs, or V2X communication to compare measurements of target vehicle with other vehicles to detect inconsistencies [18]. However, due to high cost of LIDAR, multiple LIDARs are not considered in this AV. Furthermore, there is no V2X communication in this AV example. If the vehicle

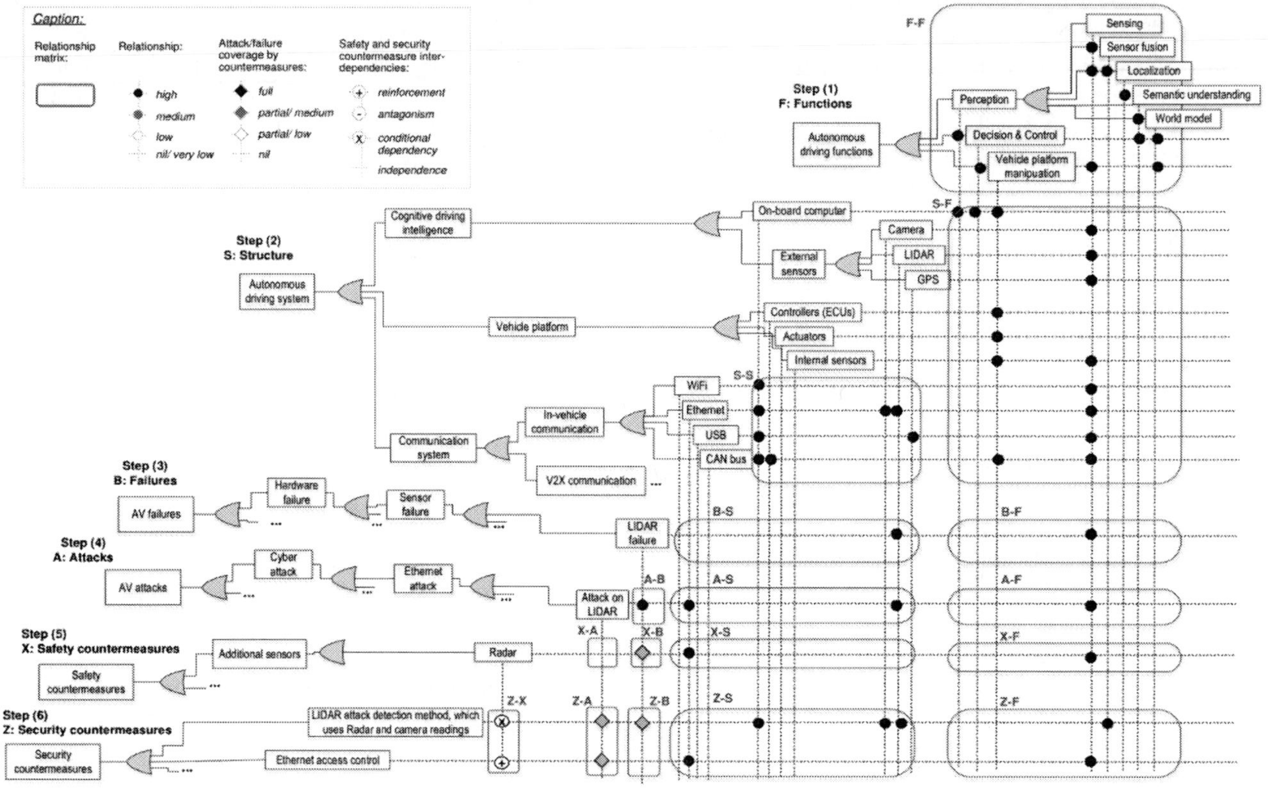

Figure 5. An example of AV Six-Step Model.

had V2X communication, LIDAR attacks could be detected by cross-comparing LIDAR reading of the nearby vehicles.

Various LIDAR attack detection and mitigation methods can be implemented inside on-board computer, e.g., LIDAR attacks can be detected by comparing LIDAR readings to Radar and camera reading, while shorter or randomized LIDAR scanning interval could help in preventing the attacks [18]. In Figure 5, a security countermeasure, "LIDAR attack detection method, which uses Radar and camera readings", is added. Additional countermeasure, "Ethernet access control", is used to prevent LIDAR attacks.

Matrices X-A, X-B, Z-A, Z-B, and Z-X are very useful for integrated safety and security analysis. X-B shows that Radar provides partial coverage of LIDAR failure, as Radar cannot fully replace LIDAR. Z-A and Z-B indicate that LIDAR attack detection method will be able to provide coverage not only for LIDAR attacks, but also failures, as it will detect corrupt LIDAR readings, which could happen in either case. Finally, Matrix Z-X shows the inter-dependencies between safety and security countermeasures. As we can see from Figure 5, Radar (safety countermeasure) and the LIDAR attack detection method (security countermeasure) share a conditional dependency (denoted by x), i.e., in order to implement the attack detection method, we need a Radar; while Radar and Ethernet access control mechanism reinforce each other.

As the new structural component, Radar, has been added to the model in Step (5), it is necessary to return to the step (2) to include it to AV structural hierarchy and to establish its relationships to the remaining elements of the model.

V. Conclusions and Future Work

In this paper, an approach for integrated autonomous vehicle safety and security analysis is proposed, which is compliant with the international standards SAE J3016, SAE J3061, and ISO 26262. It uses the Six-Step Model as a backbone for achieving and maintaining integration and alignment among safety and security artefacts throughout the entire autonomous vehicle's life-cycle. The Six-Step Model incorporates six hierarchies of autonomous vehicles, namely, functions, structure, failures, attack, safety countermeasures, and security countermeasures. An example of an autonomous vehicle Six-Step Model is included to demonstrate the usefulness of the proposed approach.

Future work will include the refinement of the proposed approach to facilitate its application in industry and the use by other researchers. We are currently building a software tool for constructing the Six-Step Model. Furthermore, we are exploring the possibility to integrate our approach with the safety analysis approach System-Theoretic Processes Analysis (STPA), which has been designed for evaluating the safety of complex systems [6]. We believe that a combination of these two approaches could help to achieve roadworthiness of the autonomous vehicles, and would contribute to the development of standards for autonomous vehicles.

REFERENCES

[1] G. Sabaliauskaite and A. P. Mathur, Aligning Cyber-Physical System Safety and Security. Cham: Springer International Publishing, 2015, pp. 41–53. [Online]. Available: https://doi.org/10.1007/978-3-319-12544-2_4

[2] L. Piètre-Cambacédès and M. Bouissou, "Cross-fertilization between safety and security engineering," Reliability Engineering & System Safety, vol. 110, 2013, pp. 110 – 126.

[3] SAE J3016: Taxonomy and Definitions for Terms Related to On-Road Motor Vehicle Automated Driving Systems. SAE International, Sep. 2016.

[4] ISO26262-2:2011, Road Vehicles – Functional Safety – Part2: Management of Functional Safety. International Organization of Standardization, ISO, 2011.

[5] F. Warg et al., Defining Autonomous Functions Using Iterative Hazard Analysis and Requirements Refinement. Cham: Springer International Publishing, 2016, pp. 286–297. [Online]. Available: https://doi.org/10.1007/978-3-319-45480-1_23

[6] A. Abdulkhaleq et al., "A systematic approach based on stpa for developing a dependable architecture for fully automated driving vehicles," Procedia Engineering, vol. 179, no. Supplement C, 2017, pp. 41 – 51.

[7] SAE J3061: Cybersecurity Guidebook for Cyber-Physical Vehicle Systems. SAE International, Jan. 2016.

[8] G. Sabaliauskaite, S. Adepu, and A. Mathur, "A six-step model for safety and security analysis of cyber-physical systems," in the 11th International Conference on Critical Information Infrastructures Security (CRITIS), Oct 2016.

[9] G. Sabaliauskaite and S. Adepu, "Integrating six-step model with information flow diagrams for comprehensive analysis of cyber-physical system safety and security," in 2017 IEEE 18th International Symposium on High Assurance Systems Engineering (HASE), Jan 2017, pp. 41–48.

[10] Automated Driving Systems 2.0. A Vision for Safety. National Highway Traffic Safety Administration, NHTSA, U.S. Department of Transportation, Sep. 2017.

[11] S. Behere and M. Törngren, "A functional reference architecture for autonomous driving," Inf. Softw. Technol., vol. 73, no. C, May 2016, pp. 136–150. [Online]. Available: http://dx.doi.org/10.1016/j.infsof.2015.12.008

[12] S. Kato, E. Takeuchi, Y. Ishiguro, Y. Ninomiya, K. Takeda, and T. Hamada, "An open approach to autonomous vehicles," IEEE Micro, vol. 35, no. 6, Nov 2015, pp. 60–68.

[13] P. Bhavsar, P. Das, M. Paugh, K. Dey, and M. Chowdhury, "Risk analysis of autonomous vehicles in mixed traffic streams," Transportation Research Record: Journal of the Transportation Research Board, vol. 2625, 2017, pp. 51–61.

[14] L. Piètre-Cambacédès and M. Bouissou, "Modeling safety and security interdependencies with bdmp (boolean logic driven markov processes)," in 2010 IEEE International Conference on Systems, Man and Cybernetics, Oct 2010, pp. 2852–2861.

[15] B. Schneier, Attack Trees. Wiley Publishing, Inc., Indianapolis, Indiana, 2015, in Book, Secrets and Lies.

[16] Z. Ma and C. Schmittner, "Threat modeling for automotive security analysis," Advanced Science and Technology Letters, vol. 139, 2016, pp. 333–339.

[17] "Beyond the Headlights: ADAS and Autonomous Sensing," 2016, URL: http://woodsidecap.com/wp-content/uploads/2016/12/20160927-Auto-Vision-Systems-Report_FINAL.pdf [accessed: 2017-09-18].

[18] J. Petit, B. Stottelaar, M. Feiri, and F. Kargl, "Remote Attacks on Automated Vehicles Sensors: Experiments on Camera and LiDAR," in Black Hat Europe, Nov. 2015.